A Book of Christian Prayer

R. Douglas Jones

the OUSE studio

DAWN

TO DARK

The House Studio
PO Box 419527
Kansas City, MO 64141

Copyright 2012 by R. Douglas Jones

ISBN 978-0-8341-2825-5
Printed in the United States of America

Editor: Kristen Allen
Interior Design: J.R. Caines/Sharon Page

www.thehousestudio.com

10 9 8 7 6 5 4 3 2 1

For Amelia Beth

CONTENTS

A Book of Christian Prayer

R. Douglas Jones

PART 1

In the Beginning

"Let's start at the very beginning—a very good place to start."[1]

from *The Sound of Music*

"In the beginning God . . ."

Genesis 1:1

The book you are holding in your hand isn't a book you read in a traditional way. What I mean is that you don't start at page one, read to the last page, and put it on a shelf to collect dust. This book is intended to be used, read, and prayed throughout the seasons of your life. At the heart of this manual is Part Two, a series of daily prayers intended to be read over and over. The rest of the book includes resources and additional guidance to make the most of the daily prayers.

However, if you have never used a prayer book before (or if you want to make the most of your *Dawn to Dark* experience), you will definitely want to start your reading right here in Part One. In this introductory section, you will find helpful background information about fixed-hour prayer and its intended benefit. You will also find some hints for using this manual to its fullest effect.

So spend some time and start reading at the beginning.

Lord, Teach Us to Pray

"One day Jesus was praying in a certain place. When he finished, one of his disciples said to him, 'Lord, teach us to pray, just as John taught his disciples.' He said to them, 'When you pray, say . . .'" (Luke 11:1-2).

Prayer is hard.

I think everyone knows this, but not everyone is willing to admit it out loud. Many people struggle to pray regularly, to find words for their hopes and fears, and to trust that the words they say are going beyond the ceiling to find God's ear. I don't think it is for lack of trying or for lack of understanding the value and power of prayer. It seems more likely that the problem for many is the way they have witnessed other people praying.

Perhaps you have had an experience like mine: you reach the point in the Sunday worship service when a person walks to the front of the church and prays a word-filled, spontaneous, and conversational prayer that you try to "join" by following along. In these moments, I often fought to stay focused on what the person was saying. I didn't always know what the pray-er was trying to pray, and I sometimes found my mind somewhere else. I was left with the impression that the problem was me; why couldn't I hang in there with the person praying? It seemed he or she was involved in the prayer, so why wasn't I?

Even though I knew praying was important, I still found it so difficult. Prayer, as I was learning it, seemed to be a rigorous mountain—one I was unable to climb. When I tried my hand at praying in this spontaneous fashion, I found doing so to be a stumbling and difficult art at which I was not particularly gifted.

Is this how prayer is supposed to be?

In many traditions, the simple answer is yes. Praying is speaking to God spontaneously, as if talking with a friend (albeit a friend tolerant of a one-way conversation).[1] The person designated to pray offers the words and ideas spoken to God while the rest of us in the room listen and "join our hearts" with the words and petitions of the designated pray-er. Prayer is modeled by communicators who are able to "pray from the heart" in front of others in a manner that is admirable.

This type of prayer was my first experience in communicating with God; maybe it was yours too. Unfortunately for many of us, praying in this way has made us feel like communicating with God is a feat that we regular folks in the pews can't attain. But what if this isn't the only way to pray? What if there is another, more accessible approach to prayer? What if prayer is more a form of exercise than art? What if there is a way to pray that is more about our heart attitude and less about our ability to put our own words to prayers?

When the disciples wanted to learn how to pray, they weren't told to "pray from their heart" or to "talk to God like a friend" (see Matthew 6 and Luke 11). The disciples had witnessed Jesus pray many times as they walked with him. On that occasion when they asked, "Lord, teach us to pray," Jesus instructed them, "Whenever you pray, say . . ." and what follows has been called the Lord's Prayer. Jesus didn't teach them prayer skills or provide them with tips. He gave the disciples *words* to pray. Notice that Jesus responded to their request by saying, "when" or "whenever you pray" or even, "whenever you pray, recite this prayer."[2] If we listen to Jesus' teaching on prayer, the Lord's Prayer is to be a part of our everyday prayer life. Prayer then becomes something that helps us focus our hearts around provided written words; we pray and recite words that are not spontaneous or coming from what we deem best, but are reflective of God's will, work, and way.

One other important point to note is that the prayer Jesus gave his disciples was entirely plural. He did not say "my Father" but "our Father," and the prayer continues to be a corporate and inclusive one from beginning to end. Jesus teaches us that whenever we pray, we are to pray these words in realization that we are praying not alone but with all of God's people.

Whenever I bring up the idea of growing our prayer life through reciting the written prayers of our common Christian history, someone generally mentions that Jesus warned us to avoid repetition. Jesus did indeed warn about such a thing, but it was not repetition Jesus was concerned with in Matthew 6:7 when he said, "And when you are praying, do not use meaningless repetition as the Gentiles do, for they suppose that they will be heard for their many words" (NASB). His concern was for a person who prays many words that don't reflect his or her true feelings and intentions. The issue at hand is *meaningless* repetition, of believing falsely that if we say the right-sounding words enough times God will be obligated to answer. When we pray we must pray with our whole person—heart, head, and hand. All of who we are needs to be in harmony with the words coming out of our mouth. Remember, Jesus himself repeated a single prayer at least three times on the last night of his life in the Garden of Gethsemane: "My Father, if it is possible, may this cup be taken from me. Yet not as I will, but as you will" (Matthew 26:39). If Jesus prayed in this manner, certainly it is not wrong for us to repeat the same words in prayer.

As a teenager I discovered that repeating or reciting a written prayer, when that prayer is heartfelt, can be a powerful and effective petition to God. One weeknight during my junior year of high school I agreed to pray with my youth pastor, Mark, in preparation for a Sunday worship service that would be led by the youth group. We desired to see God work in our hearts and lives as a result of the service. We met in the back of the church, and I followed Mark into a little chapel off the foyer of the church sanctuary.

I had never really met with someone for the sole purpose of praying, so I followed Mark's lead. He kneeled, so I kneeled. He folded his hands and rested his head on them, so I did too. He began to pray for a variety of needs that seemed appropriate, and I followed. For what seemed like a very long time we "ping-ponged" back and forth, pouring out many words. We prayed for our youth group, the pastors, the worship service, our families and friends, and a variety of other needs. I didn't let on to Mark, but our praying felt like work, and I wondered if the time we were spending talking with God was making any difference. When we ran out of words an hour or so later, we remained silent in the darkness of that little chapel. Then Mark began to recite some very familiar words: I joined him as we prayed the Lord's Prayer.

Everything changed. As we uttered those ancient words together, it seemed the space between our world and heaven evaporated and we were kneeling in the absolute presence of God. I felt embraced by God's arms as we recited the words of that familiar prayer. Lingering in the silent but tangible presence of God's Spirit in that little chapel was an amazing moment that lasted for what felt like hours.

Although I never forgot that night, my daily prayer habits didn't change after the experience. It wasn't until fifteen years later, after having a conversation about prayer with a pastor friend, that my prayer life came alive. I shared with him my frustrations regarding spontaneous, conversational prayer—how it seemed so dry and I couldn't remain focused to find the words to convey my hopes and fears, requests and thanksgivings, and prayers for those closest to me. I didn't see why prayer had to be so hard if God really wanted to have a relationship with us.

My friend listened and allowed me to run out of words (which takes a lot of patience, I can assure you) before he asked me, "Have you heard of *The Book of Common Prayer?*" He went on to explain how for many centuries Christians have stopped to pray at various points in the day for the purpose of saying their common prayer. In the morning, at midday, as the sun sets, and before going to bed, followers of Jesus have joined their voices in praying a variety of written prayers. By reading from the book of Psalms, reflecting on a passage of Scripture, and reciting the Lord's Prayer, these people have remembered God, admitted their dependency on him, and displayed an act of worship and devotion.

He explained that this manner of addressing God with words that others pray at the same time is a discipline called fixed-hour prayer.[3] Having roots in the practice of Judaism, evidence of it can be found in the Old and New Testaments. He taught me that while fixed-hour prayer is not explicitly pointed out or taught, this practice of prayer is definitely assumed in the Bible. He showed me that Daniel was thrown into the lions' den for praying facing Jerusalem three different times each day (see Daniel 6). He said that many of the psalms specifically mention praying in the morning or the evening (see Psalms 5:3; 88:13; 92:2 for morning or 17:1-3; 63:5-6; 141:2 for evening). He then pointed me to New Testament passages I knew but had never realized refer to the practice of fixed-hour prayer. For example, Pentecost happened while the disciples were gathered for morning prayer (prayer at the third hour, see Acts 2); Peter had his rooftop vision while observing midday prayer (prayer at the sixth hour, see Acts 10); and Peter and John healed a lame man on the temple steps as they were heading to gather with other believers for evening prayer (prayer at the ninth hour, see Acts 3).

Since Bible times the practice has continued. From gatherings of the early Church, to cloisters of monks, to the writings of Reformers and down through our common history, fixed-hour prayer has endured as an heirloom that has been passed on to following generations as a valuable Christian practice—a practice that helps Christians punctuate their days with meaningful prayer that both addresses God and stops to listen to him. From dawn to dark, women and men have practiced this type of prayer and found it to be an accessible and helpful way to learn how to pray. Some of the benefits of practicing fixed-hour prayer on a regular basis are:

1. Becoming saturated in Scripture
2. Joining with the Church in prayer
3. Setting aside our individualistic prayer agendas

4. Marking time as sacred
5. Finding words for our prayers
6. Learning to pray
7. Fulfilling Paul's exhortation to "pray without ceasing"
   (1 Thessalonians 5:17, KJV)

Fixed-hour prayer is an approach that engages its participants in praying Scripture. As you begin to put *Dawn to Dark* into practice, you will be praying the Psalms, praying prayers found in the Scriptures, reflecting on passages of Scripture, and declaring your faith through scriptural creeds. It won't take long to see that this ancient practice was a way for followers of God to engage the Bible both in praying it back to God and in hearing from God through its pages. Fixed-hour prayer saturates its participants in Scripture.

When you begin to pray the prayers of *Dawn to Dark*, you will find valuable what those who have passed on the tradition of fixed-hour prayer to us found valuable—the corporate nature of this practice. Whether you pray these prayers alone or in a group, you will notice that they are intentionally plural. When you are praying the Prayer at Daylight, you are joining with a host of others from the family of faith who are praying similar prayers at the same time. At first it may seem strange to pray *we, us,* and *our,* but as we continue in the practice, it is a beautiful reminder that we are not alone and that God longs to hear the Church all over the world in one voice. Fixed-hour prayer helps us join in prayer with the larger faith community.

Reciting written prayers at appointed times throughout the day challenges us and stretches us to pray about concerns and issues that we may have never considered. Our personal prayer concerns and agendas are set aside in order to rehearse authored prayers that have been prayed for thousands of years. Fixed-hour prayer demands we set aside our individualistic concerns or prayer agendas and genuinely pray in a manner that desires God's will and way rather than what seems important to us.

Praying in the manner offered in *Dawn to Dark* quickly becomes a way for followers of Jesus to practice another old tradition—observing the Christian year. As we pray the appointed words for the hours of dawn, daylight, dusk, and dark, we can also locate ourselves on the Christian calendar and pray in harmony with that time. In Part Three of this manual, we will learn more about the Christian calendar and see a variety of prayers that can enhance our prayer times. Fixed-hour prayer helps us remember and reenact God's movement and mission in our past and present. It assists us in recognizing and marking our time as sacred, touched by God, more than just passing minutes.

Praying written prayers has helped me pray more confidently, spontaneously, and conversationally. In other words, reciting prayers from the past and even contemporary written prayers has helped me find words to pray on my own when I am asked to pray for others or am seeking God's help in a crisis or a moment of joy. Now when I pray conversationally, it seems my prayers are more scriptural, more meaningful, and centered on God's will, work, and way.

Ultimately, as I have practiced fixed-hour prayer over the years, almost without my realization, I have learned how to pray. Prayer has become greater than listing requests or sharing what is on my mind: it has become something far greater than I ever imagined, integrated into ever-increasing aspects of my life. I can now see that praying without ceasing is not necessarily impossible. As we begin to pray at specific times each day with regularity, the by-product is that our awareness of God's presence and work is heightened and our likelihood to call on him, praise him, thank him, rest in him, trust him, and remember him is vastly increased. In short, fixed-hour prayer has taught me how to pray and is moving me more and more toward a life of praying without ceasing.

Prayer is hard, but it is not impossible. I hope that as you join me on this adventure of praying from dawn to dark, you will find, as I did, that we can learn to pray with greater confidence and greater capability. Let's join with Christians from all over the world and follow the example of those who came before us by praying in this manner. It takes patience. It takes perseverance. It demands our attention. It demands our whole heart. It tests our faith. But it is a worthy endeavor.

"P'ray continually . . ." (1 Thessalonians 5:17).

"Yet I am always with you; you hold me by my right hand" (Psalm 73:23).

This prayer manual might have been a gift, a bargain rack find, or a spontaneous purchase. However you came upon it, know that it was written to help those who stumble across its pages discover God, who is closer to us than we can imagine. It was toiled over and words were chosen carefully to help those who leaf through it uncover a way to pray that is helpful, meaningful, hopeful, instructive, and formative. The prayers and passages were chosen because of their place in the history of the Church and their reliance upon Scripture and the devotional tradition of our common two-thousand-year history. My hope is that this book will be a gift to all who read it, opening the door to God's goodness, presence, love, mercy, and truth.

In this chapter we will look at how you can make the most of this prayer manual and begin to experience and benefit from the practice of fixed-hour prayer. This section is meant to help you make the most of praying and using the resources found in *Dawn to Dark*. I have addressed some commonly asked questions in an effort to guide you on your way to learning how to pray in this way.

WHAT IS A PRAYER MANUAL?

Simply put, a prayer manual is an ordering of prayers, psalms, and Scripture passages to be offered in worship for various hours of the day. The intention is that this book will enable Christians from many places to join with one voice in offering their praises, prayers, and devotion to God. The prayer manual will also offer directions and resources to help the reader pray with all of God's people at various times during each day according to the Christian year.

HOW IS *DAWN TO DARK* STRUCTURED?

Dawn to Dark is a prayer manual with four parts. You are currently reading in Part One, which is designed to help you develop a clear understanding of how to make the most of this book and the practice of fixed-hour prayer. Part Two is made up of two entire weeks of prayer forms for dawn, daylight, and dusk as well as a week of prayer forms to be used at dark. This section, the heart of this prayer manual, is designed to unite your voice with the chorus of God's people praying in the tradition of morning, noon, and evening prayer. Part Three of the book is full of additional prayers for the appropriate Christian season being observed or for the personal situation in which you find yourself. In Part Four you will find a reading plan that provides a year's worth of Scripture reading to augment the prayer forms, dates for the start of various Christian seasons, as well as a listing of resources to further your experience with fixed-hour prayer.

WHAT IS THE CHRISTIAN CALENDAR?

Just as the calendar we live by has seasons and holidays, for hundreds of years the Church has observed a calendar to help followers of Jesus remember holy days and seasons with important Christian themes. The various Christian seasons are discussed at greater length in Part Three, but a brief overview of the Christian calendar is provided here:

Season	Timing	Emphasis
Advent	Four weeks before Christmas	Awaiting the coming of Jesus
Christmastide	Twelve-day period following Christmas Day	Celebrating God with us
Lent	Forty-seven days before Easter	Retreating in the wilderness with Jesus
Holy Week	Last week of Lent	Walking to the cross with Jesus
Easter	Fifty-day period following Easter Sunday	Dead to sin/New life in the Spirit
Pentecost	Last day of Easter	The birth of the body of Christ
Ordinary Time	After Pentecost until Advent	Fulfilling God's mission of restoration

THE STRUCTURE OF THE DAILY PRAYERS

Dawn to Dark has been designed to be used four times a day, praying through the Christian year. The suggested prayer times are as follows:

Prayer at Dawn:	Upon waking
Prayer at Daylight:	Between noon and 3:00 p.m.
Prayer at Dusk:	Between 5:00 p.m. and 8:00 p.m.
Prayer at Dark:	Between 9:00 p.m. and midnight

Each of the prayer services follows a similar flow (with slight variations). The basic form is:

Preparation—we slow our pace and focus our head and heart to trust in God

Invitation—we join the community of faith in inviting God to hear our prayers

Confession—we admit our lack of faith and our failures, which result in our sinning

Psalm—we read and reflect upon an appointed psalm

Praise—we join the chorus of heaven, proclaiming God's greatness and uniqueness in the universe

Declare—we affirm our faith through traditional and biblical creeds

Read—we pause to listen to the voice of God as heard through the words of Scripture

Pray—in concert with others, we offer our daily prayers and the heart of fixed-hour prayer, the Lord's Prayer

Bless—we conclude our time affirming our God, blessing his name

ADDITIONAL HINTS FOR USING *DAWN TO DARK*

Balance Routine with Variety

Fixed-hour prayer is intended to be observed at set times each day. Find a routine that allows you to keep the hours at regular times. Keep *Dawn to Dark* with your Bible so you can easily flip to suggested readings. If you want to observe the Prayers at Dawn and Dusk for a season, choose times of the day during which you generally experience the fewest interruptions and the least variation. Take advantage of the resources of Occasional Prayer (in Part Three) to bring some variety to the prayer forms and to keep you engaged in the practice. It might also help to change up the location where you observe your prayers in order to provide new vistas and scenery as you pray the hours. For example, observe dawn prayers by a window in your home, keep the prayers at daylight on your lunch hour at work, and pray on your porch or back stoop at dusk as the sun sets.

Be Patient with Yourself

Be realistic in what you are attempting to do and give yourself time to grow in this new way of prayer. Don't impose unrealistic demands upon yourself in regards to your spiritual life. There is no value in attempting to pray all the hours in this manual only to become frustrated by regular failure and put aside the book as too difficult.

One possible approach is to choose a prayer form you think will be easiest to observe in your current life stage. Then give yourself some time to "get into the routine" of praying that hour each day. In time, you will know when it is appropriate to add an additional hour to keep on a daily basis. Be patient with yourself and keep trying; join your voice with the Church, and after some time you will look back to see that your life of prayer has begun to grow.

Give Yourself Enough Time

As you start praying *Dawn to Dark*, make sure you schedule a generous amount of space to discover your pacing through the presented prayer forms. Not everyone is going to go at the same pace. There is great advantage in having enough time to slow down and be silent as you begin. The way you begin will dictate your pace; the prayers are intended to be read slowly and deliberately, so take time for reflection and "soaking" in the prayers and scriptures being offered. Some guidelines for budgeting time are as follows:

Prayer at Dawn	15 to 30 minutes
Prayer at Daylight	10 to 20 minutes
Prayer at Dusk	15 to 30 minutes
Prayer at Dark	10 to 15 minutes

Say It Aloud

It may seem strange, but for hundreds of years reading was done aloud. It is a practice that lends itself well to praying at fixed hours. I would encourage you to try it. Reading aloud will engage more of your senses— seeing the words with your eyes, forming the words with your mouth, hearing the words with your ears, and of course involving your mind will get you a long way toward involving your heart and the inner core of your emotion. If you can't get yourself to say the prayers aloud, try mouthing the words without voicing them.

Variety Within the Form

It is worth mentioning again that you should consider adding variety to the form once you have a handle on praying *Dawn to Dark*. You can do so by reviewing Part Three of this manual; then begin to add to your daily observance prayers for the appropriate Christian season or prayers that are applicable to your current situation. The Seasonal Prayers are intended to replace or supplement the Prayer of Preparation and the Closing Prayer for each service. The Situational Prayers are intended to be added to the prayer form right before the Lord's Prayer is said.

SOME SUGGESTED READING/PRAYER PLANS

A Plan for a First-Time User

Choose either the Prayer at Dawn or Dusk to observe for the next two weeks. Observe the hour, and when you come to the Scripture Reading found in the prayer form, read the Gospel passage each day. When you finish the two-week cycle, continue the practice (do one more two-week cycle), but this time read the Epistle passage during the Scripture Reading each day. When you finish this time, go to another reading plan (you can find a Scripture Reading Plan in Part Four of this manual, which lists passages to read for each day of the year).

A Plan for Observing a Prayer at Dawn and Dusk

Determine a time you will observe each of the services for Dawn and Dusk. Decide during which service you will read the Scripture. Then observe the two hours through the two-week cycle. You can choose either to read one of the passages listed in the service or to use the Scripture Reading Plan found in Part Four, which offers a listing of passages for each day of the year. I would suggest you start slowly and for your first time through the two-week cycle, read either the Gospel selection or the Epistle selection. As you continue through the cycle, add more variety (adding additional Scripture readings and either adding or substituting Occasional Prayers found in Parts Three and Four).

A Plan for a Full-Time Student

One approach for full-time students is to observe the services for Daylight and Dark. Before class or between classes, observe the Prayer at Daylight. Then between 9:00 p.m. and midnight, take time to observe the Prayer at Dark. I would recommend that prior to observing the service at Dark, you take time to quiet yourself and read a passage of Scripture: you can use the Scripture Reading Plan found in Part Four.

A Plan for a Christian Season

As a way to engage more deeply during Advent, Lent, or Easter, make room in your schedule to observe the hours of prayer for the duration of the Christian season (you can use the Guide to Christian Seasons in Part Four). To enhance your experience, use the prayers for the appropriate Christian season (found in Part Three).

A Plan for a Trip

Take your copy of *Dawn to Dark* as a companion on a trip. Take time at rest stops, places you are visiting, in your hotel room, or at your hostel or campsite to observe the appropriate hour of prayer.

A Plan for Going All In

After having some experience praying through *Dawn to Dark*, it may be time to go all in. Set a time (two weeks to two months) to observe the four hours of *Dawn to Dark*. If you are observing the hours during a Christian season, add some variety by substituting or adding the appropriate seasonal Prayers of Preparation and the Closing Prayer.

TROUBLESHOOTING

What if I Don't Have Much Time?

If you are short on time but desire to observe the service, you can make use of the "express" prayer forms found at the end of Part Two.

What if I Miss a Day?

One of the realities of life is unexpected interruption. When things seem to fall apart and you miss a day or two, don't dwell on it or give up; instead, jump to the current day and dive back in!

How Do I Figure Out When Ash Wednesday (or Any Christian Season) Is?

The Christian calendar is based on some movable feast days, which can be challenging to follow. For this reason, there is a guide in Part Four for finding the dates of Advent, Ash Wednesday, Easter, and Pentecost.

How Many Scripture Passages Should I Read at Dawn and Dusk?

To answer this question, you'll need to consider how much time you are able to budget for observing the Prayers at Dawn and at Dusk. You'll also have to determine how long you can keep your attention and focus on the practice. If you are just starting to observe both of these prayer forms, I would encourage one reading at dawn and one reading at dusk. As your experience expands and you're able to sustain your attention longer, you might expand to reading two or even three passages for one of the services and remain at one reading for the other. For example, if you tend to have more time at dawn, you can read three passages; if you have less time at dusk, you might read only the Gospel passage at that time.

How Long Should I Remain Silent?

This will look very different for each of us, but as a rule, silence is not something to gloss over. As you begin the prayer time, your ability to be still and quiet your inner voices will be the key to your ability to give attention to the prayers and readings. The rule of thumb is to take enough time to slow your pace. Become conscious of your breathing and attempt to slow it by taking deeper and less frequent breaths. Once you accomplish this, slow your mind and lessen your attention to breathing. Then, begin to focus your mind on God. You can use a simple mental prayer like, "Holy Spirit, you are welcome" or "Abba, Father, be near." Don't proceed on in the prayer form until you sense you are calm and centered on God's presence.

How Do I Use the Occasional Prayers?

In Part Three, you will notice a variety of "occasional prayers" that are of two basic varieties: Seasonal Prayers and Situational Prayers. The Seasonal Prayers are intended to be used during the observance of Christian seasons and are prayers you can either substitute for the Opening or Closing Prayer or say in addition to them. The Situational Prayers are petitions and praises that are appropriate for a variety of circumstances we all face. These prayers are intended to be said during the Prayers at Dawn and Dusk as additional prayers prior to saying the Lord's Prayer.

Before We Begin

The essence of the Latin term *peregrinatio* [*per-e-grī-nā-ti-ō*] is caught up in the ninth-century story of three Irishmen drifting over the sea from Ireland for seven days. The men, in coracles,[1] without oars, come ashore in Cornwall and are brought to the court of King Alfred. When the king asks them where they have come from and where they were going, they answer that they, "stole away because we wanted for the love of God to be on pilgrimage, we cared not where."[2]

As we begin using this primer for prayer, may we see this as an endeavor of *peregrinatio*. May we not be concerned with arriving at a destination, praying every hour, or touching every page. Instead, may we focus on using these prayers and forms as a means to allow God's Spirit to enlist us on a journey—a passage that matters, that leads us into a deeper faith and more passionate love, and ultimately a closer union with the leader of the journey.

So may we begin, caring not where the journey takes us—only that we go with God. A prayer to get us started on our *peregrinatio*:

My Lord God,
I have no idea where I am going.
I do not see the road ahead of me.
I cannot know for certain where it will end.
Nor do I really know myself,
And the fact that I think I am following your will
does not mean that I am actually doing so.
But I believe that my desire to please you
does in fact please you.
And I hope that I have that desire
in all that I am doing.
And I know that if I do this,
you will lead me by the right road
though I may know nothing about it.
Therefore will I trust you always
though I may seem to be lost
and in the shadow of death,
I will not fear, for you are ever with me
and you will never leave me
to face my perils alone.

—Thomas Merton

Prayers of Confession

In the journey of discipleship, God's grace transforms us into the likeness of Jesus (2 Corinthians 3:18). This life of Christlikeness or holiness never reaches a termination point beyond which we have no need to grow and mature. As we follow Christ, honesty and transparency remain integral to the journey. Through confession, we see ourselves and the world in which we live in a candid way. Confession is truth-telling: we look at Jesus, we look at ourselves, and we name the difference. Through the habit of honest confession, our lives remain open to the forgiving, healing, and transforming grace of God (1 John 1:5—2:2).

The Lord's Prayer

The prayer traditionally called the Lord's Prayer[1] was taught by Jesus to his disciples in response to their request, "Lord, teach us to pray." Since our great teacher taught us to recite these words, Christians have offered this prayer on a daily basis both in private devotion and in corporate worship.

TRADITIONAL

Our Father which art in heaven, Hallowed be thy name. Thy kingdom come. Thy will be done in earth, as it is in heaven. Give us this day our daily bread. And forgive us our debts, as we forgive our debtors. And lead us not into temptation, but deliver us from evil: For thine is the kingdom, and the power, and the glory, for ever. Amen.
(Matthew 6:9-13, KJV)

A CONTEMPORARY VERSION

Our Father in heaven,
Reveal who you are.
Set the world right;
Do what's best—as above, so below.
Keep us alive with three square meals.
Keep us forgiven with you and forgiving others.
Keep us safe from ourselves and the Devil.
You're in charge!
You can do anything you want!
You're ablaze in beauty!
Yes. Yes. Yes.
(Matthew 6:9-13, TM)

PART 2

Daily Prayer

WEEK ONE: REFLECTING GOD'S CHARACTER

Monday   God's Holiness

Tuesday   God's Goodness

Wednesday   God's Love

Thursday   God's Faithfulness

Friday   God's Incarnation

Saturday   God's Transcendence

Sunday   God's Mission

WEEK TWO: SHAPED BY GOD'S MISSION

Monday   Created in God's Image

Tuesday   Beloved Daughters and Sons of God

Wednesday   Called to Take Care of All God Has Made

Thursday   Invited to Be Disciples of Jesus

Friday   Made Friends of God

Saturday   Commissioned to Be God's Witnesses

Sunday   Obligated to Willingly Serve God and
                His Purposes

WEEK ONE
Reflecting God's Character

Monday

Prayer at Dawn
(Upon Waking)

PREPARE

Take time to be quiet and still. Notice your breathing and slowly greet the new day. When you are ready, continue by praying:

O Lord, open my lips that my mouth may declare your praise.
O God, make speed to save us. O Lord, make haste to help us.

INVITE

"My name will be great among the nations, from the rising to the setting of the sun. In every place incense and pure offerings will be brought to my name, because my name will be great among the nations," says the LORD Almighty. (Malachi 1:11)

Almighty God, may you be attentive to our prayers and may our words rise as fragrant incense, a pleasing aroma to you. With a oneness of heart, mind, and soul, we desire to come before you; as whole people we recognize your presence. Amen.

CONFESS

In light of God's greatness and goodness, reflect on our failings to reveal the glory of our Creator. When you are ready, continue by praying:

Almighty and most merciful God, we have strayed from your ways like lost sheep. We have left undone what we should have done, and we have done that which we should not have done. We have followed after our own ways and the desires of our own hearts. We have broken your holy laws. Good Lord, have mercy on us; restore each of us who is truly penitent, according to your promises declared to us in Jesus Christ, our Lord.

And grant, merciful Father, for Jesus' sake, that we may live a godly and obedient life, to the glory of your holy name. Amen.

PSALM 95 (NLT)

Come, let us sing to the LORD!
Let us shout joyfully to the Rock of our salvation.
Let us come to him with thanksgiving.
Let us sing psalms of praise to him.
For the LORD is a great God,
a great King above all gods.
He holds in his hands the depths of the earth
and the mightiest mountains.
The sea belongs to him, for he made it.
His hands formed the dry land, too.

Come, let us worship and bow down.
Let us kneel before the LORD our maker,
for he is our God.
We are the people he watches over,
the flock under his care.

If only you would listen to his voice today!
The LORD says, "Don't harden your hearts as Israel did at Meribah,
as they did at Massah in the wilderness.
For there your ancestors tested and tried my patience,
even though they saw everything I did.
For forty years I was angry with them, and I said,
'They are a people whose hearts turn away from me.
They refuse to do what I tell them.'
So in my anger I took an oath:
'They will never enter my place of rest.'"

Pause. Be quiet and reflect on the psalm. If necessary, read through it again.

PRAISE

Great and marvelous are your works,
O Lord God, the Almighty.
Just and true are your ways,
O King of the nations.
Who will not fear you, Lord,
and glorify your name?
For you alone are holy.
All nations will come and worship before you,
for your righteous deeds have been revealed.
(Revelation 15:3-4, NLT)

DECLARE

To whom shall we go?
You have the words of eternal life,
and we have believed and have come to know
that you are the holy one of God.
Praise to you, Lord Jesus Christ,
King of endless glory.[1]

READ

As we approach God's message today, may this prayer help us see with
fresh and new vision.

O send thy Spirit, Lord, now unto me,
that he may touch my eyes and make me see;
show me the truth concealed within thy word,
for in thy book revealed I see the Lord.[2]

Slowly and prayerfully read today's selections as found in the Devotional
Lectionary and/or in one or more of the passages below:

Exodus 15:11-18
Colossians 2:6-15
John 14:8-14

PRAY

Prayer of the Day

Almighty God and Creator, thank you for the dawn of a new day in which:

your mercies are new, overshadowing our weakness;

your provisions are more than enough to meet our needs and challenges;

your joy enriches and strengthens us;

your greatness stretches from horizon to horizon, for those with open eyes to see;

and your care extends to each of us as a parent to a child.

May we live each moment of this day knowing in our head and heart that you are ever before, behind, beside, above, and below us. Encircled by your greatness, goodness, and grace, may we reveal your glory to each person we encounter during this day. We ask this in the name of the Father, the Son, and the Holy Spirit. Amen.

The Lord's Prayer

Closing Prayer

Great God in heaven, form in us the likeness of your Son and deepen his life within us. Send us as witnesses of Gospel joy into our world of fragile peace and broken promises. Touch all hearts with your love so we may, in turn, love each other. Through Christ our Lord, Amen.[3]

BLESS

Thanks be to God. Alleluia, praise the Lord.

Monday

Prayer at Daylight
(Between noon and 3:00 p.m.)

PREPARE

Find a comfortable spot and take some moments to relax. Breathe. When you are still, focus your attention on God and pray:

The Holy Scriptures remind us that "the LORD is in his holy temple; let all the earth be silent before him" (Habakkuk 2:20).

God of heaven, may I be attentive to you in this time of prayer and silence. Amen.

REMEMBER

In a spirit of gratitude and repentance, review the past twenty-four hours. Ask God to help you become mindful of events for which you are thankful and also of those things for which you need to seek repentance, remembering that "when he, the Spirit of truth, comes, he will guide you into all truth" (John 16:13).

When you are ready, continue the remainder of the prayer.

CONFESS

Merciful God, we admit that we need your help. We confess that we have wandered from the straight and narrow path; we have done wrong, and we have failed to do what is right. You alone can help and rescue us.

Have mercy on us: wipe out our sins and teach us to forgive others. Produce in us the fruit of the Holy Spirit, that we may live as followers of Jesus. This we ask in the name of Jesus our Savior. Amen.

PSALM 121

I lift up my eyes to the hills—
where does my help come from?
My help comes from the LORD,
the Maker of heaven and earth.

He will not let your foot slip—
he who watches over you will not slumber;
indeed, he who watches over Israel
will neither slumber nor sleep.

The LORD watches over you—
the LORD is your shade at your right hand;
the sun will not harm you by day,
nor the moon by night.

The LORD will keep you from all harm—
he will watch over your life;
the LORD will watch over your coming and going
both now and forevermore.

Pause. Be quiet and reflect on the psalm. If necessary, read through it again.

PRAISE

Hark, the glad celestial hymn, angel choirs above are raising;
cherubim and seraphim in unceasing chorus praising,
fill the heavens with sweet accord: Holy, Holy, Holy Lord.

Lo! the apostolic train join thy sacred name to hallow;
prophets swell the glad refrain, and the white-robed martyrs follow,
and from morn to set of sun, through the Church the song goes on.
Amen.[4]

STOP

Re-enter the quiet and keep a few moments of silence before God, recognizing his presence and his work in our midst.

COMMIT

Teach us, dear Lord, to number our days,
that we may apply our hearts to your wisdom.
Oh, satisfy us early with your mercy,
that we may rejoice and be glad all of our days.
And let the beauty of the Lord our God be upon us
and confirm the work of our hands.
And let the beauty of the Lord our God be upon us
and confirm the work of our hands, dear Lord. Amen.

PRAY

Prayer of the Day

Almighty God and Creator, thank you for this new day in which:

your mercies are new, overshadowing our weakness;

your provisions are more than enough
to meet our needs and challenges;

your joy enriches and strengthens us;

your greatness stretches from horizon to horizon,
for those with open eyes to see;

and your care extends to each of us as a parent to a child.

May we live each moment of this day knowing in our head and heart
that you are ever before, behind, beside, above, and below us. Encircled
by your greatness, goodness, and grace, may we reveal your glory to
each person we encounter during this day. We ask this in the name of
the Father, the Son, and the Holy Spirit. Amen.

Closing Prayer

And let the beauty of the Lord our God be upon us
and confirm the work of our hands.
And let the beauty of the Lord our God be upon us
and confirm the work of our hands, dear Lord. Amen.

BLESS

For he is holy. Bless the Lord, most high. Amen.

Monday

PREPARE

Return to a quiet and still posture of heart, mind, and body. When you
are in a place of readiness, pray:

Holy God, maker of all, be near.
Lord Jesus, forgiver and friend, hear our prayer.
Holy Spirit, light and life, dwell in us.
Three in one, you are welcome; come be our guest. Amen.

PRAISE

Holy Father, holy Son,
Holy Spirit, three we name thee,
while in essence only one;
undivided God we claim thee,
and adoring, bend the knee
while we own the mystery. Amen.[5]

PSALM 42 (NLT)

As the deer longs for streams of water,
so I long for you, O God.
I thirst for God, the living God.
When can I go and stand before him?
Day and night I have only tears for food,
while my enemies continually taunt me, saying,
"Where is this God of yours?"

My heart is breaking
as I remember how it used to be:
I walked among the crowds of worshipers,
leading a great procession to the house of God,
singing for joy and giving thanks
amid the sound of a great celebration!

Why am I discouraged?
Why is my heart so sad?
I will put my hope in God!
I will praise him again—
my Savior and my God!

Now I am deeply discouraged,
but I will remember you—
even from distant Mount Hermon, the source of the Jordan,
from the land of Mount Mizar.
I hear the tumult of the raging seas
as your waves and surging tides sweep over me.
But each day the LORD pours his unfailing love upon me,
and through each night I sing his songs,
praying to God who gives me life.

"O God my rock," I cry,
"Why have you forgotten me?
Why must I wander around in grief,
oppressed by my enemies?"
Their taunts break my bones.
They scoff, "Where is this God of yours?"

Why am I discouraged?
Why is my heart so sad?
I will put my hope in God!
I will praise him again—
my Savior and my God!

Pause. Be quiet and reflect on the psalm. If necessary, read through it
again.

CONFESS

Almighty God, maker of all things, judge of all people and nations,
we admit and confess our many sins, which we have committed in
thought, word, and action.

Pause now and remember and recount those sins that come to mind.
When you're ready, continue:

We sincerely repent and turn from our misdeeds. Have mercy on us,
merciful God. For your Son our Lord Jesus Christ's sake, forgive us all
that is past and come to our help that from now on we may serve and
please you with lives that are renewed by your Holy Spirit, to the glory
of your name. Amen.

DECLARE

One of the teachers of religious law was standing there listening to the debate. He realized that Jesus had answered well, so he asked, "Of all the commandments, which is the most important?"

Jesus replied, "The most important commandment is this: 'Listen, O Israel! The LORD our God is the one and only LORD. And you must love the LORD your God with all your heart, all your soul, all your mind, and all your strength.' The second is equally important: 'Love your neighbor as yourself.' No other commandment is greater than these." (Mark 12:28-31, NLT)

READ

As we open the Bible, we pray,

God, thank you for being one who is relational and revealing. Speak now, for your servants are listening.

Slowly and prayerfully read today's selections as found in the Devotional Lectionary and/or in one or more of the passages below:

Exodus 15:19-27
Colossians 3:1-17
John 14:15-24

PRAY

Prayer of the Day

Almighty God and Creator, thank you at the close of this day in which:

your mercies are new, overshadowing our weakness;

your provisions are more than enough
to meet our needs and challenges;

your joy enriches and strengthens us;

your greatness stretches from horizon to horizon,
for those with open eyes to see;

and your care extends to each of us as a parent to a child.

May we live each moment of this day knowing in our head and heart that you are ever before, behind, beside, above, and below us. Encircled by your greatness, goodness, and grace, may we reveal your glory to each person we encounter during this day. We ask this in the name of the Father, the Son, and the Holy Spirit. Amen.

Intercede

Take a few moments to close your eyes and envision the faces of family, friends, neighbors, and others who have known needs. Take time to pray for each person and need that comes to mind. You can pray for each one in your own words or use the prayer below:

Father, Son, and Holy Spirit, three in one,

Circle around [name of individual] and encompass [him/her] on every side;

Father, Son, and Holy Spirit, embrace [him/her] in your perfect care.

The Lord's Prayer

BLESS

Holy Father, holy Son,
Holy Spirit, three we name thee,
while in essence only one;
undivided God we claim thee,
and adoring, bend the knee
while we own the mystery. Amen.[6]

PREPARE

Take time to be quiet and still. Notice your breathing and slowly greet the new day. When you are ready, continue by praying:

> This is the day the LORD has made; let us rejoice and be glad in it.
> (Psalm 118:24)

INVITE

King David invites us to "taste and see that the LORD is good. Oh, the joys of those who take refuge in him!" (Psalm 34:8, NLT). To this end, we pray,

> God of all, awaken our senses this morning to your goodness and the good things you have created for our pleasure. Today, help us learn to savor and enjoy you. Heighten our awareness and teach us to be attentive, being thankful for and enjoying your goodness and your gifts. Amen.

CONFESS

> Eternal and good God, in whom we live and move and have our being, we admit that we forget your mercy and our sin blinds us to you and your gifts. Forgive us of our evil deeds and all of our ways that offend you. Now with whole hearts, may we draw near to you, confessing the truth about ourselves and committing ourselves to your grace, that we may pursue your good way through Jesus Christ, your Son. Amen.

PSALM 31:14-24

> But I trust in you, O LORD;
> I say, "You are my God."
> My times are in your hands;
> deliver me from the hands of my enemies
> and from those who pursue me.
> Let your face shine on your servant;
> save me in your unfailing love.
> Let me not be put to shame, O LORD,
> for I have cried out to you;
> but let the wicked be put to shame
> and lie silent in the grave.
> Let their lying lips be silenced,

for with pride and contempt
they speak arrogantly against the righteous.

How great is your goodness,
which you have stored up for those who fear you,
which you bestow in the sight of men
on those who take refuge in you.
In the shelter of your presence you hide them
from the intrigues of men;
in your dwelling you keep them safe
from accusing tongues.

Praise be to the LORD,
for he showed his wonderful love to me
when I was in a besieged city.
In my alarm I said,
"I am cut off from your sight!"
Yet you heard my cry for mercy
when I called to you for help.

Love the LORD, all his saints!
The LORD preserves the faithful,
but the proud he pays back in full.
Be strong and take heart, all you who hope in the LORD.

Pause. Be quiet and reflect on the psalm. If necessary, read through it
again.

PRAISE

All people that on earth do dwell, sing to the Lord with cheerful voice;
him serve with fear, his praise forth tell, come ye before him and
rejoice.

O enter then his gates with praise, approach with joy his courts unto;
praise, laud, and bless his name always, for it is seemly so to do.

For why? The Lord our God is good, his mercy is forever sure;
his truth at all times firmly stood, and shall from age to age endure.
Amen.[7]

DECLARE

We declare our faith with the apostle Paul, who wrote the following to the church in Corinth:

> Let me now remind you, dear brothers and sisters, of the Good News I preached to you before. You welcomed it then, and you still stand firm in it. It is this Good News that saves you if you continue to believe the message I told you—unless, of course, you believed something that was never true in the first place.
>
> I passed on to you what was most important and what had also been passed on to me. Christ died for our sins, just as the Scriptures said. He was buried, and he was raised from the dead on the third day, just as the Scriptures said. He was seen by Peter and then by the Twelve. After that, he was seen by more than 500 of his followers at one time, most of whom are still alive, though some have died. Then he was seen by James and later by all the apostles. Last of all, as though I had been born at the wrong time, I also saw him. (1 Corinthians 15:1-8, NLT)

READ

As we open the Bible, we pray,

> Good seed sower, may your word find fertile and receptive hearts ready to hear and obey all that you command.

Slowly and prayerfully read today's selections as found in the Devotional Lectionary and/or in one or more of the passages below:

Exodus 15:22-27
1 Thessalonians 5:12-28
John 4:1-26

PRAY

Prayer of the Day

> Fountain of life, ever-flowing stream of life, it is through you alone that we are provided with good and perfect gifts. You are the source of all that is good and satisfying. May we learn and prove to be grateful and worthy recipients of that which flows from your throne.
>
> Keep us from seeking life from wells we attempt to dig ourselves, from sources that do not satisfy. Grow and foster in us a desire to seek only your thirst-quenching water, which flows from your side.

This day, enliven our senses to notice and be nourished by your presence all around us. Give us:

heightened taste to enjoy the food you provide—
may it remind and create in us a longing for that final banquet
in your coming kingdom;

eyes to see your presence in our neighbor
and in this world you spoke into existence;

ears attuned to your voice,
waiting to hear your promptings or notes of love;

a sense of smell that discerns the fragrance of your presence
and carries the aroma to all we meet today;

a courageous touch that is willing to reach out
and bring your mending to those we encounter
who are wounded or in pain.

Help us bring your goodness and your good gifts generously into our family, community, and world. This we ask through your Son who dwells with you and the Holy Spirit. Amen.

The Lord's Prayer

Closing Prayer

As we start out on this new day, we thank you that we are not alone, abandoned, or forgotten. Help us celebrate and enjoy your presence and goodness, which accompany us on our way. Amen.

BLESS

Thanks be to God. Alleluia, praise the Lord.

Tuesday

PREPARE

Find a comfortable spot and take some moments to relax. Breathe. When you are still, focus your attention on God and pray:

> This is the day the LORD has made; let us rejoice and be glad in it. (Psalm 118:24)

REMEMBER

In a spirit of gratitude and repentance, review the past twenty-four hours. Ask God to help you become mindful of instances you count as blessings and also of times you missed seeing God at work—remembering that "when he, the Spirit of truth, comes, he will guide you into all truth" (John 16:13).

When you are ready, continue the remainder of the prayer.

CONFESS

> Merciful God, we admit that we need your help. We recognize that we have failed to see or be grateful for your active work in our midst. We have been more ready to see others' failures and our own successes than to see your gracious hand providing for and protecting us. We confess that we have wandered from the straight and narrow path; we have done wrong, and we have failed to do what is right. You alone can help and rescue us.

> Have mercy on us: wipe out our sins and teach us to forgive others. Produce in us the fruit of the Holy Spirit, that we may live as followers of Jesus. This we ask in the name of Jesus our Savior. Amen.

PSALM 111

> Praise the LORD.

> I will extol the LORD with all my heart
> in the council of the upright and in the assembly.

> Great are the works of the LORD;
> they are pondered by all who delight in them.
> Glorious and majestic are his deeds,
> and his righteousness endures forever.
> He has caused his wonders to be remembered;

the LORD is gracious and compassionate.
He provides food for those who fear him;
he remembers his covenant forever.
He has shown his people the power of his works,
giving them the lands of other nations.
The works of his hands are faithful and just;
all his precepts are trustworthy.
They are steadfast for ever and ever,
done in faithfulness and uprightness.
He provided redemption for his people;
he ordained his covenant forever—
holy and awesome is his name.

The fear of the LORD is the beginning of wisdom;
all who follow his precepts have good understanding.
To him belongs eternal praise.

Pause. Be quiet and reflect on the psalm. If necessary, read through it again.

PRAISE

We join with all the voices of heaven and earth and say:
"Holy, holy, holy
is the Lord God Almighty,
who was, and is, and is to come. . . .
"You are worthy . . . to receive glory and honor and power" (Revelation 4:8, 11).
We praise you. Amen.

STOP

Re-enter the quiet and keep a few moments of silence before God, recognizing his presence and his work in our midst.

COMMIT

Teach us, dear Lord, to number our days,
that we may apply our hearts to your wisdom.
Oh, satisfy us early with your mercy,
that we may rejoice and be glad all of our days.
And let the beauty of the Lord our God be upon us
and confirm the work of our hands.
And let the beauty of the Lord our God be upon us
and confirm the work of our hands, dear Lord. Amen.

PRAY

Prayer of the Day

Fountain of life, ever-flowing stream of life, it is through you alone that we are provided with good and perfect gifts. You are the source of all that is good and satisfying. May we learn and prove to be grateful and worthy recipients of that which flows from your throne.

Keep us from seeking life from wells we attempt to dig ourselves, from sources that do not satisfy. Grow and foster in us a desire to seek only your thirst-quenching water, which flows from your side.

This day, enliven our senses to notice and be nourished by your presence all around us. Give us:

heightened taste to enjoy the food you provide—
may it remind and create in us a longing for that final banquet
in your coming kingdom;

eyes to see your presence in our neighbor
and in this world you spoke into existence;

ears attuned to your voice,
waiting to hear your promptings or notes of love;

a sense of smell that discerns the fragrance of your presence
and carries the aroma to all we meet today;

a courageous touch that is willing to reach out
and bring your mending to those we encounter
who are wounded or in pain.

Help us bring your goodness and your good gifts generously into our family, community, and world. This we ask through your Son who dwells with you and the Holy Spirit. Amen.

Closing Prayer

And let the beauty of the Lord our God be upon us
and confirm the work of our hands.
And let the beauty of the Lord our God be upon us
and confirm the work of our hands, dear Lord. Amen.

BLESS

For he is good, bless the Lord, most high. Amen.

Tuesday Prayer at Dusk

PREPARE

Return to a quiet and still posture of heart, mind, and body. When you are in a place of readiness, pray:

As daylight comes to a close, we are grateful to you, our God, that your goodness does not set with the sun. We thank you and are aware that your goodness extends to your children without end. As we enter into prayer this evening, we come, aware of your presence with us and mindful that you are good. Amen.

PRAISE

Praise God, from whom all blessings flow;
praise him, all creatures here below;
praise him above, ye heavenly host;
praise Father, Son, and Holy Ghost.
Amen[8]

PSALM 16

Keep me safe, O God,
for in you I take refuge.

I said to the LORD, "You are my Lord;
apart from you I have no good thing."
As for the saints who are in the land,
they are the glorious ones in whom is all my delight.
The sorrows of those will increase
who run after other gods.
I will not pour out their libations of blood
or take up their names on my lips.

LORD, you have assigned me my portion and my cup;
you have made my lot secure.
The boundary lines have fallen for me in pleasant places;
surely I have a delightful inheritance.

I will praise the LORD, who counsels me;
even at night my heart instructs me.
I have set the LORD always before me.
Because he is at my right hand,
I will not be shaken.

Therefore my heart is glad and my tongue rejoices;
my body also will rest secure,
because you will not abandon me to the grave,
nor will you let your Holy One see decay.
You have made known to me the path of life;
you will fill me with joy in your presence,
with eternal pleasures at your right hand.

Pause. Be quiet and reflect on the psalm. If necessary, read through it again.

CONFESS

Almighty God, maker of all things, judge of all people and nations, we admit and confess our many sins, which we have committed in thought, word, and action.

Pause now and remember and recount those sins that come to mind. When you're ready, continue the prayer.

We sincerely repent and turn from our misdeeds. Have mercy on us, merciful God. For your Son our Lord Jesus Christ's sake, forgive us all that is past and come to our help that from now on we may serve and please you with lives renewed by your Holy Spirit, to the glory of your name. Amen.

DECLARE

One of the teachers of religious law was standing there listening to the debate. He realized that Jesus had answered well, so he asked, "Of all the commandments, which is the most important?"

Jesus replied, "The most important commandment is this: 'Listen, O Israel! The LORD our God is the one and only LORD. And you must love the LORD your God with all your heart, all your soul, all your mind, and all your strength.' The second is equally important: 'Love your neighbor as yourself.' No other commandment is greater than these." (Mark 12:28-31, NLT)

READ

As we open the Bible, we pray,

May your words fall upon good soil in our lives, yielding a harvest of love, joy, peace, patience, kindness, goodness, faithfulness, gentleness, and self-control. Amen.

Slowly and prayerfully read today's selections as found in the Devotional Lectionary and/or in one or more of the passages below:

Exodus 16:1-18
James 1:12-18
John 6:1-14

PRAY

Prayer of the Day

Fountain of life, ever-flowing stream of life, it is through you alone that we are provided with good and perfect gifts. You are the source of all that is good and satisfying. May we learn and prove to be grateful and worthy recipients of that which flows from your throne.

Keep us from seeking life from wells we attempt to dig ourselves, from sources that do not satisfy. Grow and foster in us a desire to seek only your thirst-quenching water, which flows from your side.

This day, enliven our senses to notice and be nourished by your presence all around us. Give us:

heightened taste to enjoy the food you provide—
may it remind us and create in us a longing for that final banquet
in your coming kingdom;

eyes to see your presence in our neighbor
and in this world you spoke into existence;

ears attuned to your voice,
waiting to hear your promptings or notes of love;

a sense of smell that discerns the fragrance of your presence
and carries the aroma to all we meet;

a courageous touch that is willing to reach out
and bring your mending to those we encounter who are
wounded or in pain.

help us bring your goodness and your good gifts generously into our family, community, and world. This we ask through your Son who dwells with you and the Holy Spirit. Amen.

Intercede

Take time to remember those in need. Think of those you pass or those with whom you come in contact who are financially, relationally, or emotionally impoverished. Pray for each one in your own words or by using the simple prayer below.

Circle [name], Lord;
Above, beneath, beside, all around;
Show your goodness and greatness to my sister/brother, [name]. Amen.

Prompting: Another step in your intercession may be to write an encouraging note to one or more of the individuals that God brought to mind. Let them know of your care and concern. Write a note or an email that lets them know you are thinking of them. It does not need to be an essay; it just needs to convey your love, concern, and encouragement.

The Lord's Prayer

BLESS

Praise Father, Son, and Holy Ghost. Amen.

Wednesday Prayer at Dawn

PREPARE

Take time to be quiet and still. Notice your breathing and slowly greet the new day. When you are ready, continue by praying:

Help us rest in your love as we begin this new day.

Take a few moments to place your life in God's loving embrace. Through faith, allow your life to be surrounded and held up by God's perfect and complete kindness. Be quiet and still and remain there for a few minutes.

INVITE

The Scriptures teach us that "God is love" (1 John 4:8). We admit and confess, God of love, that we need you. We pray that your love might draw us and lead us near. We pray that your love might infuse our lives, our families, our churches, and our communities so they may reflect your goodness, kindness, mercy, sacrifice, and friendship. Love of God, rain down on us today. Amen.

CONFESS

Aware of your great love, Christ, we reflect on our failing to demonstrate your love toward our family, friends, neighbors, and enemies.

Take time to remember your lack of charity toward others. When you are ready, continue by praying:

Almighty and most merciful God, we have strayed from your ways like lost sheep. We have left undone what we should have done, and we have done that which we should not have done. We have followed after our own ways and the desires of our own hearts. We have broken your holy laws by failing to demonstrate your love toward those who are near us—toward our friend and toward our foe.

Good Lord, have mercy on us; restore each of us who is truly penitent, according to your promises declared to us in Jesus Christ, our Lord. And grant, merciful Father, for Jesus' sake, that we may live a godly and obedient life of love, to the glory of your holy name. Amen.

PSALM 63

O God, you are my God,
earnestly I seek you;
my soul thirsts for you,
my body longs for you,
in a dry and weary land
where there is no water.

I have seen you in the sanctuary
and beheld your power and your glory.
Because your love is better than life,
my lips will glorify you.
I will praise you as long as I live,
and in your name I will lift up my hands.
My soul will be satisfied as with the richest of foods;
with singing lips my mouth will praise you.

On my bed I remember you;
I think of you through the watches of the night.
Because you are my help,
I sing in the shadow of your wings.
My soul clings to you;
your right hand upholds me.

They who seek my life will be destroyed;
they will go down to the depths of the earth.
They will be given over to the sword
and become food for jackals.

But the king will rejoice in God;
all who swear by God's name will praise him,
while the mouths of liars will be silenced.

Pause. Be quiet and reflect on the psalm. If necessary, read through it
again.

PRAISE

And can it be that I should gain
an interest in the Savior's blood?
Died he for me, who caused his pain—
for me, who him to death pursued?

Amazing love! How can it be,
that thou, my God, shouldst die for me?
Amazing love! How can it be,
that thou, my God, shouldst die for me?

'Tis mystery all: th'Immortal dies:
who can explore his strange design?
In vain the firstborn seraph tries
to sound the depths of love divine.

'Tis mercy all! Let earth adore,
let angel minds inquire no more.
'Tis mercy all! Let earth adore;
let angel minds inquire no more.[9]

DECLARE

That which was from the beginning, which we have heard, which we have seen with our eyes, which we have looked at and our hands have touched—this we proclaim concerning the Word of life. The life appeared; we have seen it and testify to it, and we proclaim to you the eternal life, which was with the Father and has appeared to us. We proclaim to you what we have seen and heard, so that you also may have fellowship with us. And our fellowship is with the Father and with his Son, Jesus Christ. We write this to make our joy complete.

This is the message we have heard from him and declare to you: God is light; in him there is no darkness at all. If we claim to have fellowship with him and yet walk in the darkness, we lie and do not live by the truth. But if we walk in the light, as he is in the light, we have fellowship with one another, and the blood of Jesus, his Son, purifies us from all sin.

If we claim to be without sin, we deceive ourselves and the truth is not in us. If we confess our sins, he is faithful and just and will forgive us our sins and purify us from all unrighteousness. If we claim we have not sinned, we make him out to be a liar and his word has no place in our lives. (1 John 1:1-10)

READ

Before you continue, take time to quiet your mind and ask for the Spirit of God to allow you to hear with the ears of your heart. Ask for courage this morning to make a commitment to living out the reading's message.

Slowly and prayerfully read today's selections as found in the Devotional Lectionary and/or in one or more of the passages below:

Deuteronomy 7:6-14
Ephesians 3:14-21
John 14:15-31

PRAY

Prayer of the Day

Loving maker, redeemer, and sustainer of all things, we ask that you help us love you. On this day that has been provided to us by your perfect and unearned love, may we not lose sight of you.

Throughout this day, we ask that you will always bring us back to the light of your loving face that we might reflect your light and love to each one we meet today.

We ask this in the name of your Son, Jesus, who lives and reigns with you and the Holy Spirit, one God forever and ever. Amen.[10]

The Lord's Prayer

Closing Prayer

May the fire of Christ's love fill us, that love with which he loved us first.[11]

BLESS

Lord, you are love itself: grant that we might love you and thus be a blessing!

Wednesday   Prayer at Daylight

PREPARE

Find a comfortable spot and take some moments to relax. Breathe. When you are still, focus your attention on God and pray:

> Help us rest in your love as we continue on in this day you have pre-pared for us as a gift of love.

REMEMBER

In a spirit of gratitude and repentance, review the past twenty-four hours. Ask God to help you become mindful of instances when you sensed God's love and those times when you failed to show God's love, remembering that "when he, the Spirit of truth, comes, he will guide you into all truth" (John 16:13).

When you are ready, continue the remainder of the prayer.

CONFESS

> Merciful God, we admit that we need your help. We confess that we have wandered from the straight and narrow path; we have done wrong, and we have failed to do what is right. You alone can help and rescue us.
>
> Have mercy on us: wipe out our sins and teach us to forgive others. Produce in us the fruit of the Holy Spirit, that we may live as followers of Jesus. This we ask in the name of Jesus our Savior. Amen.

PSALM 57

> Have mercy on me, O God, have mercy on me,
> for in you my soul takes refuge.
> I will take refuge in the shadow of your wings
> until the disaster has passed.
>
> I cry out to God Most High,
> to God, who fulfills his purpose for me.
> He sends from heaven and saves me,
> rebuking those who hotly pursue me;
> God sends his love and his faithfulness.
>
> I am in the midst of lions;
> I lie among ravenous beasts—

men whose teeth are spears and arrows,
whose tongues are sharp swords.

Be exalted, O God, above the heavens;
let your glory be over all the earth.

They spread a net for my feet—
I was bowed down in distress.
They dug a pit in my path—
but they have fallen into it themselves.

My heart is steadfast, O God,
my heart is steadfast;
I will sing and make music.
Awake, my soul!
Awake, harp and lyre!
I will awaken the dawn.

I will praise you, O Lord, among the nations;
I will sing of you among the peoples.
For great is your love, reaching to the heavens;
your faithfulness reaches to the skies.

Be exalted, O God, above the heavens;
let your glory be over all the earth.

Pause. Be quiet and reflect on the psalm. If necessary, read through it
again.

PRAISE

And can it be that I should gain
an interest in the Savior's blood?
Died he for me, who caused his pain—
for me, who him to death pursued?

Amazing love! How can it be,
that thou, my God, shouldst die for me?
Amazing love! How can it be,
that thou, my God, shouldst die for me?

He left his Father's throne above
so free, so infinite his grace—
emptied himself of all but love,
and bled for Adam's helpless race:

'Tis mercy all, immense and free,
for O my God, it found out me!
'Tis mercy all, immense and free,
for O my God, it found out me![12]

STOP
Re-enter the quiet and keep a few moments of silence before God, recognizing his presence and his work in our midst.

COMMIT
Teach us, dear Lord, to number our days;
that we may apply our hearts to your wisdom.
Oh, satisfy us early with your mercy,
that we may rejoice and be glad all of our days.
And let the beauty of the Lord our God be upon us
and confirm the work of our hands.
And let the beauty of the Lord our God be upon us
and confirm the work of our hands, dear Lord. Amen.

Prompting: Today, consider how you can serve your family, your coworkers, your neighbors, or anyone else with whom you daily come in contact. Then live it out. See a need and fill it. You might sweep or vacuum a floor, prepare a meal, clear the dinner table, mow the lawn next door, pay for the order behind you in the drive-through, or wash someone's vehicle. Whatever it is, serve out of love and without being asked.

PRAY

Prayer of the Day
Loving maker, redeemer, and sustainer of all things, we ask that you help us love you. On this day that has been provided to us by your perfect and unearned love, may we not lose sight of you.

Throughout this day, we ask that you will always bring us back to the light of your loving face that we might reflect your light and love to each one we meet today.

We ask this in the name of your Son, Jesus, who lives and reigns with you and the Holy Spirit, one God forever and ever. Amen.[13]

Closing Prayer

And let the beauty of the Lord our God be upon us
and confirm the work of our hands.
And let the beauty of the Lord our God be upon us
and confirm the work of our hands, dear Lord. Amen.

BLESS

Lord, you are love itself: grant that we might love you and thus be a blessing!

Wednesday Prayer at Dusk

PREPARE

Return to a quiet and still posture of heart, mind, and body. When you are in a place of readiness, pray:

> Help us rest and rely upon your love as we continue this day, that we might demonstrate your gentleness, kindness, attention, and mercy toward others today and every day.

PRAISE

> And can it be that I should gain
> an interest in the Savior's blood?
> Died he for me, who caused his pain—
> for me, who him to death pursued?
>
> Amazing love! How can it be,
> that thou, my God, shouldst die for me?
> Amazing love! How can it be,
> that thou, my God, shouldst die for me?
>
> No condemnation now I dread;
> Jesus, and all in him, is mine;
> alive in him, my living head,
> and clothed in righteousness divine.
>
> Bold I approach th'eternal throne,
> and claim the crown, through Christ my own.
> Bold I approach th'eternal throne,
> and claim the crown, through Christ my own.[14]

PSALM 130

> Out of the depths I cry to you, O Lord;
> O Lord, hear my voice.
> Let your ears be attentive
> to my cry for mercy.
>
> If you, O Lord, kept a record of sins,
> O Lord, who could stand?
> But with you there is forgiveness;
> therefore you are feared.

I wait for the LORD, my soul waits,
and in his word I put my hope.
My soul waits for the Lord
more than watchmen wait for the morning,
more than watchmen wait for the morning.

O Israel, put your hope in the LORD,
for with the LORD is unfailing love
and with him is full redemption.
He himself will redeem Israel
from all their sins.

Pause. Be quiet and reflect on the psalm. If necessary, read through it again.

CONFESS

Almighty God, maker of all things, judge of all people and nations, we admit and confess our many sins, which we have committed in thought, word, and action.

Pause now and remember and recount those sins that come to mind.

We sincerely repent and turn from our misdeeds. Have mercy on us, merciful God. For your Son our Lord Jesus Christ's sake, forgive us all that is past and come to our help that from now on we may serve and please you with lives that are renewed by your Holy Spirit, to the glory of your name. Amen.

DECLARE

One of the teachers of religious law was standing there listening to the debate. He realized that Jesus had answered well, so he asked, "Of all the commandments, which is the most important?"

Jesus replied, "The most important commandment is this: 'Listen, O Israel! The LORD our God is the one and only LORD. And you must love the LORD your God with all your heart, all your soul, all your mind, and all your strength.' The second is equally important: 'Love your neighbor as yourself.' No other commandment is greater than these." (Mark 12:28-31, NLT)

READ

As we open the Bible, we pray,

Open our eyes, Lord. We want to see Jesus. Amen.

Slowly and prayerfully read today's selections as found in the Devotional Lectionary and/or in one or more of the passages below:

Deuteronomy 10:12-22
Ephesians 4:1-16
Luke 10:25-37

PRAY

Prayer of the Day

Loving maker, redeemer, and sustainer of all things, we ask that you help us love you. On this day that has been provided to us by your perfect and unearned love, may we not lose sight of you.

Throughout this day we ask that you will always bring us back to the light of your loving face, that we might reflect your light and love to each one we meet today.

We ask this in the name of your Son, Jesus, who lives and reigns with you and the Holy Spirit, one God, forever and ever. Amen.[15]

Intercede

For all people who confess to follow you, Almighty God, may we be of one mind, may we live and serve together in love, and may we shine your love to all of the people of your world.

For the sake of your great name, we pray.

For our nation and all of the nations of the world, we ask that you help us live in peace and lead us to respect one another and to care for each other.

Father, show us your love, we pray.

For our world, help us show a reverence for all you created and for all you have redeemed. Assist us in stewarding all you have given for the good of others and to bring you glory.

Restorer, shower down your grace, we pray.

For all the people who call us neighbor, acquaintance, friend, enemy, daughter, or son, help us see Christ in their eyes and to love them as he loves us.

Spirit of God, empower us, we pray.

For each one who is suffering this day from sickness, tragedy, or broken relationships, provide courage, mercy, and hope in the midst of their trouble, and an end to their suffering.

For the sake of your great name, loving Father, gracious restorer, and Spirit of God, we ask this prayer. Amen.

The Lord's Prayer

BLESS

Lord, you are love itself: grant that we might love you and thus be a blessing!

Thursday Prayer at Dawn

PREPARE

Take time to be quiet and still. Notice your breathing and slowly greet the new day. When you are ready, continue by praying:

O Lord, open my lips that my mouth may declare your praise.
O God, make speed to save us. O Lord, make haste to help us.

INVITE

The Bible instructs us that just as a new day follows the night, our God is true and constant, keeping his promises and sustaining all he has made.

Faithful God, turn us toward your will and way. Let our faith increase to know you are present and you hear and respond to our prayers. Amen.

CONFESS

God of life and light, in you there is no shadow and no deceit. You invite us to join you in your perfect light; yet we find ourselves crouching in the darkness with lies on our lips. May we be quick to admit our sin and not hide our faults from you. We confess that we are slow to trust you and your ways and too quick to live by sight and what seems right in our own eyes. Forgive us our sin and shortcomings. Thank you, God, that if we confess our sins, you are faithful and just to forgive us and cleanse us from our sin. Amen.[16]

PSALM 19

The heavens declare the glory of God;
the skies proclaim the work of his hands.
Day after day they pour forth speech;
night after night they display knowledge.
There is no speech or language
where their voice is not heard.
Their voice goes out into all the earth,
their words to the ends of the world.

In the heavens he has pitched a tent for the sun,
which is like a bridegroom coming forth from his pavilion,
like a champion rejoicing to run his course.
It rises at one end of the heavens

and makes its circuit to the other;
nothing is hidden from its heat.

The law of the LORD is perfect,
reviving the soul.
The statutes of the LORD are trustworthy,
making wise the simple.
The precepts of the LORD are right,
giving joy to the heart.
The commands of the LORD are radiant,
giving light to the eyes.
The fear of the LORD is pure,
enduring forever.
The ordinances of the LORD are sure
and altogether righteous.
They are more precious than gold,
than much pure gold;
they are sweeter than honey,
than honey from the comb.
By them is your servant warned;
in keeping them there is great reward.

Who can discern his errors?
Forgive my hidden faults.
Keep your servant also from willful sins;
may they not rule over me.
Then will I be blameless,
innocent of great transgression.

May the words of my mouth and the meditation of my heart
be pleasing in your sight,
O LORD, my Rock and my Redeemer.

Pause. Be quiet and reflect on the psalm. If necessary, read through it
again.

PRAISE
My hope is built on nothing less
than Jesus' blood and righteousness.
I dare not trust the sweetest frame,
but wholly lean on Jesus' name.

When darkness seems to hide his face,
I rest on his unchanging grace.
In every high and stormy gale,
my anchor holds within the veil.

His oath, his covenant, his blood,
support me in the whelming flood.
When all around my soul gives way,
he then is all my hope and stay.

On Christ, the solid rock, I stand;
all other ground is sinking sand.[17]

DECLARE

I believe in God, the Father almighty, maker of heaven and earth;
And in Jesus Christ his only Son our Lord;
   who was conceived by the Virgin Mary,
   suffered under Pontius Pilate,
   was crucified, dead and buried.
   He descended into hell.
   The third day he rose again from the dead.
   He ascended into heaven,
   and sitteth on the right hand of God the Father almighty.
From thence he shall come to judge the quick and the dead.
I believe in the Holy Ghost,
   the Church universal,
   the communion of saints,
   the forgiveness of sins,
   the resurrection of the body,
   and the life everlasting. Amen.[18]

READ

In the past God spoke to our forefathers through the prophets at many
times and in various ways, but in these last days he has spoken to us by
his Son, whom he appointed heir of all things, and through whom he
made the universe. (Hebrews 1:1-2)

Faithful one, thank you for speaking through your Son and providing
us with the Old and New Testaments. May we be faithful to listen and
joyfully submit to all of your words. Amen.

Slowly and prayerfully read today's selections as found in the Devotional Lectionary and/or in one or more of the passages below:

Joel 2:1-14
Hebrews 3:1-6
Matthew 9:1-8

PRAY

Prayer of the Day

Everlasting God, who was and is and is to come, we are grateful for your constancy, dependability, and faithfulness. You keep your word. You never fail to keep a promise. You reward those who trust in your presence, power, and provision. Help us live out the words of the author of Hebrews: "Let us hold unswervingly to the hope we profess, for he who promised is faithful. And let us consider how we may spur one another on toward love and good deeds" (Hebrews 10:23-24).

Enable your Church to become a more accurate picture of your faithfulness. Let us be a fellowship of people who are known for our love.

A community of diverse people who are kind, respectful, and gracious toward one another.

A gathering of people who are dedicated to the teachings of Jesus and the Scriptures—living them out no matter their radical demands or countercultural call.

Let us take on lives that are characterized by sharing what we have, joining in regular corporate prayer, awe-inspired worship, hospitality that welcomes neighbors and strangers, and purity of life before one another and our God.

Expand our concept of the people of God. Help us grow into a Church that is a worthy and accurate representation of your character and calling, almighty God. We ask this in the name of the one who is faithful to call and able to empower us to live out the calling—God, our maker, restorer, and comforter. Amen.[19]

The Lord's Prayer

Closing Prayer

One true promise keeper, you are the God who foretold of a deliverer and fulfilled it through Jesus' coming and living among us, through his dying and rising triumphant over sin and death. This day may our lives find their confidence, direction, hope, meaning, and contentment in your will and way. This we ask in the name of your Son, our Savior, Jesus the Christ. Amen.

BLESS

May the words of my mouth and the meditation of my heart be pleasing in your sight, O Lord, my Rock and my Redeemer. (Psalm 19:14)

PREPARE

Find a comfortable spot and take some moments to relax. Breathe. When you are still, focus your attention on God and pray:

O faithful one, keeper of promises and one true God, keep us sensitive and responsive to your promptings and cooperative with your continued activity among us, this day and every day. Amen.

REMEMBER

In a spirit of gratitude and repentance, review the past twenty-four hours. Ask God to help you become mindful of the times you were faithful to God's promptings, living in the light, and those instances when you failed to be faithful, instead following your own way toward sin and darkness. As you pray, remember that "when he, the Spirit of truth, comes, he will guide you into all truth" (John 16:13).

When you are ready, continue the remainder of the prayer.

CONFESS

Merciful God, we admit that we need your help. We confess that we have wandered from the straight and narrow path; we have done wrong, and we have failed to do what is right. You have led us toward the light, and we have gone instead toward the darkness, making our own way. You alone can help and rescue us.

Have mercy on us: wipe out our sins and teach us to forgive others. Produce in us the fruit of the Holy Spirit, that we may live as followers of Jesus. This we ask in the name of Jesus, our faithful and true God. Amen.

PSALM 43

Vindicate me, O God,
and plead my cause against an ungodly nation;
rescue me from deceitful and wicked men.
You are God my stronghold.
Why have you rejected me?
Why must I go about mourning,
oppressed by the enemy?
Send forth your light and your truth,

let them guide me;
let them bring me to your holy mountain,
to the place where you dwell.
Then will I go to the altar of God,
to God, my joy and my delight.
I will praise you with the harp,
O God, my God.

Why are you downcast, O my soul?
Why so disturbed within me?
Put your hope in God,
for I will yet praise him,
my Savior and my God.

Pause. Be quiet and reflect on the psalm. If necessary, read through it
again.

PRAISE

O God, you hold all things in space,
each star and planet in its place,
the days and years are your design,
each change of season you define.

As life's eventide draws near,
give us your light, remove our fear,
with happy death may we be blest,
and find in you eternal rest.

Hear us, O Father, gracious and forgiving,
and thou, O Christ, the coeternal Word,
who, with the Holy Spirit by all things living,
now and to endless ages are adored. Amen.[20]

STOP

Re-enter the quiet and keep a few moments of silence before God, recognizing his presence and his work in our midst.

COMMIT

Teach us, dear Lord, to number our days,
that we may apply our hearts to your wisdom.
Oh, satisfy us early with your mercy,
that we may rejoice and be glad all of our days.
And let the beauty of the Lord our God be upon us
and confirm the work of our hands.
And let the beauty of the Lord our God be upon us
and confirm the work of our hands, dear Lord. Amen.

PRAY

Prayer of the Day

Everlasting God, who was and is and is to come, we are grateful for your constancy, dependability, and faithfulness. You keep your word. You never fail to keep a promise. You reward those who trust in your presence, power, and provision. Help us live out the words of the author of Hebrews: "Let us hold unswervingly to the hope we profess, for he who promised is faithful. And let us consider how we may spur one another on toward love and good deeds" (Hebrews 10:23-24).

Enable your Church to become a more accurate picture of your faithfulness. Let us be a fellowship of people who are known for our love.

A community of diverse people who are kind, respectful, and gracious toward one another.

A gathering of people who are dedicated to the teachings of Jesus and the Scriptures—living them out no matter their radical demands or countercultural call.

Let us take on lives that are characterized by sharing what we have, joining in regular corporate prayer, awe-inspired worship, hospitality that welcomes neighbors and strangers, and purity of life before one another and our God.

Expand our concept of the people of God. Help us grow into a Church that is a worthy and accurate representation of your character and calling, almighty God. We ask this in the name of the one who is faithful to call and able to empower us to live out the calling—God, our maker, restorer, and comforter. Amen.[21]

Closing Prayer

And let the beauty of the Lord our God be upon us
and confirm the work of our hands.
And let the beauty of the Lord our God be upon us
and confirm the work of our hands, dear Lord. Amen.

BLESS

We bless thee, O God, the maker of ways!
And boldly ask of thee a blessing, this day.
One more grace would I implore,
that many souls this day,
because of me, may love thee more. Amen.[22]

Thursday Prayer at Dusk

PREPARE

Return to a quiet and still posture of heart, mind, and body. When you are in a place of readiness, continue by praying:

> In the beginning, out of the silence, God, you spoke and there was light. In this moment of silence meet with us. If it is in your plan, break the silence with your voice. Open our ears that we might hear and soften our hearts that we might obey quickly, completely, and joyfully. Amen.

Remain quiet and listen. When you are ready, continue the prayer.

PRAISE

> O gracious Light,
> pure brightness of the ever-living Father in heaven,
> O Jesus Christ, holy and blessed!
> Now as we come to the setting of the sun,
> and our eyes behold the vesper light,
> we sing your praises, O God: Father, Son, and Holy Spirit.
> You are worthy at all times to be praised by happy voices,
> O Son of God, O giver of life,
> and to be glorified through all the worlds.[23]

PSALM 115

> Not to us, O Lord, not to us
> but to your name be the glory,
> because of your love and faithfulness.
>
> Why do the nations say,
> "Where is their God?"
> Our God is in heaven;
> he does whatever pleases him.
> But their idols are silver and gold,
> made by the hands of men.
> They have mouths, but cannot speak,
> eyes, but they cannot see;
> they have ears, but cannot hear,
> noses, but they cannot smell;
> they have hands, but cannot feel,

feet, but they cannot walk;
nor can they utter a sound with their throats.
Those who make them will be like them,
and so will all who trust in them.

O house of Israel, trust in the LORD—
he is their help and shield.
O house of Aaron, trust in the LORD—
he is their help and shield.
You who fear him, trust in the LORD—
he is their help and shield.

The LORD remembers us and will bless us:
He will bless the house of Israel,
he will bless the house of Aaron,
he will bless those who fear the LORD—
small and great alike.

May the LORD make you increase,
both you and your children.
May you be blessed by the LORD,
the Maker of heaven and earth.

The highest heavens belong to the LORD,
but the earth he has given to man.
It is not the dead who praise the LORD,
those who go down to silence;
it is we who extol the LORD,
both now and forevermore.

Praise the LORD.

Pause. Be quiet and reflect on the psalm. If necessary, read through it again.

CONFESS

Almighty God, maker of all things, judge of all people and nations, we admit and confess our many sins, which we have committed in thought, word, and action.

Pause now and remember and recount those sins that come to mind.

We sincerely repent and turn from our misdeeds. Have mercy on us, merciful God. For your Son our Lord Jesus Christ's sake, forgive us all that is past and come to our help that from now on we may serve and please you with lives that are renewed by your Holy Spirit, to the glory of your name. Amen.

DECLARE

One of the teachers of religious law was standing there listening to the debate. He realized that Jesus had answered well, so he asked, "Of all the commandments, which is the most important?"

Jesus replied, "The most important commandment is this: 'Listen, O Israel! The LORD our God is the one and only LORD. And you must love the LORD your God with all your heart, all your soul, all your mind, and all your strength.' The second is equally important: 'Love your neighbor as yourself.' No other commandment is greater than these." (Mark 12:28-31, NLT)

READ

As we open the Bible, we pray,

O Word of God incarnate,
O Wisdom from on high,
O Truth unchanged, unchanging,
O Light of our dark sky:
we praise you for the radiance
that from the hallowed page,
a lantern to our footsteps,
shines on from age to age.[24]

Slowly and prayerfully read today's selections as found in the Devotional Lectionary and/or in one or more of the passages below:

Joel 2:15-32
Hebrews 3:7-19
Matthew 9:18-26

PRAY

Prayer of the Day

Everlasting God, who was and is and is to come, we are grateful for your constancy, dependability, and faithfulness. You keep your word. You never fail to keep a promise. You reward those who trust in your presence, power, and provision. Help us live out the words of the author of Hebrews: "Let us hold unswervingly to the hope we profess, for he who promised is faithful. And let us consider how we may spur one another on toward love and good deeds" (Hebrews 10:23-24).

Enable your Church to become a more accurate picture of your faithfulness. Let us be a fellowship of people who are known for our love.

A community of diverse people who are kind, respectful, and gracious toward one another.

A gathering of people who are dedicated to the teachings of Jesus and the Scriptures—living them out no matter their radical demands or countercultural call.

Let us take on lives that are characterized by sharing what we have, joining in regular corporate prayer, awe-inspired worship, hospitality that welcomes neighbors and strangers, and purity of life before one another and our God.

Expand our concept of the people of God. Help us grow into a Church that is a worthy and accurate representation of your character and calling, almighty God. We ask this in the name of the one who is faithful to call and able to empower us to live out the calling—God, our maker, restorer, and comforter. Amen.[25]

Intercede

Take time to remember your local faith community in prayer:

That God's people will acknowledge God's glory not only with their lips but with their lives.

For a hunger among the congregation to fulfill God's will and mission in their community.

That the people will become followers who will know, receive, and obey the Holy Christian Scriptures.

For unity among God's people.

That the leaders and body of believers may be humble toward one another and willing to listen to one another and for God's voice.

For the members of your congregation to consistently share the gospel through their actions and their words.

That joy would characterize the lives and gatherings of the people of God.

The Lord's Prayer

BLESS

Thanks be to God. Alleluia, praise the Lord.

Friday   Prayer at Dawn

PREPARE

Take time to be quiet and still. Notice your breathing and slowly greet the new day. When you are ready, continue:

> For this is what the high and lofty One says—
> he who lives forever, whose name is holy:
> "I live in a high and holy place,
> but also with him who is contrite and lowly in spirit,
> to revive the spirit of the lowly
> and to revive the heart of the contrite."
> (Isaiah 57:15)

INVITE

> Most holy one, we ask, humbly, that you would come near and that your presence would both guide and guard us on this new day. Amen.

CONFESS

> Most merciful God, we confess that we have sinned against you in thought, word, and deed by what we have done and by what we have left undone. We have not loved you with our whole heart; we have not loved our neighbors as ourselves. We are truly sorry and we humbly repent. For the sake of your Son Jesus Christ, have mercy on us and forgive us, that we may delight in your will and walk in your ways to the glory of your name. Amen.[26]

PSALM 23

> The LORD is my shepherd, I shall not be in want.
> He makes me lie down in green pastures,
> he leads me beside quiet waters,
> he restores my soul.
> He guides me in paths of righteousness
> for his name's sake.
> Even though I walk
> through the valley of the shadow of death,
> I will fear no evil,
> for you are with me;
> your rod and your staff,
> they comfort me.

You prepare a table before me
in the presence of my enemies.
You anoint my head with oil;
my cup overflows.
Surely goodness and love will follow me
all the days of my life,
and I will dwell in the house of the LORD
forever.

Pause. Be quiet and reflect on the psalm. If necessary, read through it again.

PRAISE

Unto thee I cry, my Savior
Don't be silent long, O, my Lord
Hear the voice of my troubled heart
When I lift my hands to thee
Be my hiding place in times of trouble
Compass me about with songs of deliverance

Blessed are you Lord, my Savior
My heart will trust in you, my strength
My soul will rise again, rejoicing
And I will praise your name, my God
Be my hiding place in times of trouble
Compass me about with songs of deliverance[27]

DECLARE

There is one body and one Spirit—just as you were called to one hope when you were called—one Lord, one faith, one baptism; one God and Father of all, who is over all and through all and in all.
(Ephesians 4:4-6)

READ

As we approach God's message today, may this prayer help us recognize the nearness of our God.

God Almighty, you laid aside your majesty that you might reveal yourself and your kingdom to us. May we not take your presence for granted. As we approach the Scriptures you have given to us, create in us a desire to commune with you, face to face. Amen.

Slowly and prayerfully read today's selections as found in the Devotional Lectionary and/or in one or more of the passages below:

Joshua 3:1-8

Acts 17:22-34

John 16:1-15

PRAY

Prayer of the Day

As we awake this day, we awake in your world and in your presence. Help us rise from the slumber of our own selfish whims and willful ways to a new alertness, being more fully aware of your purposes for this day. Help us desire to stay near to your heart, your concerns, and your love.

Through the power and prompting of your presence:

Help our hearts beat with the same love and compassion for our friends, neighbors, and enemies. Through the power of your Holy Spirit, may we be quick to listen to others, forgive wrongs, and serve when we see a need.

May we be concerned about what concerns you. Make us passionate about those who are perceived as the least, lonely, or lost—those you came to free, to fill, and to befriend. Help us share your loving presence with those we come across today, and every day, who are poor, alone, or searching for meaning in this life. Help us embrace them with the same grace, mercy, love, and hope with which you have embraced us.

Fill us with the love you demonstrated by being willing to come and live among us through your Son, Jesus, and by sending the Holy Spirit to be with us, indwell us, and empower us. In the same manner, may we demonstrate a love that is tangible, that serves and forgives, listens and shares, thinks the best and goes the second mile, and befriends and faithfully supports.

Thank you for being present with us, God, our maker, restorer, and comforter. Help us be a very real example and expression of your presence to those we meet today. Amen.

The Lord's Prayer

Closing Prayer

Lord Jesus Christ, you stretched out your arms of love on the hard wood of the cross, that everyone might come within the reach of your saving embrace.

So clothe us in your Spirit that we, reaching forth our hands in love, may bring those who do not know you to the knowledge and love of you; for the honor of your name. Amen.[28]

BLESS

May God be gracious to us and bless us and make his face shine upon us, that your ways may be known on earth, your salvation among all nations. May the peoples praise you, O God; may all the peoples praise you. May the nations be glad and sing for joy, for you rule the peoples justly and guide the nations of the earth. (Psalm 67:1-4)

Friday   ## Prayer at Daylight

PREPARE

Find a comfortable spot and take some moments to relax. Breathe. When you are still, focus your attention on God and pray:

"From one man he made every nation of men, that they should inhabit the whole earth; and he determined the times set for them and the exact places where they should live. God did this so that men would seek him and perhaps reach out for him and find him, though he is not far from each one of us" (Acts 17:26-27).

In light of this truth, we ask, humbly, that you would draw us near and that your presence would both guide and guard us as we continue this day. Amen.

REMEMBER

In a spirit of gratitude and repentance, review the past twenty-four hours. Ask God to help you become mindful of those times you were aware, alert, and attentive to God's presence and then of those times you were hiding or avoiding God's presence, remembering that "when he, the Spirit of truth, comes, he will guide you into all truth" (John 16:13).

When you are ready, continue the remainder of the prayer.

CONFESS

Merciful God, we admit that we need your help. We confess that we have wandered from the straight and narrow path; we have done wrong, and we have failed to do what is right. Like our ancestors Adam and Eve, you have come calling for us and we have tried to hide from your presence and avoid your provisions. Forgive us, for you alone are able to help and rescue us. You alone are able to lead us to true love and authentic life.

Have mercy on us: wipe out our sins and teach us to forgive others. Produce in us the fruit of the Holy Spirit, that we may live as followers of Jesus. This we ask in the name of Jesus our Savior. Amen.

PSALM 46

God is our refuge and strength,
an ever-present help in trouble.
Therefore we will not fear, though the earth give way

and the mountains fall into the heart of the sea,
though its waters roar and foam
and the mountains quake with their surging.

There is a river whose streams make glad the city of God,
the holy place where the Most High dwells.
God is within her, she will not fall;
God will help her at break of day.
Nations are in uproar, kingdoms fall;
he lifts his voice, the earth melts.

The LORD Almighty is with us;
the God of Jacob is our fortress.

Come and see the works of the LORD,
the desolations he has brought on the earth.
He makes wars cease to the ends of the earth;
He breaks the bow and shatters the spear,
he burns the shields with fire.
"Be still, and know that I am God;
I will be exalted among the nations,
I will be exalted in the earth."

The LORD Almighty is with us;
the God of Jacob is our fortress.

Pause. Be quiet and reflect on the psalm. If necessary, read through it again.

PRAISE

You, O Christ, are the king of glory, Son of the eternal Father. You overcame the power of death, opening the Father's kingdom to all who believe in you.

Day by day we praise you; we acclaim you now and to all eternity. In your goodness, Lord, keep us from sin. Have mercy on us, Lord. Have mercy.

May your mercy always be with us, Lord, for we have hoped in you. In you, Lord, we put our trust: we shall not be put to shame.[29]

STOP

Re-enter the quiet and keep a few moments of silence before God, recognizing his presence and his work in our midst.

COMMIT

Blessed Savior, at this hour you hung upon the cross, stretching out your willing arms: grant that all the peoples of the earth may look to you and be saved. Let us join with you and extend your embrace, reflecting your love, truth, mercy, joy, and compassion to all those we meet today. Amen.

Prompting: It was on a Friday that the Lord was humiliated, punished, and crucified on our behalf. As a way to enter into his suffering and remember that we have been bought with a price, consider fasting a meal today. As you fast from eating, you can commemorate this great event of our history by meditating on a passage of Scripture. (Isaiah 53; Matthew 27:27-56; Luke 23:26-49; John 19:1-37; and Philippians 2:1-11, among others, are suitable for meditating on the death of Jesus.) Take time to seek the Lord in prayer and silence.

PRAY

Prayer of the Day

As we work and live this day, we work and live in your world and in your presence. Help us break free from our own selfish whims and willful ways to embrace a new alertness, being more fully aware of your purposes for this day. Help us desire to stay near to your heart, your concerns, and your love.

Through the power and prompting of your presence:

Help our hearts beat with the same love and compassion for our friends, neighbors, and enemies. May we be quick to listen to others, forgive wrongs, and serve when we see a need through the power of your Holy Spirit.

May we be concerned about what concerns you. Make us passionate about those who are perceived as the least, lonely, or lost—those who you came to free, to fill, and to befriend. Help us share your loving presence with those we come across today, and every day, who are poor, alone, or searching for meaning in this life. Help us embrace them with the same grace, mercy, love, and hope with which you have embraced us.

Fill us with the love that you demonstrated by being willing to come and live among us through your Son, Jesus, and by sending the Holy

Spirit to be with us, indwell us, and empower us. In the same manner, may we demonstrate a love that is tangible—a love that serves and forgives, listens and shares, thinks the best and goes the second mile, and befriends and faithfully supports.

Thank you for being present with us, God, our maker, restorer, and comforter. Help us be a very real example and expression of your presence to those we meet today. Amen.

Closing Prayer

Day by day we praise you; we acclaim you now and for all eternity. In your goodness, Lord, keep us from sin. Have mercy on us, Lord, have mercy.

May your mercy always be with us, Lord, for we have hoped in you. In you, Lord, we put our trust: we shall not be put to shame.[30]

BLESS

May God be gracious to us and bless us
and make his face shine upon us,
that your ways may be known on earth,
your salvation among all nations.

May the peoples praise you, O God;
may all the peoples praise you.
May the nations be glad and sing for joy,
for you rule the peoples justly
and guide the nations of the earth.
(Psalm 67:1-4)

Friday   Prayer at Dusk

PREPARE

Return to a quiet and still posture of heart, mind, and body. When you are in a place of readiness, pray:

> Most holy and exalted one, we ask, humbly, that you would come near and that your presence would both guide and guard us as we near the end of this day. Amen.

PRAISE

> At the close of day and rising of the moon, we pause to praise you, Almighty God.

> Maker and originator of all there is, we praise you for staying near to all you have made.

> Restorer and revealer who became God with us, we praise you for kneeling to our place; by doing so, you have revealed your true nature and taught us how to live as fully human beings.

> Spirit of God and comforter, we praise you that you have indwelled your Church, empowered the people of God, and are molding us to reveal your image to all we meet.

> For this and more than words can express, we magnify and exalt you our Lord, our God, our only hope. Amen.

PSALM 139

> O Lord, you have searched me
> and you know me.
> You know when I sit and when I rise;
> you perceive my thoughts from afar.
> You discern my going out and my lying down;
> you are familiar with all my ways.
> Before a word is on my tongue
> you know it completely, O Lord.
>
> You hem me in—behind and before;
> you have laid your hand upon me.
> Such knowledge is too wonderful for me,
> too lofty for me to attain.

Where can I go from your Spirit?
Where can I flee from your presence?
If I go up to the heavens, you are there;
if I make my bed in the depths, you are there.
If I rise on the wings of the dawn,
if I settle on the far side of the sea,
even there your hand will guide me,
your right hand will hold me fast.

If I say, "Surely the darkness will hide me
and the light become night around me,"
even the darkness will not be dark to you;
the night will shine like the day,
for darkness is as light to you.

For you created my inmost being;
you knit me together in my mother's womb.
I praise you because I am fearfully and wonderfully made;
your works are wonderful,
I know that full well.
My frame was not hidden from you
when I was made in the secret place.
When I was woven together in the depths of the earth,
your eyes saw my unformed body.
All the days ordained for me
were written in your book
before one of them came to be.

How precious to me are your thoughts, O God!
How vast is the sum of them!
Were I to count them,
they would outnumber the grains of sand.
When I awake,
I am still with you.

If only you would slay the wicked, O God!
Away from me, you bloodthirsty men!
They speak of you with evil intent;
your adversaries misuse your name.
Do I not hate those who hate you, O Lord,
and abhor those who rise up against you?
I have nothing but hatred for them;
I count them my enemies.

Search me, O God, and know my heart;
test me and know my anxious thoughts.
See if there is any offensive way in me,
and lead me in the way everlasting.

Pause. Be quiet and reflect on the psalm. If necessary, read through it again.

CONFESS

Almighty God, maker of all things, judge of all people and nations, we admit and confess our many sins, which we have committed in thought, word, and action.

Pause now and remember and recount those sins that come to mind.

We sincerely repent and turn from our misdeeds. Have mercy on us, merciful God. For your Son our Lord Jesus Christ's sake, forgive us all that is past and come to our help that from now on we may serve and please you with lives that are renewed by your Holy Spirit, to the glory of your name. Amen.

DECLARE

One of the teachers of religious law was standing there listening to the debate. He realized that Jesus had answered well, so he asked, "Of all the commandments, which is the most important?"

Jesus replied, "The most important commandment is this: 'Listen, O Israel! The Lord our God is the one and only Lord. And you must love the Lord your God with all your heart, all your soul, all your mind, and all your strength.' The second is equally important: 'Love your neighbor as yourself.' No other commandment is greater than these." (Mark 12:28-31, NLT)

READ

As we open the Bible, we pray,

God Almighty, you laid aside your majesty that you might reveal yourself and your kingdom to us. May we not take your presence for granted. As we approach the Scriptures you have given to us, create in us a desire to commune with you, face to face. Amen.

Slowly and prayerfully read today's selections as found in the Devotional Lectionary and/or in one or more of the passages below:

Joshua 3:9-17

2 Corinthians 6:14-18

John 16:16-33

PRAY

Prayer of the Day

As we close out this day, we do so in the midst of your world and in your presence. Forgive us for catering to our own selfish whims and willful ways. Help us embrace a new alertness, being more fully aware of your presence and your promptings. Help us desire to stay near to your heart, your concerns, and your love.

Through the power and prompting of your presence:

Help our hearts beat with the same love and compassion for our friends, neighbors, and enemies. May we be quick to listen to others, forgive wrongs, and serve when we see a need, through the power of your Holy Spirit.

May we be concerned about what concerns you. Make us passionate about those who are perceived as the least, lonely, or lost—those you came to free, to fill, and to befriend. Help us share your loving presence with those we come across today, and every day, who are poor, alone, or searching for meaning in this life. Help us embrace them with the same grace, mercy, love, and hope with which you have embraced us.

Fill us with the love you demonstrated by being willing to come and live among us through your Son, Jesus, and by sending the Holy Spirit to be with us, indwell us, and empower us. In the same manner, may we demonstrate a love that is tangible—that serves and forgives, listens and shares, thinks the best and goes the second mile, and befriends and faithfully supports.

Thank you for being present with us, God, our maker, restorer, and comforter. Help us be a very real example and expression of your presence to those we meet today. Amen.

Intercede

Lord, this evening, we pray for the poor and exploited, for the unemployed and the needy, for the prisoner and the forgotten, for the widow and the orphan, and for ourselves. May we remember and care for the least, lost, and lonely. Have mercy on us, Lord. Amen.

Take a moment and wait to see if the Lord brings anyone to mind you can pray for specifically who is poor, alone, or spiritually searching.

The Lord's Prayer

BLESS

Search me, O God, and know my heart;
test me and know my anxious thoughts.
See if there is any offensive way in me,
and lead me in the way everlasting.
(Psalm 139:23-24)

We ask that through your power and presence, our thoughts, words, and deeds would reflect your image as we finish this day and every day. All glory to God. Amen.

Saturday Prayer at Dawn

PREPARE

Each of the four living creatures had six wings and was covered with eyes all around, even under his wings. Day and night they never stop saying:

"Holy, holy, holy
is the Lord God Almighty,
who was, and is, and is to come."
(Revelation 4:8)

Take time to be quiet and still. Notice your breathing and slowly greet the new day. When you are ready, continue by praying,

With the creatures of heaven, we join in declaring that you alone are God; there is no one like you in all of heaven or earth. We praise you and bow before you today. Amen.

INVITE

Great God in whom there is no shadow, this morning we are struck by the truth that you are God and we are definitely not. This morning we come to you aware that you alone are capable of coming to our assistance. We need you. We depend upon you. Help us have the faith to trust in your will, your ways, and your provision. We ask this through your Son who came to save us. Amen.

CONFESS

Almighty and most merciful God, we have strayed from your ways like lost sheep. We have left undone what we should have done, and we have done that which we should not have done. We have followed after our own will and the desires of our own hearts. We have broken your holy laws by failing to trust your commands to live as aliens and strangers in this world. We have been more willing to accommodate and fit into this world than to obey your command to be holy as you are holy.

Forgive us and fill us afresh with faith and power to live in such a way as to reflect your image in this world of your creation.

Great God and Lord of all, have mercy on us; restore each of us who is truly penitent, according to your promises declared to us in Jesus Christ, our Lord.

Thank you for life, for second chances, and for your presence and guidance this day. Amen.

PSALM 90

Lord, you have been our dwelling place
throughout all generations.
Before the mountains were born
or you brought forth the earth and the world,
from everlasting to everlasting you are God.

You turn men back to dust,
saying, "Return to dust, O sons of men."
For a thousand years in your sight
are like a day that has just gone by,
or like a watch in the night.
You sweep men away in the sleep of death;
they are like the new grass of the morning—
though in the morning it springs up new,
by evening it is dry and withered.

We are consumed by your anger
and terrified by your indignation.
You have set our iniquities before you,
our secret sins in the light of your presence.
All our days pass away under your wrath;
we finish our years with a moan.
The length of our days is seventy years—
or eighty, if we have the strength;
yet their span is but trouble and sorrow,
for they quickly pass, and we fly away.

Who knows the power of your anger?
For your wrath is as great as the fear that is due you.
Teach us to number our days aright,
that we may gain a heart of wisdom.

Relent, O Lord! How long will it be?
Have compassion on your servants.
Satisfy us in the morning with your unfailing love,
that we may sing for joy and be glad all our days.
Make us glad for as many days as you have afflicted us,
for as many years as we have seen trouble.
May your deeds be shown to your servants,
your splendor to their children.

May the favor of the Lord our God rest upon us;
establish the work of our hands for us—
yes, establish the work of our hands.

Pause. Be quiet and reflect on the psalm. If necessary, read through it again.

PRAISE

Immortal, invisible, God only wise,
in light inaccessible hid from our eyes,
most blessed, most glorious, the Ancient of Days,
Almighty, victorious, thy great name we praise.

Great Father of glory, pure Father of light,
thine angels adore thee, all veiling their sight;
all praise we would render; O help us to see
'tis only the splendor of light hideth thee! Amen.[31]

DECLARE

With our ancient Christian ancestors we declare this to be the substance of our faith:

The Church, though dispersed throughout the whole world, even to the ends of the earth, has received from the apostles and their disciples this faith:

The Church believes in one God, the Father Almighty,
who made the heaven and the earth and the seas
and all the things that are in them;
and in one Christ Jesus, the Son of God,
who was made flesh for our salvation;
and in the Holy Spirit, who made known
through the prophets the plan of salvation,
and the coming, and the birth from a virgin, and the passion,

and the resurrection from the dead,
and the bodily ascension into heaven
of the beloved Christ Jesus, our Lord,
and his future appearing from heaven in the glory of the Father
to sum up all things and to raise anew all flesh
of the whole human race.[32]

READ

As we approach God's message, let us continue in an attitude of prayerful listening. Let us pray:

Good and great God, after you raised your Son Jesus from the grave, he opened up the Scriptures to pilgrims on the Emmaus way; in the same manner, we ask that you would reveal your message for us this day as we look to the Bible and that just as Luke recorded, we might join that fellowship of burning hearts. Refine our faith and trust that we might become more reliable witnesses of all that we have seen and heard of your great acts. Amen.

Slowly and prayerfully read today's selections as found in the Devotional Lectionary and/or in one or more of the passages below:

Isaiah 55:6-13
Romans 11:13-36
Matthew 14:13-21

PRAY

Prayer of the Day

God of mystery, God of paradox, help us grow in our trust and faith in you. Your ways are unique and different from ours. You call us to die to self in order to find abundant life in you. You call us to give up all we have in order to gain what is priceless.

You remind us that the way to greatness is the way of humility and serving. To be first we must take the position of least or last. Help us embrace this mystery and grow in our trust of this "upside down" way of viewing our world and our place in it.

Cause our faith in you to be expanded. May it mark us as followers of the most high God and citizens of your kingdom.

Creator God, we encounter you in the beauty of creation. Help us learn to trust you in both the splendor of a sunset and in the power of a thunderstorm.

Companion God, we encounter you in our human relationships. Grow our faith to know your presence is with us in the warmth of a friend-ship and in the loneliness of the betrayal of a former friend.

Loving God, we encounter you in the embrace of a loved one. May we also know your power to forgive and show grace to the cold shoulder of a friend turned foe.

Merciful God, we encounter you in the search for justice. Put a desire and determination within us to partner with your mission to see peace among nations, peace in our homes, and peace in our hearts.

Mysterious God, in our restlessness we search for you; we desire you. Grow our confidence in your presence—whether or not we feel it— now and forever. Amen.

The Lord's Prayer

Prompting: Prayer is ultimately waking up to the presence of God no matter where we are or what we are up to. One way to exercise this ability is through awareness. We practice this art by choosing a spot outside or by a window and being still and alert to the moment we are in, by being attentive to whatever is in front of us. Living in this moment, we become fully aware that we are fully alive and we can take time to notice the presence of God in each moment.

Closing Prayer

Most high, glorious God,
enlighten the darkness of my heart;
give me right faith, sure hope, and perfect charity.
Fill me with understanding and knowledge, that I may fulfill your commands. Amen.

BLESS

Oh, the depth of the riches of the wisdom and knowledge of God!
How unsearchable his judgments,
and his paths beyond tracing out!
"Who has known the mind of the Lord?
Or who has been his counselor?"
"Who has ever given to God,
that God should repay him?"
For from him and through him and to him are all things.
To him be the glory forever! Amen.
(Romans 11:33-36)

Saturday

Prayer at Daylight

PREPARE

Find a comfortable spot and take some moments to relax. Breathe. When you are still, focus your attention on God and pray:

God Almighty, in whom we live and move and have our being, may we not forget that in all our work and interactions this day, we are ever walking under your gaze. Amen.

REMEMBER

In a spirit of gratitude and repentance, review the past seven days. Ask God to help you become mindful of themes or a consistent message from the way you have been living over the last week. What might God be trying to reveal or share with you as you review before God your interactions and failings? Remember that "when he, the Spirit of truth, comes, he will guide you into all truth" (John 16:13).

When you are ready, continue the remainder of the prayer.

CONFESS

Merciful God, we admit that we need your help. We confess that we have wandered from the straight and narrow path; we have done wrong, and we have failed to do what is right. You alone can help and rescue us.

Have mercy on us: wipe out our sins and teach us to forgive others. Produce in us the fruit of the Holy Spirit, that we may live as followers of Jesus. This we ask in the name of Jesus our Savior. Amen.

PSALM 147:1-11

Praise the LORD.

How good it is to sing praises to our God,
how pleasant and fitting to praise him!

The LORD builds up Jerusalem;
he gathers the exiles of Israel.
He heals the brokenhearted
and binds up their wounds.
He determines the number of the stars
and calls them each by name.

Great is our Lord and mighty in power;
his understanding has no limit.
The LORD sustains the humble
but casts the wicked to the ground.

Sing to the LORD with thanksgiving;
make music to our God on the harp.
He covers the sky with clouds;
he supplies the earth with rain
and makes grass grow on the hills.
He provides food for the cattle
and for the young ravens when they call.

His pleasure is not in the strength of the horse,
nor his delight in the legs of a man;
the LORD delights in those who fear him,
who put their hope in his unfailing love.

Pause. Be quiet and reflect on the psalm. If necessary, read through it
again.

PRAISE

O worship the King, all glorious above,
and gratefully sing his wonderful love;
our shield and defender, the Ancient of Days,
pavilioned in splendor and girded with praise.

O tell of his might, and sing of his grace,
whose robe is the light, whose canopy space;
his chariots of wrath the deep thunderclouds form,
and dark is his path on the wings of the storm.

Frail children of dust, and feeble as frail,
in thee do we trust, nor find thee to fail;
thy mercies how tender! How firm to the end!
Our maker, defender, redeemer and friend.

O worship the King, all glorious above,
and gratefully sing his wonderful love. Amen.[33]

STOP

Re-enter the quiet and keep a few moments of silence before God, recognizing his presence and his work in our midst.

COMMIT

Teach us, dear Lord, to number our days,
that we may apply our hearts to your wisdom.
Oh, satisfy us early with your mercy,
that we may rejoice and be glad all of our days.
And let the beauty of the Lord our God be upon us
and confirm the work of our hands.
And let the beauty of the Lord our God be upon us
and confirm the work of our hands, dear Lord. Amen.

PRAY

Prayer of the Day

God of mystery, God of paradox, help us grow in our trust and faith in you. Your ways are unique and different from ours. You call us to die to self in order to find abundant life in you. You call us to give up all we have in order to gain what is priceless.

You remind us that the way to greatness is the way of humility and serving. To be first we must take the position of least or last. Help us embrace this mystery and grow in our trust of this upside down way of viewing our world and our place in it. Cause our faith in you to be expanded. May our faith mark us as followers of the most high God and as citizens of your kingdom.

Creator God, we encounter you in the beauty of creation. Help us learn to trust you in both the splendor of a sunset and in the power of a thunderstorm.

Companion God, we encounter you in our human relationships. Grow our faith to know your presence is with us in the warmth of a friendship and in the loneliness of the betrayal of a former friend.

Loving God, we encounter you in the embrace of a loved one. May we also know your power to forgive and show grace to the cold shoulder of a friend turned foe.

Merciful God, we encounter you in the search for justice. Put a desire and determination within us to partner with your mission to see peace among nations, peace in our homes, and peace in our hearts.

Mysterious God, in our restlessness we search for you; we desire you. Grow our confidence in your presence—whether or not we feel it— now and forever. Amen.

Closing Prayer

And let the beauty of the Lord our God be upon us
and confirm the work of our hands.
And let the beauty of the Lord our God be upon us
and confirm the work of our hands, dear Lord. Amen.

BLESS

Glory to the Father, and to the Son, and to the Holy Spirit: as it was in the beginning, is now, and will be for ever. Amen.[34]

PREPARE

Return to a quiet and still posture of heart, mind, and body. When you are in a place of readiness, pray:

Great God, who has called us to be your people, you dwell in unapproachable light. Come near to us, we pray.

Jesus, who bowed to the earth and who has been exalted to the highest place, hear our prayer today.

Spirit of God, sent to guide, empower, and correct us, gather our voices in one accord that we might be found in heaven as fragrant incense rising in your presence. Amen.

PRAISE

We have come to the setting of the sun
and we look to the evening light.
We sing to God, the Father, Son, and Holy Spirit.
You are worthy of being praised with pure voices forever.
O Son of God, O giver of life,
the universe proclaims your glory.

Let us give thanks to the Lord our God.
It is right to give him thanks and praise. Amen.[35]

PSALM 76

In Judah God is known;
his name is great in Israel.
His tent is in Salem,
his dwelling place in Zion.
There he broke the flashing arrows,
the shields and the swords, the weapons of war.

You are resplendent with light,
more majestic than mountains rich with game.
Valiant men lie plundered,
they sleep their last sleep;
not one of the warriors
can lift his hands.
At your rebuke, O God of Jacob,

both horse and chariot lie still.
You alone are to be feared.
Who can stand before you when you are angry?
From heaven you pronounced judgment,
and the land feared and was quiet—
when you, O God, rose up to judge,
to save all the afflicted of the land.
Surely your wrath against men brings you praise,
and the survivors of your wrath are restrained.

Make vows to the Lord your God and fulfill them;
let all the neighboring lands
bring gifts to the One to be feared.
He breaks the spirit of rulers;
he is feared by the kings of the earth.

Pause. Be quiet and reflect on the psalm. If necessary, read through it again.

CONFESS

Almighty God, maker of all things, judge of all people and nations, we admit and confess our many sins, which we have committed in thought, word, and action.

Pause now and remember and recount those sins that come to mind.

We sincerely repent and turn from our misdeeds. Have mercy on us, merciful God. For your Son our Lord Jesus Christ's sake, forgive us all that is past and come to our help that from now on we may serve and please you with lives that are renewed by your Holy Spirit, to the glory of your name. Amen.

DECLARE

One of the teachers of religious law was standing there listening to the debate. He realized that Jesus had answered well, so he asked, "Of all the commandments, which is the most important?"

Jesus replied, "The most important commandment is this: 'Listen, O Israel! The Lord our God is the one and only Lord. And you must love the Lord your God with all your heart, all your soul, all your mind, and all your strength.' The second is equally important: 'Love your neighbor as yourself.' No other commandment is greater than these." (Mark 12:28-31, NLT)

READ

As we open the Bible, we pray,

> Blessed are you, O Lord our God, king of the universe, who led your people Israel by a pillar of cloud by day and a pillar of fire by night. Enlighten our darkness by the light of your Christ; may his word be a lamp to our feet and a light to our path. Amen.

Slowly and prayerfully read today's selections as found in the Devotional Lectionary and/or in one or more of the passages below:

Isaiah 6:1-8
Hebrews 1
Matthew 14:22-33

PRAY

Prayer of the Day

God of mystery, God of paradox, help us grow in our trust and faith in you. Your ways are unique and different from ours. You call us to die to self in order to find abundant life in you. You call us to give up all we have in order to gain what is priceless.

You remind us that the way to greatness is the way of humility and serving. To be first we must take the position of least or last. Help us embrace this mystery and grow in our trust of this upside down way of viewing our world and our place in it.

Cause our faith in you to be expanded. May it mark us as followers of the most high God and citizens of your kingdom.

Creator God, we encounter you in the beauty of creation. Help us learn to trust you in both the splendor of a sunset and in the power of a thunderstorm.

Companion God, we encounter you in our human relationships. Grow our faith to know your presence is with us in the warmth of a friendship and in the loneliness of the betrayal of a former friend.

Loving God, we encounter you in the embrace of a loved one. May we also know your power to forgive and show grace to the cold shoulder of a friend turned foe.

Merciful God, we encounter you in the search for justice. Put a desire and determination within us to partner with your mission to see peace among nations, peace in our homes, and peace in our hearts.

Mysterious God, in our restlessness we search for you; we desire you. Grow our confidence in your presence—whether or not we feel it— now and forever. Amen.

Intercede

Make us worthy, Lord, to serve our fellow men throughout the world, who live and die in poverty and hunger.
Give them through our hands, this day, their daily bread
and by our understanding love give peace and joy.

Lord, make me a channel of thy peace:
that where there is hatred, I may bring love;
that where there is wrong, I may bring the spirit of forgiveness;
that where there is discord, I may bring harmony;
that where there is error, I may bring truth;
that where there is doubt, I may bring faith;
that where there is despair, I may bring hope;
that where there are shadows, I may bring light;
that where there is sadness, I may bring joy.

Lord, grant that I may seek rather to comfort than to be comforted;
to understand than to be understood;
to love than to be loved.
For it is by forgetting self that one finds;
it is by forgiving that one is forgiven;
it is by dying that one awakens to eternal life. Amen.[36]

The Lord's Prayer

BLESS

Oh, the depth of the riches of the wisdom and knowledge of God!
How unsearchable his judgments,
and his paths beyond tracing out!
"Who has known the mind of the Lord?
Or who has been his counselor?"
"Who has ever given to God,
that God should repay him?"
For from him and through him and to him are all things.
To him be the glory forever! Amen.
(Romans 11:33-36)

Sunday   Prayer at Dawn

PREPARE

Take time to be quiet and still. Notice your breathing and slowly greet
the new day. When you are ready, continue by praying:

> Glory be to the Father, and to the Son, and to the Holy Ghost;
> as it was in the beginning, is now, and ever shall be,
> world without end. Amen.[37]

INVITE

> Come, let us sing for joy to the LORD;
> let us shout aloud to the Rock of our salvation.
> (Psalm 95:1)

> Our Rock, our God and only Savior, who walked out of the tomb, may
> we know afresh and reflect faithfully the love, joy, and hope that you
> have shown to us and the entire world. Amen.

CONFESS

In light of God's work that restores us to reflect the most high among
creation, let us remember our failure to reveal God's image and to participate in God's mission.

When you are ready, continue by praying:

> Maker and Messiah, we recognize your hand has both made us and
> made a way for us to return to you. We are your workmanship created
> for good works that will continue to reveal your kingdom reign. Yet in
> our everyday lives we have been more concerned with our own passions
> and pursuits, our own dreams and desires. We confess that we have
> sinned against you by putting our ways above your ways.

Pause here and name specific ways you have offended God.

> God, we need you to change our minds and mold our lives that we
> might again chase your heart and handiwork. Thank you, gracious and
> good God, our Savior. Amen.

PSALM 24:1-6

The earth is the LORD's, and everything in it,
the world, and all who live in it;
for he founded it upon the seas
and established it upon the waters.

Who may ascend the hill of the LORD?
Who may stand in his holy place?
He who has clean hands and a pure heart,
who does not lift up his soul to an idol
or swear by what is false.
He will receive blessing from the LORD
and vindication from God his Savior.
Such is the generation of those who seek him,
who seek your face, O God of Jacob.

Pause. Be quiet and reflect on the psalm. If necessary, read through it again.

PRAISE

Blessed are you, Lord God of Israel, for you have visited us, bought us back, and made us your people.

From out of your servant David's family you have raised up a mighty rescuer and restorer to provide us with a way and a hope. Since the world began, you spoke through the prophets, declaring:

> that we would be saved from our enemies and from all who desire our demise;

> that you would demonstrate your merciful acts, which you promised to all those who came before us;

> that you would remember the promises you swore to Abraham, which he passed down to us;

> that as a result of your acting, we might be able to serve you without fear and live before you, holy and righteous, all the days of our life.

You gave us John the Baptist, who was called a prophet of the most high because he went before the Lord and prepared the way. He told his people how to find a new and restored life through the forgiveness of their sins.

We praise you for your tender mercy, for the light of heaven, which has dawned before us, giving light to we who live in darkness and in the shadow of death, guiding us to a path of wholeness and well-being.[38]

DECLARE

I believe in God, the Father Almighty, maker of heaven and earth;
And in Jesus Christ his only Son our Lord;
   who was conceived by the Virgin Mary,
   suffered under Pontius Pilate,
   was crucified, dead and buried.
   He descended into hell.
   The third day he rose again from the dead.
   He ascended into heaven,
   and sitteth on the right hand of God the Father Almighty.
From thence he shall come to judge the quick and the dead.
I believe in the Holy Ghost,
   the Church universal,
   the communion of saints,
   the forgiveness of sins,
   the resurrection of the body,
   and the life everlasting. Amen.[39]

READ

As we open the Bible, we pray:

Almighty God, may we read and mark in the Holy Scriptures the tale of your loving purposes—from the beginning of our disobedience, to the promise of your restoration, to the coming of your holy child, who made it possible to become your adopted daughters and sons. Soften our hearts and minds to hear afresh these words; help us honor them in our words, actions, and attitudes. Amen.

Slowly and prayerfully read today's selections as found in the Devotional Lectionary and/or in one or more of the passages below:
Genesis 2
Colossians 1:15-23
John 1:1-18

PRAY

Prayer of the Day

Holy and great Father, who has made all of heaven and earth good;

Jesus, the anointed one, through whom we are all restored and made children of God;

Holy Spirit, whose presence and power again fill our lives and churches;

Have mercy upon us all and refresh us with:

minds that dwell and rest in you and your kingdom priorities;

eyes touched by your hand,
that we might see and join your mission in our midst;

ears open to hear the voices of others
who hunger for hope and restoration;

mouths unashamed to share how you have transformed
the story of our lives;

hands ready and able to accomplish the work set before us today;

feet that gladly and promptly walk where you direct us.

We ask this in the name of the Father, the Son, and the Holy Spirit. Amen.

The Lord's Prayer

Closing Prayer

Today we rejoice in Jesus being raised from the dead. Because he was obedient and overcame sin and death, all things can be restored. We ask that we might be worthy and faithful witnesses and workers on behalf of the risen Christ and his coming kingdom—a kingdom so wonderful no eye has seen, no ear has heard, no imagination has fathomed how wonderful it is! Thank you for the privilege of representing you and your mission today. May your grace and power keep us following after you this day and every day. Amen.

BLESSING

Great are you, O God of the universe; there is no one like you.
You alone are God; there is no one like you.
May you and your kingdom be revealed through our lives today.

Sunday Prayer at Daylight

PREPARE

Find a comfortable spot and take some moments to relax and breathe.
When you are still, focus your attention on God and pray:

Glory be to the Father, and to the Son, and to the Holy Ghost;
as it was in the beginning, is now, and ever shall be,
world without end. Amen.[40]

REMEMBER

If you have been baptized, for the next few minutes remember your
baptism. Consider the prayer below a renewal of the vow you took (or
your parents took on your behalf) when you "went under the waters" of
baptism.

If you haven't been baptized, consider this a prayer of your intention and
aspiration to follow Christ into the waters of baptism.

Almighty and everlasting God, who in mercy saved Noah and his family in the days of the flood, led the children of Israel through the waters
of the Red Sea, and by the baptism of your Son, Jesus Christ, sanctified
water to represent the washing away of sin, look upon us with mercy.
Assist us in keeping our vows to:

renounce the devil and all his works;

trust in God the Father Almighty, maker of heaven and earth;

trust in Jesus Christ, who was crucified for our sins, rose from the
dead, and is the only way to salvation;

trust in the Holy Spirit, who enables us to receive God's word, repent, and believe the good news of the gospel.

Trusting the help of the Holy Spirit, I will keep God's holy will and
commandments all the days of my life. Amen.[41]

CONFESS

Merciful God, we admit that we need your help. We confess that
we have wandered from the straight and narrow path; we have done
wrong, and we have failed to do what is right. You alone can help and
rescue us.

Have mercy on us: wipe out our sins and teach us to forgive others.
Produce in us the fruit of the Holy Spirit, that we may live as followers
of Jesus. This we ask in the name of Jesus our Savior. Amen.

PSALM 148

Praise the LORD.

Praise the LORD from the heavens,
praise him in the heights above.
Praise him, all his angels,
praise him, all his heavenly hosts.
Praise him, sun and moon,
praise him, all you shining stars.
Praise him, you highest heavens
and you waters above the skies.
Let them praise the name of the LORD,
for he commanded and they were created.
He set them in place for ever and ever;
he gave a decree that will never pass away.

Praise the LORD from the earth,
you great sea creatures and all ocean depths,
lightning and hail, snow and clouds,
stormy winds that do his bidding,
you mountains and all hills,
fruit trees and all cedars,
wild animals and all cattle,
small creatures and flying birds,
kings of the earth and all nations,
you princes and all rulers on earth,
young men and maidens,
old men and children.

Let them praise the name of the LORD,
for his name alone is exalted;
his splendor is above the earth and the heavens.
He has raised up for his people a horn,
the praise of all his saints,
of Israel, the people close to his heart.

Praise the LORD.

Pause. Be quiet and reflect on the psalm. If necessary, read through it again.

PRAISE

Praise God, from whom all blessings flow;
praise him, all creatures here below;
praise him above, ye heavenly host;
praise Father, Son, and Holy Ghost. Amen.[42]

STOP

Re-enter the quiet and keep a few moments of silence before God, recognizing his presence and his work in our midst.

COMMIT

Teach us, dear Lord, to number our days,
that we may apply our hearts to your wisdom.
Oh, satisfy us early with your mercy,
that we may rejoice and be glad all of our days.
And let the beauty of the Lord our God be upon us
and confirm the work of our hands.
And let the beauty of the Lord our God be upon us
and confirm the work of our hands, dear Lord. Amen.

PRAY

Prayer of the Day

Holy and great Father, who has made all of heaven and earth good;

Jesus, the anointed one, through whom we are all restored and made children of God;

Holy Spirit, whose presence and power again fill our lives and churches;

Have mercy upon us all and refresh us with:
minds that dwell and rest in you and your kingdom priorities;
eyes touched by your hand,
that we might see and join your mission in our midst;
ears open to hear the voices of others
who hunger for hope and restoration;
mouths unashamed to share how you have transformed
the story of our lives;

hands ready and able to accomplish the work set before us today;
feet that gladly and promptly walk where you direct us.

We ask this in the name of the Father, the Son, and the Holy Spirit.
Amen.

Closing Prayer
And let the beauty of the Lord our God be upon us
and confirm the work of our hands.
And let the beauty of the Lord our God be upon us
and confirm the work of our hands, dear Lord. Amen.

BLESS
Praise Father, Son, and Holy Ghost. Amen.

Sunday

PREPARE

Return to a quiet and still posture of heart, mind, and body. When you are in a place of readiness, pray:

Glory be to the Father, and to the Son, and to the Holy Ghost;
as it was in the beginning, is now, and ever shall be,
world without end. Amen.[43]

PRAISE

We proclaim that you are a great God; we rejoice in your gift of life
found in giving your Son, Jesus the Christ.

We praise you for the mercy you have shown to us and to each generation.

We praise you, Almighty God, because:
you have shown the strength of your arm
by scattering the proud in their conceit;

you have cast down the mighty from their high places
and lifted up the lowly;

you have filled those who hunger with the best thing
and sent away the wealthy with nothing;

you remembered and kept your promises to your people;

your promise and your mercy have extended
from Abraham to Mary and even to our generation.

We proclaim that you are a great God; we rejoice in God our Savior!
Amen.[44]

PSALM 67

May God be gracious to us and bless us
and make his face shine upon us,
that your ways may be known on earth,
your salvation among all nations.

May the peoples praise you, O God;
may all the peoples praise you.
May the nations be glad and sing for joy,
for you rule the peoples justly
and guide the nations of the earth.
May the peoples praise you, O God;
may all the peoples praise you.

Then the land will yield its harvest,
and God, our God, will bless us.
God will bless us,
and all the ends of the earth will fear him.

Pause. Be quiet and reflect on the psalm. If necessary, read through it again.

CONFESS

Almighty God, maker of all things, judge of all people and nations, we admit and confess our many sins, which we have committed in thought, word, and action.

Pause now and remember and recount those sins that come to mind. When you are ready, continue by praying:

We sincerely repent and turn from our misdeeds. Have mercy on us, merciful God. For your Son our Lord Jesus Christ's sake, forgive us all that is past and come to our help that from now on we may serve and please you with lives that are renewed by your Holy Spirit, to the glory of your name. Amen.

DECLARE

One of the teachers of religious law was standing there listening to the debate. He realized that Jesus had answered well, so he asked, "Of all the commandments, which is the most important?"

Jesus replied, "The most important commandment is this: 'Listen, O Israel! The Lord our God is the one and only Lord. And you must love the Lord your God with all your heart, all your soul, all your mind, and all your strength.' The second is equally important: 'Love your neighbor as yourself.' No other commandment is greater than these." (Mark 12:28-31, NLT)

READ

As we open the Bible, we pray:

> Almighty God, may we read and mark in the Holy Scriptures the tale
> of your loving purposes—from the beginning of our disobedience, to
> the promise of your restoration, to the coming of your holy child, who
> made it possible to become your adopted daughters and sons. Soften
> our hearts and minds to hear afresh these words; help us honor them in
> our words, actions, and attitudes. Amen.

Slowly and prayerfully read today's selections as found in the Devotional
Lectionary and/or in one or more of the passages below:

Genesis 12:1-6
Galatians 3:1-14
Luke 4:14-21

PRAY

Prayer of the Day

> Holy and great Father, who has made all of heaven and earth good;
>
> Jesus, the anointed one, through whom we are all restored and made
> children of God;
>
> Holy Spirit, whose presence and power again fill our lives and churches;
>
> Have mercy upon us all and refresh us with:
>> minds that dwell and rest in you and your kingdom priorities;
>> eyes touched by your hand,
>> that we might see and join your mission in our midst;
>> ears open to hear the voices of others
>> who hunger for hope and restoration;
>> mouths unashamed to share how you have transformed
>> the story of our lives;
>> hands ready and able to accomplish the work set before us today;
>> feet that gladly and promptly walk where you direct us.
>
> We ask this in the name of the Father, the Son, and the Holy Spirit.
> Amen.

Intercede

Gracious God, who called out a people to be your body on earth, we pray for the one, holy, and universal Church. Fill it with all truth and peace. Where the Church is impure, purify it; where it is in error, correct it; and where in any way it is unpleasing to you, reform it. Where the Church is right, strengthen it; where it is in need, provide; and where it is divided, reunite it, for the greatness of your fame and the sake of Jesus Christ your Son, our Lord and Savior. Amen.[45]

The Lord's Prayer

BLESS

"God will bless us, and all the ends of the earth will fear him" (Psalm 67:7). Amen.

WEEK TWO

Shaped by God's Mission

Monday Prayer at Dawn

PREPARE

Take time to be quiet and still. Notice your breathing and slowly greet the new day. When you are ready, continue by praying:

> As the sun has risen today, we rise to you today; you are the one who never tires and never sleeps. Help us be alert to your presence, promises, and promptings as we meet the challenges and opportunities of this new day. Amen.

INVITE

The author of Genesis declares, "So God created man in his own image, in the image of God he created him; male and female he created them" (Genesis 1:27).

> God, we are grateful that we were made to reflect your image in all of creation. Thank you for making us in a manner so we can commune with you. We pray that you will meet with us this morning as we spend the next moments in prayer. Amen.

CONFESS

> Lord God, our rock and our refuge, help us in our weakness. Chase out of us all of the evil desires that drain us and strengthen our feet to walk in the way of your will and commands.
>
> May your grace and mercy triumph when our selfishness and willfulness to rule our decisions and choices surface. Empower us to live as your children in all of our actions and to conquer our sinful natures. Renew our faith. Show us your glorious face, that we might reflect your image as we were made to do. Amen.[1]

PSALM 143

> O LORD, hear my prayer,
> listen to my cry for mercy;
> in your faithfulness and righteousness
> come to my relief.
> Do not bring your servant into judgment,
> for no one living is righteous before you.
>
> The enemy pursues me,
> he crushes me to the ground;

he makes me dwell in darkness
like those long dead.
So my spirit grows faint within me;
my heart within me is dismayed.

I remember the days of long ago;
I meditate on all your works
and consider what your hands have done.
I spread out my hands to you;
my soul thirsts for you like a parched land.

Answer me quickly, O LORD;
my spirit fails.
Do not hide your face from me
or I will be like those who go down to the pit.
Let the morning bring me word of your unfailing love,
for I have put my trust in you.
Show me the way I should go,
for to you I lift up my soul.
Rescue me from my enemies, O LORD,
for I hide myself in you.
Teach me to do your will,
for you are my God;
may your good Spirit
lead me on level ground.

For your name's sake, O LORD, preserve my life;
in your righteousness, bring me out of trouble.
In your unfailing love, silence my enemies;
destroy all my foes,
for I am your servant.

Pause. Be quiet and reflect on the psalm. If necessary, read through it
again.

PRAISE

O Lord my God! When I in awesome wonder
consider all the worlds thy hands have made,
I see the stars, I hear the rolling thunder,
thy pow'r throughout the universe displayed.

And when I think that God his Son not sparing,
sent him to die, I scarce can take it in;

that on the cross, my burden gladly bearing,
he bled and died to take away my sin.

Then sings my soul, my Savior God to thee;
how great thou art, how great thou art!
Then sings my soul, my Savior God to thee;
how great thou art, how great thou art! Amen.[2]

DECLARE

With Paul we remember and declare,

Beyond all question, the mystery of godliness is great: He appeared in
a body, was vindicated by the Spirit, was seen by angels, was preached
among the nations, was believed on in the world, was taken up in
glory. (1 Timothy 3:16)

READ

As we approach God's message today, may this prayer direct us to view
ourselves in light of the reality and truth God reveals in the Scriptures:

Lord of creation, we were made to reflect your image throughout the
world, but we have fallen short of this purpose. We pray that as we approach the Bible this morning, you will mold and form us, restoring us
to our original identity and calling. Amen.

Slowly and prayerfully read today's selections as found in the Devotional
Lectionary and/or in one or more of the passages below:

Genesis 1
2 Corinthians 5:16-21
Matthew 21:28-44

Prompting: As you go throughout your day, ask God to help you love someone as Jesus loves. Be conscious of any individual to whom you can demonstrate a generous and unconditional love through serving, listening, or just being with that person. Then, faithfully and actively follow through by showing a genuine, selfless expression of God's love.

PRAY

Prayer of the Day

O God, you made us in your own image and redeemed us through Jesus your Son. Remember your whole human family with compassion. We pray that you will take away the arrogance and hatred that infect our hearts. Break down the walls that separate us and instead unite us, making us one as you God are one with the Holy Spirit and the Son. As we continue throughout this day, help us value all people we meet as image bearers and treat all people with respect and dignity. Keep us tenderhearted toward the image of God in each person who crosses our paths. For this we pray through Jesus Christ our Lord. Amen.[3]

The Lord's Prayer

Closing Prayer

Thank you, God, for bringing light into our darkness and making your love known to us. Guide us in your paths today and assist us in bearing your image to all we meet. May all of your creatures bless your name in your kingdom, where with your Son and the Holy Spirit you live and reign, now and forever. Amen.

BLESS

Then sings my soul, my Savior God to thee;
how great thou art, how great thou art!
Then sings my soul, my Savior God to thee;
how great thou art, how great thou art! Amen.[4]

Monday

Prayer at Daylight

PREPARE

Find a comfortable spot and take some moments to relax. Breathe. When you are still, focus your attention on God and pray:

> With the sun high in the sky, we are reminded that you are reigning over us. We thank you that you are our shade and rest from the labors of this day. Refresh us with your Holy Spirit that we can continue to serve you today. Amen.

REMEMBER

In a spirit of gratitude and repentance, review the past twenty-four hours. Ask God to help you become mindful of instances when you were aware of God's love and nearness and those times when you felt far from God. Remember that "when he, the Spirit of truth, comes, he will guide you into all truth" (John 16:13).

When you are ready, continue the remainder of the prayer.

CONFESS

> Merciful God, we admit that we need your help. We confess that we have wandered from the straight and narrow path; we have done wrong, and we have failed to do what is right. You alone can help and rescue us.

> Have mercy on us: wipe out our sins and teach us to forgive others. Produce in us the fruit of the Holy Spirit, that we may live as followers of Jesus. This we ask in the name of Jesus our Savior. Amen.

PSALM 146

> Praise the LORD.

> Praise the LORD, O my soul.
> I will praise the LORD all my life;
> I will sing praise to my God as long as I live.

> Do not put your trust in princes,
> in mortal men, who cannot save.
> When their spirit departs, they return to the ground;
> on that very day their plans come to nothing.

Blessed is he whose help is the God of Jacob,
whose hope is in the LORD his God,
the Maker of heaven and earth,
the sea, and everything in them—
the LORD, who remains faithful forever.
He upholds the cause of the oppressed
and gives food to the hungry.
The LORD sets prisoners free,
the LORD gives sight to the blind,
the LORD lifts up those who are bowed down,
the LORD loves the righteous.
The LORD watches over the alien
and sustains the fatherless and the widow,
but he frustrates the ways of the wicked.

The LORD reigns forever,
your God, O Zion, for all generations.

Praise the LORD.

Pause. Be quiet and reflect on the psalm. If necessary, read through it again.

PRAISE
Glory to God in the highest,
and on earth peace to the people of good will.
We praise you, maker of all.
We bless you, redeemer of sinners.
We adore you, Spirit sent to comfort.
We glorify you, three in one.
We are your people, the flock of your pasture.
We give thanks to you for your great glory. Amen.

STOP
Re-enter the quiet and keep a few moments of silence before God, recognizing his presence and his work in our midst.

COMMIT
Teach us, dear Lord, to number our days,
that we may apply our hearts to your wisdom.
Oh, satisfy us early with your mercy,
that we may rejoice and be glad all of our days.

And let the beauty of the Lord our God be upon us
and confirm the work of our hands.
And let the beauty of the Lord our God be upon us
and confirm the work of our hands, dear Lord. Amen.

PRAY

Prayer of the Day

O God, you made us in your own image and redeemed us through
Jesus your Son. Remember your whole human family with compassion.
We pray that you will take away the arrogance and hatred that infect
our hearts. Break down the walls that separate us and instead unite us,
making us one as you God are one with the Holy Spirit and the Son.
As we continue throughout this day, help us value all people we meet
as image bearers and treat all people with respect and dignity. Keep us
tenderhearted toward the image of God in each person who crosses our
paths. For this we pray through Jesus Christ our Lord. Amen.[5]

Closing Prayer

And let the beauty of the Lord our God be upon us
and confirm the work of our hands.
And let the beauty of the Lord our God be upon us
and confirm the work of our hands, dear Lord. Amen.

BLESS

We praise you, maker of all.
We bless you, redeemer of sinners.
We adore you, Spirit sent to comfort.
We glorify you, three in one. Amen.

PREPARE

Return to a quiet and still posture of heart, mind, and body. When you are in a place of readiness, pray:

> As another day comes to a close, help me keep it from being just another day and grow my love for you and for that which you have made, especially my neighbor. Amen.

PRAISE

> Another moon is up, another day is spent
> Don't let the sun go down on anger or dissent
> When we enter heaven as the Lord's own bride
> We will dance together, sanctified
>
> Don't put your brother down
> Don't wanna make your sister cry
> And when you look at me
> Please lend a gracious eye
> 'Cos we are all forgiven
> That's why Jesus died
> We will live forever, sanctified
> We're gonna live forever, sanctified[6]

PSALM 133

> How good and pleasant it is
> when brothers live together in unity!
> It is like precious oil poured on the head,
> running down on the beard,
> running down on Aaron's beard,
> down upon the collar of his robes.
> It is as if the dew of Hermon
> were falling on Mount Zion.
> For there the LORD bestows his blessing,
> even life forevermore.

Pause. Be quiet and reflect on the psalm. If necessary, read through it again.

CONFESS

Almighty God, maker of all things, judge of all people and nations, we admit and confess our many sins, which we have committed in thought, word, and action.

Pause now and remember and recount those sins that come to mind.

We sincerely repent and turn from our misdeeds. Have mercy on us, merciful God. For your Son our Lord Jesus Christ's sake, forgive us all that is past and come to our help that from now on we may serve and please you with lives that are renewed by your Holy Spirit, to the glory of your name. Amen.

DECLARE

One of the teachers of religious law was standing there listening to the debate. He realized that Jesus had answered well, so he asked, "Of all the commandments, which is the most important?"

Jesus replied, "The most important commandment is this: 'Listen, O Israel! The LORD our God is the one and only LORD. And you must love the LORD your God with all your heart, all your soul, all your mind, and all your strength.' The second is equally important: 'Love your neighbor as yourself.' No other commandment is greater than these." (Mark 12:28-31, NLT)

READ

As we open the Bible, we pray:

Lord of creation, we were made to reflect your image throughout the world, but we have fallen short of this purpose. We pray that as we approach the Bible this evening, you will mold us and form us, restoring us to our original identity and calling. Amen.

Slowly and prayerfully read today's selections as found in the Devotional Lectionary and/or in one or more of the passages below:

Ezekiel 37:1-14
1 Peter 2:1-10
Matthew 12:46-50

PRAY

Prayer of the Day

O God, you made us in your own image and redeemed us through Jesus your Son. Remember your whole human family with compassion. We pray that you will take away the arrogance and hatred that infect our hearts. Break down the walls that separate us and instead unite us, making us one as you God are one with the Holy Spirit and the Son. As we continue throughout this day, help us value all people we meet as image bearers and treat all people with respect and dignity. Keep us tenderhearted toward the image of God in each person who crosses our paths. For this we pray through Jesus Christ our Lord. Amen.[7]

Intercede

Reflect on the events of today and remember people with whom you interacted or those you particularly noticed. As each one comes to mind, pray for them in your own words or use the simple prayer below.

God, in whose image we have been created,
circle around [person's name];
encompass [him/her] with your presence that [he/she] may trust you more. Amen.

The Lord's Prayer

BLESS

God created man in his own image, in the image of God he created them. (Genesis 1:27)

We bless you and declare that our maker is greatly to be praised, for he has made us, pursued us, loved us, and restored us. Amen.

Tuesday **Prayer at Dawn**

PREPARE

Take time to be quiet and still. Notice your breathing and slowly greet the new day. When you are ready, continue by praying:

God of love, as we open our eyes to a new day, may we view this world through the lens of your beloved Son, our king and Lord. Amen.

INVITE

This is my Son, whom I love; with him I am well pleased. Listen to him! (Matthew 17:5)

Great God, who spoke from the cloud, as you have throughout history continue to reveal your will and way, and give us ears that hear today. Amen.

CONFESS

Eternal and good God, in whom we live and move and have our being, we admit that we forget your mercy and become blinded to your love for us as your beloved children. Forgive us for our forgetfulness and for all the ways we offend you. Make us clean. With whole hearts may we draw near to you, confessing the truth about ourselves and committing ourselves to your grace, that we may pursue your good way through Jesus Christ, your Son. Amen.

PSALM 8

O Lord, our Lord,
how majestic is your name in all the earth!

You have set your glory
above the heavens.
From the lips of children and infants
you have ordained praise
because of your enemies,
to silence the foe and the avenger.

When I consider your heavens,
the work of your fingers,
the moon and the stars,
which you have set in place,
what is man that you are mindful of him,

the son of man that you care for him?
You made him a little lower than the heavenly beings
and crowned him with glory and honor.

You made him ruler over the works of your hands;
you put everything under his feet:
all flocks and herds,
and the beasts of the field,
the birds of the air,
and the fish of the sea,
all that swim the paths of the seas.

O Lord, our Lord,
how majestic is your name in all the earth!

Pause. Be quiet and reflect on the psalm. If necessary, read through it again.

PRAISE

All people that on earth do dwell,
sing to the Lord with cheerful voice.
Him serve with fear, his praise forth tell;
come ye before him and rejoice.

The Lord, ye know, is God indeed;
without our aid he did us make;
we are his flock, he doth us feed,
and for his sheep he doth us take.

O enter then his gates with praise;
approach with joy his courts unto;
praise, laud, and bless his name always,
for it is seemly so to do.[8]

DECLARE

With the apostle Paul we affirm our faith by declaring that "yet for us there is but one God, the Father, from whom all things came and for whom we live; and there is but one Lord, Jesus Christ, through whom all things came and through whom we live" (1 Corinthians 8:6).

READ

As we approach God's message today, may this prayer help us refresh our understanding of our identity and calling:

Lord, again we pray, give us ears to hear today. Help us listen to and obey your beloved Son, Jesus, in whose name we pray. Amen.

Slowly and prayerfully read today's selections as found in the Devotional Lectionary and/or in one or more of the passages below:

Deuteronomy 33:12
Ephesians 1:3-14
Matthew 3:13-17

PRAY

Prayer of the Day

God of the beloved, you chose and took your Son, blessed and broke him that he might be given to redeem and restore the people of the earth. May we follow your beloved Son's path as your beloved children, pleased to be taken, blessed, and broken to be given for your cause.

God of Abraham, Isaac, and Jacob, show your love to us by choosing us as your own unique people; help us claim this reality into which you have taken us and accept us as part of your family. Today may we trust you to support and uphold us as your chosen children.

God the living word, show your love to us by blessing us and speaking well about us, telling the truth about who we are and how you have made us. Help us listen to your voice today and hear the blessing of your words spoken over us.

Loving maker who disciplines his children, show your love to us by breaking us that we might turn from our stubbornness and willfulness and instead live depending on you under your blessing. Help us stop hiding our brokenness as a curse that causes bitterness and instead befriend it as a gift that moves us toward you.

Father who sent his Son and the Holy Spirit, show your love to us by giving us to the needs, hurts, and concerns of others. Help us see that it is only as we are given to others that our chosen-ness, blessedness, and brokenness are ultimately lived to their fullest significance. May we live as the beloved today—living for the sake of those who have not yet accepted their beloved-ness. Amen.[9]

The Lord's Prayer

Closing Prayer

Almighty Lord, amid the grandeur of your creation, you sought us out. In the coming of your Son, you adorned us with glory and honor, raising us in him above the heavens. Enable us to care for the earth that all creation may radiate the splendor of your Son, Jesus Christ our Lord. Amen.[10]

BLESS

To Father, Son, and Holy Ghost,
the God whom heaven and earth adore,
from men and from the angel host
be praise and glory evermore.[11]

Tuesday

PREPARE

Find a comfortable spot and take some moments to relax and breathe. When you are still, focus your attention on God and pray:

> God of love, as we continue throughout this day, may we see and serve our world through the strength, compassion, and love of your beloved Son, our king and Lord. Amen.

REMEMBER

In a spirit of gratitude and repentance, review the past twenty-four hours. Ask God to help you become mindful of moments when you sensed you were "most alive." Now think of those times when you were allowing the curse of sin to reign in your life. Remember that "when he, the Spirit of truth, comes, he will guide you into all truth" (John 16:13).

When you are ready, continue the remainder of the prayer.

CONFESS

> Merciful God, we admit that we need your help. We confess that we have wandered from the straight and narrow path; we have done wrong, and we have failed to do what is right. You alone can help and rescue us.

> Have mercy on us: wipe out our sins and teach us to forgive others. Produce in us the fruit of the Holy Spirit, that we may live as followers of Jesus. This we ask in the name of Jesus our Savior. Amen.

PSALM 126

> When the Lord brought back the captives to Zion,
> we were like men who dreamed.
> Our mouths were filled with laughter,
> our tongues with songs of joy.
> Then it was said among the nations,
> "The Lord has done great things for them."
> The Lord has done great things for us,
> and we are filled with joy.
> Restore our fortunes, O Lord,
> like streams in the Negev.
> Those who sow in tears

will reap with songs of joy.
He who goes out weeping,
carrying seed to sow,
will return with songs of joy,
carrying sheaves with him.

Pause. Be quiet and reflect on the psalm. If necessary, read through it again.

PRAISE

Arise, my soul, arise! Shake off the guilty fears;
the bleeding sacrifice in my behalf appears.
Before the throne my surety stands;
my name is written on his hands,
my name is written on his hands.

The Father hears him pray, his dear anointed one;
he cannot turn away the presence of his Son:
his Spirit answers to the blood,
and tells me I am born of God,
and tells me I am born of God. Amen.[12]

We praise you for choosing us as your own and revealing to us that we are your beloved children, born from above. May we live to please and praise your great name. Amen.

STOP

Re-enter the quiet and keep a few moments of silence before God, recognizing his presence and his work in our midst.

COMMIT

Teach us, dear Lord, to number our days,
that we may apply our hearts to your wisdom.
Oh, satisfy us early with your mercy,
that we may rejoice and be glad all of our days.
And let the beauty of the Lord our God be upon us
and confirm the work of our hands.
And let the beauty of the Lord our God be upon us
and confirm the work of our hands, dear Lord. Amen.

PRAY

Prayer of the Day

God of the beloved, you chose and took your Son, blessed and broke him that he might be given to redeem and restore the people of the earth. May we follow your beloved Son's path as your beloved children, pleased to be taken, blessed, and broken to be given for your cause.

God of Abraham, Isaac, and Jacob, show your love to us by choosing us as your own unique people; help us claim this reality into which you have taken us and accept us as part of your family. Today may we trust you to support and uphold us as your chosen children.

God the living word, show your love to us by blessing us and speaking well about us, telling the truth about who we are and how you have made us. Help us listen to your voice today and hear the blessing of your words spoken over us.

Loving maker who disciplines his children, show your love to us by breaking us that we might turn from our stubbornness and willful-ness and instead live depending on you under your blessing. Help us stop hiding our brokenness as a curse that causes bitterness and instead befriend it as a gift that moves us toward you.

Father who sent his Son and the Holy Spirit, show your love to us by giving us to the needs, hurts, and concerns of others. Help us see that it is only as we are given to others that our chosen-ness, blessedness, and brokenness are ultimately lived to their fullest significance. May we live as the beloved today—living for the sake of those who have not yet accepted their beloved-ness. Amen.[13]

Closing Prayer

And let the beauty of the Lord our God be upon us
and confirm the work of our hands.
And let the beauty of the Lord our God be upon us
and confirm the work of our hands, dear Lord. Amen.

BLESS

My God is reconciled, his pard'ning voice I hear;
he owns me for his child, I can no longer fear;
with confidence I now draw nigh,
and "Father, Abba, Father" cry,
and "Father, Abba, Father" cry.[14]

PREPARE

Return to a quiet and still posture of heart, mind, and body. When you are in a place of readiness, pray:

> God of love, as the sun is setting at the close of day, may we love one another through the strength, compassion, and love of your beloved Son, our king and Lord. Amen.

PRAISE

> Loved with everlasting love, led by grace that love to know;
> gracious Spirit from above, thou hast taught me it is so!
> O this full and perfect peace! O this transport all divine!
> In a love which cannot cease, I am his, and he is mine.

> Things that once were wild alarms cannot now disturb my rest;
> closed in everlasting arms, pillowed on the loving breast.
> O to lie forever here, doubt and care and self resign,
> while he whispers in my ear, I am his, and he is mine.[15]

PSALM 131

> My heart is not proud, O Lord,
> my eyes are not haughty;
> I do not concern myself with great matters
> or things too wonderful for me.
> But I have stilled and quieted my soul;
> like a weaned child with its mother,
> like a weaned child is my soul within me.

> O Israel, put your hope in the Lord
> both now and forevermore.

Pause. Be quiet and reflect on the psalm. If necessary, read through it again.

CONFESS

> Almighty God, maker of all things, judge of all people and nations, we admit and confess our many sins, which we have committed in thought, word, and action.

Pause now and remember and recount those sins that come to mind.

We sincerely repent and turn from our misdeeds. Have mercy on us, merciful God. For your Son our Lord Jesus Christ's sake, forgive us all that is past and come to our help that from now on we may serve and please you with lives that are renewed by your Holy Spirit, to the glory of your name. Amen.

DECLARE

One of the teachers of religious law was standing there listening to the debate. He realized that Jesus had answered well, so he asked, "Of all the commandments, which is the most important?"

Jesus replied, "The most important commandment is this: 'Listen, O Israel! The LORD our God is the one and only LORD. And you must love the LORD your God with all your heart, all your soul, all your mind, and all your strength.' The second is equally important: 'Love your neighbor as yourself.' No other commandment is greater than these." (Mark 12:28-31, NLT)

READ

As we open the Bible, we pray:

Lord, again we pray, give us ears to hear and help us listen to and obey your beloved Son, Jesus, in whose name we pray. Amen.

Slowly and prayerfully read today's selections as found in the Devotional Lectionary and/or in one or more of the passages below:

Hosea 2
Romans 5:1-11
Matthew 17:1-11

PRAY

Prayer of the Day

God of the beloved, you chose and took your Son, blessed and broke him that he might be given to redeem and restore the people of the earth. May we follow your beloved Son's path as your beloved children, pleased to be taken, blessed, and broken to be given for your cause.

God of Abraham, Isaac, and Jacob, show your love to us by choosing us as your own unique people; help us claim this reality into which you have taken us and accept us as part of your family. Today may we trust you to support and uphold us as your chosen children.

God the living word, show your love to us by blessing us and speaking well about us, telling the truth about who we are and how you have made us. Help us listen to your voice today and hear the blessing of your words spoken over us.

Loving maker who disciplines his children, show your love to us by breaking us that we might turn from our stubbornness and willfulness and instead live depending on you under your blessing. Help us stop hiding our brokenness as a curse that causes bitterness and instead befriend it as a gift that moves us toward you.

Father who sent his Son and the Holy Spirit, show your love to us by giving us to the needs, hurts, and concerns of others. Help us see that it is only as we are given to others that our chosen-ness, blessedness, and brokenness are ultimately lived to their fullest significance.[16]

Intercede

Grant us, Jesus, that tender, indestructible love which asks forgiveness for its executioners and gives hope to the thief on the cross. Keep us compassionate when the way is hard and gentle with all who oppose us.[17]

In this spirit, pray for your enemies. Ask God to show them mercy and to help you demonstrate an indestructible love toward them. When you are ready, pray:

Gentle God, give us, we pray, a mind forgetful of past injury, a will to seek the good of others, and a heart of love. Amen.[18]

The Lord's Prayer

BLESS

We place our hope in the Lord, both now and forevermore. Amen.

Wednesday   Prayer at Dawn

PREPARE

Take time to be quiet and still. Notice your breathing and slowly greet the new day. When you are ready, continue by praying:

> We worship you for the beauty of a new day and join with all of creation proclaiming you are God, the maker and sustainer of all things.

INVITE

> O Lord, what a variety of things you have made!
> In wisdom you have made them all.
> The earth is full of your creatures.
> (Psalm 104:24, NLT)

> Hear our prayers today. Be honored by our words, be pleased with our thoughts, and prosper the works of our hands that we might partner with you in caring for all you have made. Amen.

CONFESS

In light of God's act of creation and our being placed in the garden to care for and steward all that was made, reflect on our failings to fulfill our purpose and reflect the glory of our Creator. When you are ready, continue by praying:

> Almighty and most merciful God, we have strayed from your path like lost sheep. We have left undone what we should have done, and we have done that which we should not have done. We have followed after our own ways and the desires of our own hearts. We have broken your holy laws and neglected the good works, which you have assigned us in caring for all that you made. Good Lord, have mercy on us; restore each of us who is truly penitent, according to your promises declared to us in Jesus Christ our Lord.

> And grant, merciful Father, for Jesus' sake, that we may live a godly and obedient life, to the glory of your holy name. Amen.

PSALM 96

Sing to the LORD a new song;
sing to the LORD, all the earth.
Sing to the LORD, praise his name;
proclaim his salvation day after day.
Declare his glory among the nations,
his marvelous deeds among all peoples.

For great is the LORD and most worthy of praise;
he is to be feared above all gods.
For all the gods of the nations are idols,
but the LORD made the heavens.
Splendor and majesty are before him;
strength and glory are in his sanctuary.

Ascribe to the LORD, O families of nations,
ascribe to the LORD glory and strength.
Ascribe to the LORD the glory due his name;
bring an offering and come into his courts.
Worship the LORD in the splendor of his holiness;
tremble before him, all the earth.

Say among the nations, "The LORD reigns."
The world is firmly established, it cannot be moved;
he will judge the peoples with equity.
Let the heavens rejoice, let the earth be glad;
let the sea resound, and all that is in it;
let the fields be jubilant, and everything in them.
Then all the trees of the forest will sing for joy;
they will sing before the LORD, for he comes,
he comes to judge the earth.
He will judge the world in righteousness
and the peoples in his truth.

Pause. Be quiet and reflect on the psalm. If necessary, read through it again.

PRAISE

Fairest Lord Jesus, ruler of all nature,
O thou of God and man the Son,
thee will I cherish, thee will I honor,
thou, my soul's glory, joy, and crown.

Fair are the meadows, fairer still the woodlands,
robed in the blooming garb of spring;
Jesus is fairer, Jesus is purer,
who makes the woeful heart to sing.

All fairest beauty, heavenly and earthly,
wondrously, Jesus, is found in thee;
none can be nearer, fairer, or dearer,
than thou, my Savior, art to me.[19]

DECLARE
We believe that:

apart from God, no one is holy. Holy people are set apart for God's purpose in the world. Empowered by the Holy Spirit, holy people live and love like Jesus Christ. Holiness is both gift and response, renewing and transforming, personal and communal, ethical and missional. The holy people of God follow Jesus Christ in engaging all the cultures of the world and drawing all peoples to God.

Holy people are not legalistic or judgmental. They do not pursue an exclusive, private state of being better than others. Holiness is not flawlessness but the fulfillment of God's intention for us. The pursuit of holiness can never cease because love can never be exhausted.

God wants us to be, think, speak, and act in the world in a Christ-like manner. We invite all to embrace God's call to:

be filled with all the fullness of God in Jesus Christ—Holy Spirit-endowed co-workers for the reign of God;

live lives that are devout, pure, and reconciled, thereby being Jesus Christ's agents of transformation in the world;

live as a faithful covenant people, building accountable community, growing up into Jesus Christ, embodying the spirit of God's law in holy love;

exercise for the common good an effective array of ministries and callings, according to the diversity of the gifts of the Holy Spirit;

practice compassionate ministries, solidarity with the poor, advocacy for equality, justice, reconciliation, and peace;

care for the earth, God's gift in trust to us, working in faith, hope, and confidence for the healing and care of all creation.

By the grace of God, let us covenant together to be a holy people.[20]

READ

As we approach God's message today, we pray:

Lord our Father, each morning you welcome us as we are; give us a heart that is pure and free, to receive your Word, and discover in our brothers and sisters the message of life that you bring us, through Jesus, the Christ, our Lord. Amen.[21]

Slowly and prayerfully read today's selections as found in the Devotional Lectionary and/or in one or more of the passages below:

Ruth 2
Colossians 3:12-17
Matthew 6:1-4

Prompting: As you move about today, take note of God's grace and creative fingerprints in the midst of nature. Spend time contemplating what you notice in our world and what it might reveal about God as the maker of everything. Allow these thoughts to prompt you to praise: take time to care for our world as well by picking up litter, tending a garden, or volunteering at an animal shelter.

PRAY

Prayer of the Day

God Almighty, our Creator and caretaker, our curer and coming king, you alone are our source, our salvation, and our future satisfaction! Today we pray that our hearts will be full of praise and gratitude and kept far from greed and a sense of privilege. As we go through this day, move us toward you and draw from us an offering of praise.

There is no plant in the ground but tells of your beauty, O Christ.

There is no creature on the sea but proclaims your goodness.

There is no bird on the wing, there is no star in the sky, there is nothing beneath the sun but is full of your blessing.

Lighten our understanding of your presence all around, O Christ.

Quicken our will to be caring for creation, today and each day, we pray for the sake of the mission, name, and glory of the one true God. Amen.[22]

The Lord's Prayer

Closing Prayer

Lord Jesus, the word made flesh when you consented to dwell with us, the heavens were glad and the earth rejoiced. With hope and love we await your return.

Help us partner with your work and will in caring for all of creation—earth, water, sky, creature, and each human being—until the whole earth sings a new song of praise to you and the Father and the Holy Spirit, one God, now and forever. Amen.[23]

BLESS

Beautiful Savior! Lord of all the nations!
Son of God and Son of man!
Glory and honor, praise, adoration,
now and forevermore be thine.[24]

PREPARE

Find a comfortable spot and take some moments to relax and breathe. When you are still, focus your attention on God and pray:

> We worship you for the beauty of this day, in which we can partner with your will, work, and way. We join with all you have made, proclaiming you are God, the maker and sustainer of all things. Amen.

REMEMBER

In a spirit of gratitude and repentance, review the past twenty-four hours. Ask God to help you become mindful of events for which you are thankful and also for those things for which you need to seek repentance, remembering that "when he, the Spirit of truth, comes, he will guide you into all truth" (John 16:13).

When you are ready, continue the remainder of the prayer.

CONFESS

> Merciful God, we admit that we need your help. We confess that we have wandered from the straight and narrow path; we have done wrong, and we have failed to do what is right. You alone can help and rescue us.

> Have mercy on us: wipe out our sins and teach us to forgive others. Produce in us the fruit of the Holy Spirit, that we may live as followers of Jesus. This we ask in the name of Jesus our Savior. Amen.

PSALM 84

> How lovely is your dwelling place,
> O Lord Almighty!
> My soul yearns, even faints,
> for the courts of the Lord;
> my heart and my flesh cry out
> for the living God.

> Even the sparrow has found a home,
> and the swallow a nest for herself,
> where she may have her young—
> a place near your altar,
> O Lord Almighty, my King and my God.

Blessed are those who dwell in your house;
they are ever praising you.

Blessed are those whose strength is in you,
who have set their hearts on pilgrimage.
As they pass through the Valley of Baca,
they make it a place of springs;
the autumn rains also cover it with pools.
They go from strength to strength,
till each appears before God in Zion.

Hear my prayer, O Lord God Almighty;
listen to me, O God of Jacob.
Look upon our shield, O God;
look with favor on your anointed one.

Better is one day in your courts
than a thousand elsewhere;
I would rather be a doorkeeper in the house of my God
than dwell in the tents of the wicked.
For the Lord God is a sun and shield;
the Lord bestows favor and honor;
no good thing does he withhold
from those whose walk is blameless.

O Lord Almighty,
blessed is the man who trusts in you.

Pause. Be quiet and reflect on the psalm. If necessary, read through it
again.

PRAISE

God of the earth, the sky, the sea,
maker of all above, below,
creation lives and moves in thee,
thy present life through all doth flow.

Thy love is in the sunshine's glow,
thy life is in the quickening air;
when lightning flashes and storm winds blow,
there is thy power; thy law is there.[25]

We join with all you have made, proclaiming you are God, the maker
and sustainer of all things, and we praise you. Amen.

STOP

Re-enter the quiet and keep a few moments of silence before God, recognizing his presence and his work in our midst.

COMMIT

Teach us, dear Lord, to number our days,
that we may apply our hearts to your wisdom.
Oh, satisfy us early with your mercy,
that we may rejoice and be glad all of our days.
And let the beauty of the Lord our God be upon us
and confirm the work of our hands.
And let the beauty of the Lord our God be upon us
and confirm the work of our hands, dear Lord. Amen.

PRAY

Prayer of the Day

God Almighty, our Creator and caretaker, our curer and coming king,
you alone are our source, our salvation, and our future satisfaction!
Today we pray that our hearts will be full of praise and gratitude and
kept far from greed and a sense of privilege. As we go through this day,
move us toward you and draw from us an offering of praise.

There is no plant in the ground but tells of your beauty, O Christ.

There is no creature on the sea but proclaims your goodness.

There is no bird on the wing, there is no star in the sky, there is
nothing beneath the sun but is full of your blessing.

Lighten our understanding of your presence all around, O Christ.

Quicken our will to be caring for creation, today and each day, we
pray, for the sake of the mission, name, and glory of the one true
God. Amen.[26]

Closing Prayer

And let the beauty of the Lord our God be upon us
and confirm the work of our hands.
And let the beauty of the Lord our God be upon us
and confirm the work of our hands, dear Lord. Amen.

BLESS

But higher far, and far more clear,
thee in man's spirit we behold;
thine image and thyself are there,
th'indwelling God, proclaimed of old.[27]

May we bless thee, by being a blessing to all you have made today, God of all. Amen.

Wednesday Prayer at Dusk

PREPARE

Return to a quiet and still posture of heart, mind, and body. When you are in a place of readiness, pray:

At the close of day, we worship you for the beauty of being in your presence and surrounded by all you have made. We join with your creation, proclaiming you are God, the maker and sustainer of all things. Amen.

PRAISE

We bend our knee
in the eye of the God who created us
in the eye of the Son who died for us
in the eye of the Spirit who moves us
in love and in desire.
For the many gifts you have bestowed on us
each day and night
each sea and land
each weather fair
each calm, each wild
thanks be to you, O God.[28]

PSALM 65

Praise awaits you, O God, in Zion;
to you our vows will be fulfilled.
O you who hear prayer,
to you all men will come.
When we were overwhelmed by sins,
you forgave our transgressions.
Blessed are those you choose
and bring near to live in your courts!
We are filled with the good things of your house,
of your holy temple.

You answer us with awesome deeds of righteousness,
O God our Savior,
the hope of all the ends of the earth
and of the farthest seas,
who formed the mountains by your power,

having armed yourself with strength,
who stilled the roaring of the seas,
the roaring of their waves,
and the turmoil of the nations.
Those living far away fear your wonders;
where morning dawns and evening fades
you call forth songs of joy.

You care for the land and water it;
you enrich it abundantly.
The streams of God are filled with water
to provide the people with grain,
for so you have ordained it.
You drench its furrows
and level its ridges;
you soften it with showers
and bless its crops.
You crown the year with your bounty,
and your carts overflow with abundance.
The grasslands of the desert overflow;
the hills are clothed with gladness.
The meadows are covered with flocks
and the valleys are mantled with grain;
they shout for joy and sing.

Pause. Be quiet and reflect on the psalm. If necessary, read through it again.

CONFESS

Almighty God, maker of all things, judge of all people and nations, we admit and confess our many sins, which we have committed in thought, word, and action.

Pause now and remember and recount those sins that come to mind.

We sincerely repent and turn from our misdeeds. Have mercy on us, merciful God. For your Son our Lord Jesus Christ's sake, forgive us all that is past and come to our help that from now on we may serve and please you with lives that are renewed by your Holy Spirit, to the glory of your name. Amen.

DECLARE

One of the teachers of religious law was standing there listening to the debate. He realized that Jesus had answered well, so he asked, "Of all the commandments, which is the most important?"

Jesus replied, "The most important commandment is this: 'Listen, O Israel! The Lord our God is the one and only Lord. And you must love the Lord your God with all your heart, all your soul, all your mind, and all your strength.' The second is equally important: 'Love your neighbor as yourself.' No other commandment is greater than these." (Mark 12:28-31, NLT)

READ

As we open the Bible, we pray:

Guide me, O thou great Jehovah,
pilgrim through this barren land.
I am weak, but thou art mighty,
hold me with thy powerful hand.
Bread of heaven, bread of heaven,
feed me till I want no more;
feed me till I want no more.[29]

Slowly and prayerfully read today's selections as found in the Devotional Lectionary and/or in one or more of the passages below:

Leviticus 19:1-18
Romans 13:8-10
Matthew 5:43-48

PRAY

Prayer of the Day

God Almighty, our Creator and caretaker, our curer and coming king, you alone are our source, our salvation, and our future satisfaction! Today we pray that our hearts will be full of praise and gratitude and kept far from greed and a sense of privilege. As we go through this day, move us toward you and draw from us an offering of praise.

There is no plant in the ground but tells of your beauty, O Christ.

There is no creature on the sea but proclaims your goodness.

There is no bird on the wing, there is no star in the sky, there is nothing beneath the sun but is full of your blessing.

Lighten our understanding of your presence all around, O Christ.

Quicken our will to be caring for creation, today and each day, we pray for the sake of the mission, name, and glory of the one true God. Amen.[30]

Intercede

Our only God and maker, in giving us dominion over things on earth, you made us your fellow workers in creation: give us wisdom and reverence to care for and make use of all you have made, that no one may suffer from our abuse of nature and that generations yet to come may continue to praise you for your bounty, through Jesus Christ our Lord. Amen.[31]

The Lord's Prayer

BLESS

We bend our knee
in the eye of the God who created us
in the eye of the Son who died for us
in the eye of the Spirit who moves us
in love and in desire.[32]

PREPARE

Take time to be quiet and still. Notice your breathing and slowly greet the new day. When you are ready, continue by praying:

"Holy, holy, holy
is the Lord God Almighty,
who was, and is, and is to come. . . .

"You are worthy . . . to receive glory and honor and power" (Revelation 4:8, 11).

We praise you. Amen.

INVITE

Then he called the crowd to him along with his disciples and said: "If anyone would come after me, he must deny himself and take up his cross and follow me." (Mark 8:34)

Great teacher, we thank you for the grace that allows us to be called your disciples. Today we pray that you might fill us with your power and strength so we might follow you closely and faithfully. Amen.

CONFESS

Almighty and most merciful God, we have strayed from your path like lost sheep. We have left undone what we should have done, and we have done that which we should not have done. We have called ourselves "Christians" and "Christ followers" but too often have been following our own ways. We have misrepresented you by being vengeful rather than merciful, impatient, lacking in compassion, and overly concerned with what others think about us.

Good Lord, have mercy on us; restore each of us who is truly penitent, according to your promises declared to us in Jesus Christ, our Lord.

And grant, merciful Father, for Jesus' sake, that we may live as faithful followers of you, to the glory of your holy name. Amen.

PSALM 1

Blessed is the man
who does not walk in the counsel of the wicked
or stand in the way of sinners
or sit in the seat of mockers.
But his delight is in the law of the LORD,
and on his law he meditates day and night.
He is like a tree planted by streams of water,
which yields its fruit in season
and whose leaf does not wither.
Whatever he does prospers.

Not so the wicked!
They are like chaff
that the wind blows away.
Therefore the wicked will not stand in the judgment,
nor sinners in the assembly of the righteous.

For the LORD watches over the way of the righteous,
but the way of the wicked will perish.

Pause. Be quiet and reflect on the psalm. If necessary, read through it again.

PRAISE

Our God, who sent us a leader to follow and a teacher to form us, we join in praising you that Jesus has made it possible to live as your children and obey your calling.

With one voice we praise you, God of all, that through Jesus:

his worthiness makes us worthy;
his sinlessness covers our transgressions;
his purity transforms our uncleanliness;
his sincerity replaces our masks;
his truth corrects our deceit;
his love banishes our hate;
his faithfulness converts our treason;
his devotedness overcomes our waywardness;
his holiness overshadows our imperfection;
his death gives us life and life in you, O God!

We praise you for all you have done to restore us to our place of purpose in creation—to bear your image amid all you have made. We praise you for your Son, our teacher, who has made a way for us to join you in your work! Amen.

DECLARE

When Jesus came to the region of Caesarea Philippi, he asked his disciples, "Who do people say the Son of Man is?"

They replied, "Some say John the Baptist; others say Elijah; and still others, Jeremiah or one of the prophets."

"But what about you?" he asked. "Who do you say I am?"

Simon Peter answered, "You are the Christ, the Son of the living God." (Matthew 16:13-16)

READ

As we approach God's message today, may this prayer help us value with greater devotion the revelation of Scripture and the one it reveals.

God of heaven, you sent your Son, Jesus, to reveal your character and your calling to us. May we desire to listen and to obey your words; may we faithfully reflect their truth as we grow as your devoted disciples. Amen.

Slowly and prayerfully read today's selections as found in the Devotional Lectionary and/or in one or more of the passages below:

Deuteronomy 8
Ephesians 4:17-32
Matthew 4:18-25

PRAY

Prayer of the Day

We pray with the apostle Paul today for the deepening of the roots and the widening of the embrace of your Church, Lord. We kneel before the God from whom every person in heaven and on earth derives his or her name. We thank you for our earthly family into which we have been born, but we are also grateful that you have invited us to follow you as disciples and have adopted us into your heavenly family as your children.

We ask that out of your abundant riches and by the power of your Holy Spirit, your Church and her individual members might be strengthened to better represent you here on earth. Through your power may our faith grow and our trust deepen so that we can more immediately rely upon and follow faithfully the head of the Church, Jesus, and know that he resides in our hearts.

We ask that the example of your Son, Jesus, and the privilege of being his disciple would draw us to grow roots deeply planted in your love that we might follow after him in faithfulness and with joy. Help us take in the amazing and mind-boggling expanse of Christ's love, experiencing its breadth, attempting to come to the end of its length, plumbing its depths, and rising to its heights! Surrounded and encased in such love, may we know to the core of our being the security, life, and richness of such love. Help us lavishly share this love with all we meet today.

Filled with your power to follow after you and with your love to share, let us faithfully go forward demonstrating the living God to our communities and world. Amen.[33]

The Lord's Prayer

Closing Prayer

Our Lord and our God, in your loving wisdom you have set us beside the fountain of life, like a tree planted by living streams. We ask that we might grow as your disciples to faithfully bear the cross of your Son in this world and that many would find in it a tree of life. Let your kingdom come, we ask in Jesus' name. Amen.

BLESS

Now to him who is able to do immeasurably more than all we ask or imagine, according to his power that is at work within us, to him be glory in the church and in Christ Jesus throughout all generations, for ever and ever! Amen. (Ephesians 3:20-21)

PREPARE

Find a comfortable spot and take some moments to relax and breathe. When you are still, focus your attention on God and pray:

One and only God of all, your Son invited us,

Come to me, all you who are weary and burdened, and I will give you rest. Take my yoke upon you and learn from me, for I am gentle and humble in heart, and you will find rest for your souls. For my yoke is easy and my burden is light. (Matthew 11:28-30)

We pray that we might faithfully follow after you, diligently and joyfully bearing the easy yoke and light burden of being disciples and friends of your Son and our Savior, Jesus the Christ, in whose name we pray. Amen.

REMEMBER

In a spirit of gratitude and repentance, review the past twenty-four hours. Ask God to help you become mindful of those times you followed Christ on the narrow path. Now recount your day and remember instances when you left the narrow path for the way that is broad and leads to destruction, remembering that "when he, the Spirit of truth, comes, he will guide you into all truth" (John 16:13).

When you are ready, continue the remainder of the prayer.

CONFESS

Merciful God, we admit that we need your help. We confess that we have wandered from the straight and narrow path; we have done wrong, and we have failed to do what is right. You alone can help and rescue us.

Have mercy on us: wipe out our sins and teach us to forgive others. Produce in us the fruit of the Holy Spirit, that we may live as followers of Jesus. This we ask in the name of Jesus our Savior. Amen.

PSALM 16

Keep me safe, O God,
for in you I take refuge.

I said to the LORD, "You are my Lord;
apart from you I have no good thing."
As for the saints who are in the land,
they are the glorious ones in whom is all my delight.
The sorrows of those will increase
who run after other gods.
I will not pour out their libations of blood
or take up their names on my lips.

LORD, you have assigned me my portion and my cup;
you have made my lot secure.
The boundary lines have fallen for me in pleasant places;
surely I have a delightful inheritance.

I will praise the LORD, who counsels me;
even at night my heart instructs me.
I have set the LORD always before me.
Because he is at my right hand,
I will not be shaken.

Therefore my heart is glad and my tongue rejoices;
my body also will rest secure,
because you will not abandon me to the grave,
nor will you let your Holy One see decay.
You have made known to me the path of life;
you will fill me with joy in your presence,
with eternal pleasures at your right hand.

Pause. Be quiet and reflect on the psalm. If necessary, read through it again.

PRAISE

Savior, teach me, day by day, thine own lesson to obey;
better lesson cannot be, loving him who first loved me.

With a child's glad heart of love at thy bidding may I move;
prompt to serve and follow thee, loving him who first loved me.

Teach me thus thy steps to trace, strong to follow in thy grace,
learning how to love from thee, loving him who first loved me.

Thus may I rejoice to show that I feel the love I owe;
singing, till thy face I see, of his love who first loved me.[34]

We rejoice in the privilege of bearing your love and following you
wherever you may lead. We praise you, God, that we might be called
disciples and friends of the one who loved us first. Amen.

STOP

Re-enter the quiet and keep a few moments of silence before God, recognizing his presence and his work in our midst.

COMMIT

Teach us, dear Lord, to number our days,
that we may apply our hearts to your wisdom.
Oh, satisfy us early with your mercy,
that we may rejoice and be glad all of our days.
And let the beauty of the Lord our God be upon us
and confirm the work of our hands.
And let the beauty of the Lord our God be upon us
and confirm the work of our hands, dear Lord. Amen.

PRAY

Prayer of the Day

We pray with the apostle Paul today for the deepening of the roots and the widening of the embrace of your Church, Lord. We kneel before the God from whom every person in heaven and on earth derives his or her name. We thank you for our earthly family into which we have been born, but we are also grateful that you have invited us to follow you as disciples and have adopted us into your heavenly family as your children.

We ask that out of your abundant riches and by the power of your Holy Spirit, your Church and her individual members might be strengthened to better represent you here on earth. Through your power may our faith grow and our trust deepen so that we can more immediately rely upon and follow faithfully the head of the Church, Jesus, and know that he resides in our hearts.

We ask that the example of your Son, Jesus, and the privilege of being his disciple would draw us to grow roots deeply planted in your love that we might follow after him in faithfulness and with joy. Help us take in the amazing and mind-boggling expanse of Christ's love, experiencing its breadth, attempting to come to the end of its length, plumbing its depths, and rising to its heights! Surrounded and encased in such love, may we know to the core of our being the security, life, and richness of such love. Help us lavishly share this love with all we meet today.

Filled with your power to follow after you and with your love to share, let us faithfully go forward demonstrating the living God to our communities and world. Amen.[35]

Closing Prayer

And let the beauty of the Lord our God be upon us
and confirm the work of our hands.
And let the beauty of the Lord our God be upon us
and confirm the work of our hands, dear Lord. Amen.

BLESS

Now to him who is able to do immeasurably more than all we ask or imagine, according to his power that is at work within us, to him be glory in the church and in Christ Jesus throughout all generations, for ever and ever! Amen. (Ephesians 3:20-21)

Thursday **Prayer at Dusk**

PREPARE

Return to a quiet and still posture of heart, mind, and body. When you are in a place of readiness, pray:

> Holy, holy, holy
> is the Lord God Almighty,
> who was, and is, and is to come. (Revelation 4:8)

PRAISE

> Praise, my soul, the King of heaven;
> to his feet thy tribute bring.
> Ransomed, healed, restored, forgiven,
> evermore his praises sing.
> Alleluia! Alleluia! Praise the everlasting King.
>
> Praise him for his grace and favor
> to our fathers in distress.
> Praise him still the same as ever,
> slow to chide, and swift to bless.
> Alleluia! Alleluia! Glorious in his faithfulness.
>
> Fatherlike he tends and spares us;
> well our feeble frame he knows.
> In his hands he gently bears us,
> rescues us from all our foes.
> Alleluia! Alleluia! Widely yet his mercy flows.
>
> Frail as summer's flower we flourish,
> blows the wind and it is gone;
> but while mortals rise and perish
> our God lives unchanging on.
> Praise him! Praise him! Hallelujah! Praise the high eternal One!
>
> Angels, help us to adore him;
> ye behold him face to face;
> sun and moon, bow down before him,
> dwellers all in time and space.
> Alleluia! Alleluia! Praise with us the God of grace.[36]

PSALM 92

It is good to praise the LORD
and make music to your name, O Most High,
to proclaim your love in the morning
and your faithfulness at night,
to the music of the ten-stringed lyre
and the melody of the harp.

For you make me glad by your deeds, O LORD;
I sing for joy at the works of your hands.
How great are your works, O LORD,
how profound your thoughts!
The senseless man does not know,
fools do not understand,
that though the wicked spring up like grass
and all evildoers flourish,
they will be forever destroyed.

But you, O LORD, are exalted forever.

For surely your enemies, O LORD,
surely your enemies will perish;
all evildoers will be scattered.
You have exalted my horn like that of a wild ox;
fine oils have been poured upon me.
My eyes have seen the defeat of my adversaries;
my ears have heard the rout of my wicked foes.

The righteous will flourish like a palm tree,
they will grow like a cedar of Lebanon;
planted in the house of the LORD,
they will flourish in the courts of our God.
They will still bear fruit in old age,
they will stay fresh and green,
proclaiming, "The LORD is upright;
he is my Rock, and there is no wickedness in him."

Pause. Be quiet and reflect on the psalm. If necessary, read through it
again.

CONFESS

Almighty God, maker of all things, judge of all people and nations, we admit and confess our many sins, which we have committed in thought, word, and action.

Pause now and remember and recount those sins that come to mind.

We sincerely repent and turn from our misdeeds. Have mercy on us, merciful God. For your Son our Lord Jesus Christ's sake, forgive us all that is past and come to our help that from now on we may serve and please you with lives that are renewed by your Holy Spirit, to the glory of your name. Amen.

DECLARE

One of the teachers of religious law was standing there listening to the debate. He realized that Jesus had answered well, so he asked, "Of all the commandments, which is the most important?"

Jesus replied, "The most important commandment is this: 'Listen, O Israel! The Lord our God is the one and only Lord. And you must love the Lord your God with all your heart, all your soul, all your mind, and all your strength.' The second is equally important: 'Love your neighbor as yourself.' No other commandment is greater than these." (Mark 12:28-31, NLT)

READ

As we open the Bible, we pray,

God of heaven you sent your Son, Jesus, to reveal your character and your calling to us. May we desire to listen and obey your words and may we faithfully reflect its truth as we grow as your devoted disciples. Amen.

Slowly and prayerfully read today's selections as found in the Devotional Lectionary and/or in one or more of the passages below:

Micah 6:1-8
1 Corinthians 1:10-31
Matthew 9:9-13

PRAY

Prayer of the Day

We pray with the apostle Paul today for the deepening of the roots and the widening of the embrace of your Church, Lord. We kneel before the God from whom every person in heaven and on earth derives his or her name. We thank you for our earthly family into which we have been born, but we are also grateful that you have invited us to follow you as disciples and have adopted us into your heavenly family as your children.

We ask that out of your abundant riches and by the power of your Holy Spirit, your Church and her individual members might be strengthened to better represent you here on earth. Through your power may our faith grow and our trust deepen so that we can more immediately rely upon and follow faithfully the head of the Church, Jesus, and know that he resides in our hearts.

We ask that the example of your Son, Jesus, and the privilege of being his disciple would draw us to grow roots deeply planted in your love that we might follow after him in faithfulness and with joy. Help us take in the amazing and mind-boggling expanse of Christ's love, experiencing its breadth, attempting to come to the end of its length, plumbing its depths, and rising to its heights! Surrounded and encased in such love, may we know to the core of our being the security, life, and richness of such love. Help us lavishly share this love with all we meet today.

Filled with your power to follow after you and with your love to share, let us faithfully go forward demonstrating the living God to our communities and world. Amen.[37]

Intercede

O gracious and holy Father,
give us wisdom to perceive you,
intelligence to understand you,
diligence to seek you,
patience to wait for you,
eyes to behold you,
a heart to meditate upon you,
and a life to proclaim you,
through the power of the Spirit of our Lord Jesus Christ. Amen.[38]

The Lord's Prayer

BLESS

Now to him who is able to do immeasurably more than all we ask or imagine, according to his power that is at work within us, to him be glory in the church and in Christ Jesus throughout all generations, for ever and ever! Amen. (Ephesians 3:20-21)

PREPARE

Take time to be quiet and still. Notice your breathing and slowly greet the new day. When you are ready, continue by praying:

O Lord, open my lips that my mouth may declare your praise.
O God, make speed to save us. O Lord, make haste to help us.

INVITE

Now that we have actually received this amazing friendship with God, we are no longer content to simply say it in plodding prose. We sing and shout our praises to God through Jesus, the Messiah! (Romans 5:11, TM)

Friend of saints and sinners, take pleasure in our offering of prayer and praise this morning! We are profoundly grateful to be included in your circle of friends. Amen.

CONFESS

Most merciful God, we confess that we have sinned against you in thought, word, and deed by what we have done and by what we have left undone. We have not loved you with our whole heart; we have not loved our neighbors as ourselves. We are truly sorry and we humbly repent. For the sake of your Son Jesus Christ, have mercy on us and forgive us, that we may delight in your will and walk in your ways to the glory of your name. Amen.[39]

PSALM 5

Give ear to my words, O LORD,
consider my sighing.
Listen to my cry for help,
my King and my God,
for to you I pray.
In the morning, O LORD, you hear my voice;
in the morning I lay my requests before you
and wait in expectation.

You are not a God who takes pleasure in evil;
with you the wicked cannot dwell.
The arrogant cannot stand in your presence;
you hate all who do wrong.
You destroy those who tell lies;
bloodthirsty and deceitful men
the LORD abhors.

But I, by your great mercy,
will come into your house;
in reverence will I bow down
toward your holy temple.
Lead me, O LORD, in your righteousness
because of my enemies—
make straight your way before me.

Not a word from their mouth can be trusted;
their heart is filled with destruction.
Their throat is an open grave;
with their tongue they speak deceit.
Declare them guilty, O God!
Let their intrigues be their downfall.
Banish them for their many sins,
for they have rebelled against you.

But let all who take refuge in you be glad;
let them ever sing for joy.
Spread your protection over them,
that those who love your name may rejoice in you.
For surely, O LORD, you bless the righteous;
you surround them with your favor as with a shield.

Pause. Be quiet and reflect on the psalm. If necessary, read through it again.

PRAISE

I am thine, O Lord, I have heard thy voice, and it told thy love to me;
but I long to rise in the arms of faith, and be closer drawn to thee.

Consecrate me now to thy service, Lord, by the power of grace divine;
let my soul look up with a steadfast hope, and my will be lost in thine.

Draw me nearer, nearer, blessed Lord, to the cross where thou hast died;
draw me nearer, nearer, nearer, blessed Lord, to thy precious, bleeding side.

O the pure delight of a single hour that before thy throne I spend, when I kneel in prayer, and with thee, my God, I commune as friend with friend!

There are depths of love that I cannot know till I cross the narrow sea; there are heights of joy that I may not reach till I rest in peace with thee.

Draw me nearer, nearer, blessed Lord, to the cross where thou hast died; draw me nearer, nearer, nearer, blessed Lord, to thy precious, bleeding side. Amen.[40]

DECLARE

We believe in:

One God, the Father, by whom are all things, and we in him;

And one Lord Jesus Christ, through whom are all things, and we through him; who was manifested in the flesh, justified in the spirit, seen of angels, preached among the nations, believed on in the world, received up into glory;

And one Spirit of truth, proceeding from the Father, bearing witness of Christ, guiding us into all truth, declaring unto us the things that are to come, bearing witness with our spirit that we are the children of God, having fruit in all goodness, righteousness, and truth.[41]

READ

As we approach God's message today, may this prayer help us see with fresh and new vision:

Dear God and lover of our souls, we ask that as we come to read and understand the revelation found in the Christian Scriptures, we will demonstrate our love for you not only by knowing your commands, but also by obeying them. May our friendship with Jesus deepen and may our devotion be evident to all we meet today. Amen.

Slowly and prayerfully read today's selections as found in the Devotional Lectionary and/or in one or more of the passages below:

Exodus 33:7-11
John 15:1-17
James 1:19-27

PRAY

Prayer of the Day

Our God who calls us friends, we come this morning with an offering of praise because you invite us to be a part of your family and to enter into friendship with you. We praise you and worship you because you do not forget us though we are unworthy sinners. We thank you that you deem us worthy of your love and not only tell us of your love but demonstrated it by sending your very own Son to us that he might show us your love.

Jesus revealed your love in word, in compassionate acts, in his way with people, and ultimately in his willingness to walk toward Jerusalem and die on a cross as a sinless sacrifice for our guilt. We know we neither desire nor deserve this honor, but because you pursued us and made a way, we can now enter into this unmerited, unparalleled relationship. Help us rest in this place of being completely known and, despite this, completely loved and regarded as close friends.

This day may we live as ones who are friends of God. Help us be marked by the love, mercy, compassion, patience, faithfulness, and truth that marked your Son, our Savior and friend, Jesus. May we walk in humility as he walked, speak the truth in love as he modeled, and live as he did—friend of saints and sinners. May we be known today as friends of God. Amen.

The Lord's Prayer

Closing Prayer

Holy Lord and friend of sinners, all good things come from your hand and all that is wrong will be made right under your reign. Today help us reflect mercy and justice with all the people we meet. Help us extend mercy to the weak and burdened and bring justice and truth to places where inequity and wrongs have gone unchallenged. We ask that we might be filled with your wisdom, strength, and grace as we approach and live out this new day in front of us. Amen.

BLESS

O the pure delight of a single hour that before thy throne I spend, when I kneel in prayer, and with thee, my God, I commune as friend with friend![42]

PREPARE

Find a comfortable spot and take a few moments to relax. Breathe. When you are still, focus your attention on God and pray:

> Thank you for moments of stillness; in this time of quiet may we be more aware of your friendship, God, and may we have a greater trust and confidence in your love, concern, care, provision, power, and plan. Amen.

Take a few more moments to be quiet and listen for God's voice as you trust in his attentiveness toward his children.

REMEMBER

In a spirit of gratitude and repentance, review the past twenty-four hours. Ask God to help you become mindful of times you have been known as a friend of God. Take time to thank God for those times. In the same way, reflect on those times when you have failed to live up to the calling to be a friend of God. Remember that "when he, the Spirit of truth, comes, he will guide you into all truth" (John 16:13).

When you are ready, continue the remainder of the prayer.

CONFESS

> Merciful God, we admit that we need your help. We confess that we have wandered from the straight and narrow path; we have done wrong, and we have failed to do what is right. You alone can help and rescue us.

> Have mercy on us: wipe out our sins and teach us to forgive others. Produce in us the fruit of the Holy Spirit, that we may live as followers of Jesus. This we ask in the name of Jesus our Savior. Amen.

PSALM 14

> The fool says in his heart,
> "There is no God."
> They are corrupt, their deeds are vile;
> there is no one who does good.
> The Lord looks down from heaven
> on the sons of men
> to see if there are any who understand,

any who seek God.
All have turned aside,
they have together become corrupt;
there is no one who does good,
not even one.

Will evildoers never learn—
those who devour my people as men eat bread
and who do not call on the LORD?
There they are, overwhelmed with dread,
for God is present in the company of the righteous.
You evildoers frustrate the plans of the poor,
but the LORD is their refuge.

Oh, that salvation for Israel would come out of Zion!
When the LORD restores the fortunes of his people,
let Jacob rejoice and Israel be glad!

Pause. Be quiet and reflect on the psalm. If necessary, read through it
again.

PRAISE

Jesus! What a friend for sinners!
Jesus! Lover of my soul;
friends may fail me, foes assail me,
he, my Savior, makes me whole.

Hallelujah! What a Savior!
Hallelujah! What a friend!
Saving, helping, keeping, loving,
he is with me to the end.[43]

STOP

Re-enter the quiet and keep a few moments of silence before God, recognizing his presence and his work in our midst.

COMMIT

Blessed Savior, at this hour you hung upon the cross, stretching out
your willing arms. Grant that all the peoples of the earth may look to
you and be saved.

Let us join with you and extend your embrace, reflecting your love,
truth, mercy, joy, and compassion to all we meet today. Amen.

Prompting: As you continue throughout this day, ask God to assist you in listening more than speaking, understanding more than being understood, and being a true friend who freely gives rather than befriending for what you can gain. Try putting this exercise into practice today by speaking less and really listening to others when they speak to you. Don't try to formulate answers or think about what you are going to say until you first take time to listen closely to what others are saying with their words and actions. Keep your ears open to the voices of your friends today.

PRAY

Prayer of the Day

Our God who calls us friends, we come this morning with an offering of praise because you invite us to be a part of your family and to enter into friendship with you. We praise you and worship you because you do not forget us though we are unworthy sinners. We thank you that you deem us worthy of your love and not only tell us of your love but demonstrated it by sending your very own Son to us that he might show us your love.

Jesus revealed your love in word, in compassionate acts, in his way with people, and ultimately in his willingness to walk toward Jerusalem and die on a cross as a sinless sacrifice for our guilt. We know we neither desire nor deserve this honor, but because you pursued us and made a way, we can now enter into this unmerited, unparalleled relationship. Help us rest in this place of being completely known and, despite this, completely loved and regarded as close friends.

This day may we live as ones who are friends of God. Help us be marked by the love, mercy, compassion, patience, faithfulness, and truth that marked your Son, our Savior and friend, Jesus. May we walk in humility as he walked, speak the truth in love as he modeled, and live as he did—friend of saints and sinners. May we be known today as friends of God. Amen.

Closing Prayer

God of wisdom and truth, without you neither truth nor holiness can survive. Show your mighty presence among us, and make us glad in proclaiming your deliverance in Jesus Christ our Lord. Amen.[44]

BLESS

Hallelujah! What a Savior!
Hallelujah! What a friend!
Saving, helping, keeping, loving,
he is with me to the end.[45]

PREPARE

Return to a quiet and still posture of heart, mind, and body. When you are in a place of readiness, pray:

Father, at the end of another day, we gratefully acknowledge our need for your help and your hand of provision. We offer these prayers, petitions, and praises admitting our gratitude, our dependence, and our faith in you. Hear our prayer. Amen.

PRAISE

Jesus! What a strength in weakness!
Let me hide myself in him.
Tempted, tried, and sometimes failing,
he, my strength, my victory wins.

Jesus! I do now adore him,
more than all in him I find.
He hath granted me forgiveness,
I am his, and he is mine.

Hallelujah! What a savior!
Hallelujah! What a friend!
Saving, helping, keeping, loving,
he is with me to the end.[46]

PSALM 141

O Lord, I call to you; come quickly to me.
Hear my voice when I call to you.
May my prayer be set before you like incense;
may the lifting up of my hands be like the evening sacrifice.

Set a guard over my mouth, O Lord;
keep watch over the door of my lips.
Let not my heart be drawn to what is evil,
to take part in wicked deeds
with men who are evildoers;
let me not eat of their delicacies.

Let a righteous man strike me—it is a kindness;
let him rebuke me—it is oil on my head.
My head will not refuse it.

Yet my prayer is ever against the deeds of evildoers;
their rulers will be thrown down from the cliffs,
and the wicked will learn that my words were well spoken.
They will say, "As one plows and breaks up the earth,
so our bones have been scattered at the mouth of the grave."

But my eyes are fixed on you, O Sovereign LORD;
in you I take refuge—do not give me over to death.
Keep me from the snares they have laid for me,
from the traps set by evildoers.
Let the wicked fall into their own nets,
while I pass by in safety.

Pause. Be quiet and reflect on the psalm. If necessary, read through it again.

CONFESS

Almighty God, maker of all things, judge of all people and nations, we admit and confess our many sins, which we have committed in thought, word, and action.

Pause now and remember and recount those sins that come to mind.

We sincerely repent and turn from our misdeeds. Have mercy on us, merciful God. For your Son our Lord Jesus Christ's sake, forgive us all that is past and come to our help that from now on we may serve and please you with lives that are renewed by your Holy Spirit, to the glory of your name. Amen.

DECLARE

One of the teachers of religious law was standing there listening to the debate. He realized that Jesus had answered well, so he asked, "Of all the commandments, which is the most important?"

Jesus replied, "The most important commandment is this: 'Listen, O Israel! The Lord our God is the one and only Lord. And you must love the Lord your God with all your heart, all your soul, all your mind, and all your strength.' The second is equally important: 'Love your neighbor as yourself.' No other commandment is greater than these." (Mark 12:28-31, NLT)

READ

As we open the Bible, we pray,

> Dear God and lover of our souls, we ask that as we come to read and understand the revelation found in the Christian Scriptures, we will demonstrate our love for you not only by knowing your commands, but also by obeying them. May our friendship with Jesus deepen and may our devotion be evident to all we meet today. Amen.

Slowly and prayerfully read today's selections as found in the Devotional Lectionary and/or in one or more of the passages below:

Joshua 1:1-9
1 John 4:7-21
Luke 10:38-41

PRAY

Prayer of the Day

> Our God who calls us friends, we come this morning with an offering of praise because you invite us to be a part of your family and to enter into friendship with you. We praise you and worship you because you do not forget us though we are unworthy sinners. We thank you that you deem us worthy of your love and not only tell us of your love but demonstrated it by sending your very own Son to us that he might show us your love.

> Jesus revealed your love in word, in compassionate acts, in his way with people, and ultimately in his willingness to walk toward Jerusalem and die on a cross as a sinless sacrifice for our guilt. We know we neither desire nor deserve this honor, but because you pursued us and made a way, we can now enter into this unmerited, unparalleled relationship. Help us rest in this place of being completely known and, despite this, completely loved and regarded as close friends.

> This day may we live as ones who are friends of God. Help us be marked by the love, mercy, compassion, patience, faithfulness, and truth that marked your Son, our Savior and friend, Jesus. May we walk in humility as he walked, speak the truth in love as he modeled, and live as he did—friend of saints and sinners. May we be known today as friends of God. Amen.

Intercede

Take a few moments and focus on friends, praying for their needs, their relationships, and their futures. Next, ask God to bring to mind friends who are hurting or whom you have hurt; pray for these friends. Pray that God would allow you to be a friend who helps bring healing and hope back into their lives. Finally, pray for those you know who are distant from God; pray that you might be a partner with God in helping your friends see God in a new light and with fresh insight.

The Lord's Prayer

BLESS

Hallelujah! What a Savior!
Hallelujah! What a friend!
Saving, helping, keeping, loving,
he is with me to the end.[47]

PREPARE

Take time to be quiet and still. Notice your breathing and slowly greet the new day. When you are ready, continue by praying:

In the name of the Father of all, in the name of the Son who came, lived, died, and rose, and in the name of the Spirit who empowers the Church. Amen.

INVITE

You will receive power when the Holy Spirit comes on you; and you will be my witnesses in Jerusalem, and in all Judea and Samaria, and to the ends of the earth. (Acts 1:8)

Thank you, Father, for including us in your mission of restoring all you have made. We pray that we might be filled afresh with your Spirit so our lives may witness to the reality of your love for all you have made and that we might reliably relay your invitation for all to be a part of the family of God. In the name of the Father, Son, and Holy Spirit. Amen.

CONFESS

Eternal and good God, in whom we live and move and have our being, we admit that we forget your mercy and by our sin we become blinded to you and your gifts. We confess that we take for granted your loving pursuit of us and too easily fail to remember your active presence in our lives made possible by your Son, Jesus. Forgive us our evil deeds and all of our ways that offend you. Now with whole hearts may we again draw near to you, committing ourselves to your grace and your good works, through Jesus Christ, your Son. Amen.

PSALM 20

May the LORD answer you when you are in distress;
may the name of the God of Jacob protect you.
May he send you help from the sanctuary
and grant you support from Zion.
May he remember all your sacrifices
and accept your burnt offerings.
May he give you the desire of your heart
and make all your plans succeed.

We will shout for joy when you are victorious
and will lift up our banners in the name of our God.
May the LORD grant all your requests.

Now I know that the LORD saves his anointed;
he answers him from his holy heaven
with the saving power of his right hand.
Some trust in chariots and some in horses,
but we trust in the name of the LORD our God.
They are brought to their knees and fall,
but we rise up and stand firm.

O LORD, save the king!
Answer us when we call!

Pause. Be quiet and reflect on the psalm. If necessary, read through it
again.

PRAISE

Tell me the story of Jesus, write on my heart every word;
tell me the story most precious, sweetest that ever was heard.
Tell how the angels in chorus sang as they welcomed his birth,
"Glory to God in the highest! Peace and good tidings to earth."

Fasting alone in the desert, tell of the days that are past,
how for our sins he was tempted, yet was triumphant at last.
Tell of the years of his labor, tell of the sorrow he bore,
he was despised and afflicted, homeless, rejected and poor.

Tell of the cross where they nailed him, writhing in anguish and pain;
tell of the grave where they laid him, tell how he liveth again.
Love in that story so tender, clearer than ever I see:
stay, let me weep while you whisper, love paid the ransom for me.[48]

We praise you, God, for this story that restores us; we are blessed that
we might be a blessing by sharing with others how love has paid our
ransom. Amen.

DECLARE

We affirm that Christ sends his redeemed people into the world as the Father sent him, and that this calls for a similar deep and costly penetration of the world. We need to break out of our ecclesiastical ghettos and permeate non-Christian society. In the Church's mission of sacrificial service evangelism is primary. World evangelization requires the whole Church to take the whole gospel to the whole world. The Church is at the very center of God's cosmic purpose and is his appointed means of spreading the gospel. But a church which preaches the cross must itself be marked by the cross. It becomes a stumbling block to evangelism when it betrays the gospel or lacks a living faith in God, a genuine love for people, or scrupulous honesty in all things including promotion and finance. The church is the community of God's people rather than an institution, and must not be identified with any particular culture, social or political system, or human ideology.[49]

READ

As we approach God's message today, may this prayer help us see with fresh and new vision:

Almighty God, may we read and mark in the Holy Scriptures the tale of your loving purposes—from the beginning of our disobedience, to the promise of your restoration, to the coming of your holy child, who made it possible to become your adopted daughters and sons. Soften our hearts and minds to hear afresh these words; help us honor them in our words, actions, and attitudes. Amen.

Slowly and prayerfully read today's selections as found in the Devotional Lectionary and/or in one or more of the passages below:

Exodus 3
1 Thessalonians 1:2-10
John 3:5-21

PRAY

Prayer of the Day

Good and gracious eternal God, we pray this morning that we might share your story of love and restoration with all those we meet. Since we sinned with Adam and Eve, you have been pursuing us and preparing a way for us to be your image once again among creation. Your love for us moved you to send your very own Son to be among us and ultimately to die on our behalf.

By hanging on a cross, your Son, our savior, declared to us your unmatched love and your willingness to forgive. Beside him hung a thief, beneath him waited Mary the forgiven, and all around watched so many people to whom you gave hope and a chance for forgiveness and restoration.

To us you are a restored life and hope. As forgiven sinners, we become your body and a part of your Church, joining the mission of restoring your creation to its intended purpose. May this hope and this story we now embody bring your good news to all the world.

Eternal God, by your power we are created and by your love we are redeemed and restored; guide and strengthen us by your Spirit, that we may give ourselves to your service and live this day loving you and each other.

Jesus, you knew rejection and disappointment. Help and empower us if our work seems distasteful or if a task seems too demanding; help us decide what best to do, what next to do, or what to do at all. Give us courage and cheerfulness to go the second mile and all the miles ahead as your followers and witnesses. Amen.[50]

The Lord's Prayer

Closing Prayer

Lord God, you accepted the perfect sacrifice of your Son upon the cross. Hear us during the times of trouble and protect us by the power of his name, that we who share his struggle on earth may share in his victory in the life to come, where he lives and reigns with you and the Holy Spirit, one God, now and forever. Amen.[51]

BLESS

To God the Father, who first loved us, and made us acceptable in the beloved Son;

To God the Son, who loved us and washed us from our sins in his own blood;

To God the Holy Spirit, who sheds abroad the love of God in our hearts;

To the one true God be all love and all glory for time and eternity. Amen.[52]

Saturday

PREPARE

Find a comfortable spot and take some moments to relax. Breathe. When you are still, focus your attention on God and pray:

> In the name of the Father of all, in the name of the Son who came, lived, died and rose, and in the name of the Spirit who empowers the Church. Amen.

REMEMBER

In a spirit of gratitude and repentance, review the past twenty-four hours. Ask God to help you become mindful of moments when you were living in harmony with God and God's plan to restore all of creation. Then ask God to reveal those times when you were more focused on your own agenda rather than on God's mission of restoration. Remember that "when he, the Spirit of truth, comes, he will guide you into all truth" (John 16:13).

When you are ready, continue the remainder of the prayer.

CONFESS

> Merciful God, we admit that we need your help. We confess that we have wandered from the straight and narrow path; we have done wrong, and we have failed to do what is right. You alone can help and rescue us.

> Have mercy on us: wipe out our sins and teach us to forgive others. Produce in us the fruit of the Holy Spirit, that we may live as followers of Jesus. This we ask in the name of Jesus our Savior. Amen.

PSALM 51:10-19

> Create in me a pure heart, O God,
> and renew a steadfast spirit within me.
> Do not cast me from your presence
> or take your Holy Spirit from me.
> Restore to me the joy of your salvation
> and grant me a willing spirit, to sustain me.

> Then I will teach transgressors your ways,
> and sinners will turn back to you.
> Save me from bloodguilt, O God,

the God who saves me,
and my tongue will sing of your righteousness.
O Lord, open my lips,
and my mouth will declare your praise.
You do not delight in sacrifice, or I would bring it;
you do not take pleasure in burnt offerings.
The sacrifices of God are a broken spirit;
a broken and contrite heart,
O God, you will not despise.

In your good pleasure make Zion prosper;
build up the walls of Jerusalem.
Then there will be righteous sacrifices,
whole burnt offerings to delight you;
then bulls will be offered on your altar.

Pause. Be quiet and reflect on the psalm. If necessary, read through it again.

PRAISE

I love to tell the story of unseen things above,
of Jesus and his glory, of Jesus and his love.
I love to tell the story, because I know 'tis true;
it satisfies my longings as nothing else can do.

I love to tell the story, 'twill be my theme in glory,
to tell the old, old story of Jesus and his love.
I love to tell the story; 'tis pleasant to repeat
what seems, each time I tell it, more wonderfully sweet.
I love to tell the story, for some have never heard
the message of salvation from God's own Holy Word.[53]

STOP

Re-enter the quiet and keep a few moments of silence before God, recognizing his presence and his work in our midst.

COMMIT

Teach us, dear Lord, to number our days,
that we may apply our hearts to your wisdom.
Oh, satisfy us early with your mercy,
that we may rejoice and be glad all of our days.
And let the beauty of the Lord our God be upon us
and confirm the work of our hands.
And let the beauty of the Lord our God be upon us
and confirm the work of our hands, dear Lord. Amen.

PRAY

Prayer of the Day

Good and gracious eternal God, we pray this afternoon that we might share your story of love and restoration with all those we meet. Since we sinned with Adam and Eve, you have been pursuing us and preparing a way for us to be your image once again among creation. Your love for us moved you to send your very own Son to be among us and ultimately to die on our behalf.

By hanging on a cross, your Son, our savior, declared to us your unmatched love and your willingness to forgive. Beside him hung a thief, beneath him waited Mary the forgiven, and all around watched so many people to whom you gave hope and a chance for forgiveness and restoration.

To us you are a restored life and hope. As forgiven sinners, we become your body and a part of your Church, joining the mission of restoring your creation to its intended purpose. May this hope and this story we now embody bring your good news to all the world.

Eternal God, by your power we are created and by your love we are redeemed and restored; guide and strengthen us by your Spirit, that we may give ourselves to your service and live this day loving you and each other.

Jesus, you knew rejection and disappointment. Help and empower us if our work seems distasteful or if a task seems too demanding; help us decide what best to do, what next to do, or what to do at all. Give us courage and cheerfulness to go the second mile and all the miles ahead as your followers and witnesses. Amen.[54]

Closing Prayer

And let the beauty of the Lord our God be upon us
and confirm the work of our hands.
And let the beauty of the Lord our God be upon us
and confirm the work of our hands, dear Lord. Amen.

BLESS

Glory to the Father, and to the Son, and to the Holy Spirit: as it was in
the beginning, is now, and will be for ever. Amen.[55]

Saturday Prayer at Dusk

PREPARE

Return to a quiet and still posture of heart, mind, and body. When you are in a place of readiness, pray:

> Thank you, Father, for including us in your mission of restoring all you have made. We pray that we might be filled afresh with your Spirit so our lives may witness to the reality of your love for all you have made and that we might reliably relay your invitation for all to be a part of the family of God. In the name of the Father, Son, and Holy Spirit. Amen.

PRAISE

> Who is he in yonder stall, at whose feet the shepherds fall?
> Who is he in deep distress, fasting in the wilderness?
>
> Who is he the people bless for his words of gentleness?
> Who is he to whom they bring all the sick and sorrowing?
>
> Who is he that stands and weeps at the grave where Lazarus sleeps?
> Who is he the gath'ring throng greet with loud triumphant song?
>
> Lo! at midnight, who is he prays in dark Gethsemane?
> Who is he on yonder tree dies in grief and agony?
>
> Who is he that from the grave comes to heal and help and save?
> Who is he that from his throne rules through all the world alone?
>
> 'Tis the Lord! O wondrous story!
> 'Tis the Lord! The King of glory!
> At his feet we humbly fall,
> crown Him! Crown him, Lord of all![56]

PSALM 107:1-16

> Give thanks to the LORD, for he is good;
> his love endures forever.
> Let the redeemed of the LORD say this—
> those he redeemed from the hand of the foe,
> those he gathered from the lands,
> from east and west, from north and south.

Some wandered in desert wastelands,
finding no way to a city where they could settle.
They were hungry and thirsty,
and their lives ebbed away.
Then they cried out to the LORD in their trouble,
and he delivered them from their distress.
He led them by a straight way
to a city where they could settle.
Let them give thanks to the LORD for his unfailing love
and his wonderful deeds for men,
for he satisfies the thirsty
and fills the hungry with good things.

Some sat in darkness and the deepest gloom,
prisoners suffering in iron chains,
for they had rebelled against the words of God
and despised the counsel of the Most High.
So he subjected them to bitter labor;
they stumbled, and there was no one to help.
Then they cried to the LORD in their trouble,
and he saved them from their distress.
He brought them out of darkness and the deepest gloom
and broke away their chains.
Let them give thanks to the LORD for his unfailing love
and his wonderful deeds for men,
for he breaks down gates of bronze
and cuts through bars of iron.

Pause. Be quiet and reflect on the psalm. If necessary, read through it again.

CONFESS

Almighty God, maker of all things, judge of all people and nations, we admit and confess our many sins, which we have committed in thought, word, and action.

Pause now and remember and recount those sins that come to mind.

We sincerely repent and turn from our misdeeds. Have mercy on us, merciful God. For your Son our Lord Jesus Christ's sake, forgive us all that is past and come to our help that from now on we may serve and please you with lives that are renewed by your Holy Spirit, to the glory of your name. Amen.

DECLARE

One of the teachers of religious law was standing there listening to the debate. He realized that Jesus had answered well, so he asked, "Of all the commandments, which is the most important?"

Jesus replied, "The most important commandment is this: 'Listen, O Israel! The Lord our God is the one and only Lord. And you must love the Lord your God with all your heart, all your soul, all your mind, and all your strength.' The second is equally important: 'Love your neighbor as yourself.' No other commandment is greater than these." (Mark 12:28-31, NLT)

READ

As we open the Bible, we pray,

Almighty God, may we read and mark in the Holy Scriptures the tale of your loving purposes—from the beginning of our disobedience, to the promise of your restoration, to the coming of your holy child, who made it possible to become your adopted daughters and sons. Soften our hearts and minds to hear afresh these words; help us honor them in our words, actions, and attitudes. Amen.

Slowly and prayerfully read today's selections as found in the Devotional Lectionary and/or in one or more of the passages below:

Jonah 3
Romans 10:5-15
Matthew 5:1-16

PRAY

Prayer of the Day

Good and gracious eternal God, we pray this evening that we might share your story of love and restoration with all those we meet. Since we sinned with Adam and Eve, you have been pursuing us and preparing a way for us to be your image once again among creation. Your love for us moved you to send your very own Son to be among us and ultimately to die on our behalf.

By hanging on a cross, your Son, our savior, declared to us your unmatched love and your willingness to forgive. Beside him hung a thief, beneath him waited Mary the forgiven, and all around watched so many people to whom you gave hope and a chance for forgiveness and restoration.

To us you are a restored life and hope. As forgiven sinners, we become your body and a part of your Church, joining the mission of restoring your creation to its intended purpose. May this hope and this story we now embody bring your good news to all the world.

Eternal God, by your power we are created and by your love we are redeemed and restored; guide and strengthen us by your Spirit, that we may give ourselves to your service and live this day loving you and each other.

Jesus, you knew rejection and disappointment. Help and empower us if our work seems distasteful or if a task seems too demanding; help us decide what best to do, what next to do, or what to do at all. Give us courage and cheerfulness to go the second mile and all the miles ahead as your followers and witnesses. Amen.[57]

Intercede

God of heaven and earth, your desire is for not one to perish but for all to come into a relationship that restores us to our intended purpose. May you bring new life to our churches so they may hear afresh your heart and be infused by your Holy Spirit to act in accordance with your will and way.

God, may I surrender my good ideas and plans to you and by your strength and grace participate instead in your plans; may I share in your mission by faithfully declaring with my words, actions, and attitudes your radical love and transforming truth.

In your own words, share with God your fears and your desire to be a trustworthy witness of what you have seen and heard God doing in your midst to those people who are a part of your life.

The Lord's Prayer

BLESS

To God the Father, who first loved us, and made us acceptable in the beloved Son;

To God the Son, who loved us and washed us from our sins in his own blood;

To God the Holy Spirit, who sheds abroad the love of God in our hearts;

To the one true God be all love and all glory for time and eternity. Amen.[58]

Sunday Prayer at Dawn

PREPARE

Take time to be quiet and still. Notice your breathing and slowly greet the new day. When you are ready, continue by praying:

Each of the four living creatures had six wings and was covered with eyes all around, even under his wings. Day and night they never stop saying:

"Holy, holy, holy
is the Lord God Almighty,
who was, and is, and is to come." (Revelation 4:8)

With the creatures of heaven, we join in declaring that you alone are God and there is no one like you in all of heaven or earth. We praise you and bow before you today. Amen.

INVITE

Our Lord and our God, who has opened the way for us to be recipients of your grace and extended an invitation to participate in your mission of restoration, we invite you to receive the offering of our prayers as we begin this day. In your mercy hear our prayers. Amen.

CONFESS

Maker and Messiah, we recognize your hand has both made us and made a way for us to return to you. We are your workmanship, created for good works that will continue to reveal your kingdom reign. Yet in our everyday lives we have been more concerned with our own passions and pursuits, our own dreams and desires. We confess that we have sinned against you by putting our will above your perfect will.

Pause here and name specific ways you have offended God.

God, change our minds and mold our lives that we might again chase your heart and handiwork. Shape our lives and fill us with your Spirit that we might be your willing servants. Thank you, gracious and good God, for making a way for us to serve you. Amen.

PSALM 108

My heart is steadfast, O God;
I will sing and make music with all my soul.
Awake, harp and lyre!
I will awaken the dawn.
I will praise you, O LORD, among the nations;
I will sing of you among the peoples.
For great is your love, higher than the heavens;
your faithfulness reaches to the skies.
Be exalted, O God, above the heavens,
and let your glory be over all the earth.

Save us and help us with your right hand,
that those you love may be delivered.
God has spoken from his sanctuary:
"In triumph I will parcel out Shechem
and measure off the Valley of Succoth.
Gilead is mine, Manasseh is mine;
Ephraim is my helmet,
Judah my scepter.
Moab is my washbasin,
upon Edom I toss my sandal;
over Philistia I shout in triumph."

Who will bring me to the fortified city?
Who will lead me to Edom?
Is it not you, O God, you who have rejected us
and no longer go out with our armies?
Give us aid against the enemy,
for the help of man is worthless.
With God we will gain the victory,
and he will trample down our enemies.

Pause. Be quiet and reflect on the psalm. If necessary, read through it
again.

PRAISE

Blessed are you, Lord God of Israel, for you have visited us and bought us back and made us your people. From out of your servant David's family, you have raised up a mighty rescuer and restorer to provide us a way and a hope. Since the world began, you spoke through the prophets, declaring that:

> we would be saved from our enemies
> and from all who desire our demise;
>
> you would demonstrate your merciful acts,
> which you promised to all those who came before us;
>
> you would remember the promises you swore to Abraham,
> which he passed down to us;
>
> as a result of your acting, we might be able to serve you without fear;
>
> we might be able to live before you, holy and righteous,
> all the days of our life.

You gave us John the Baptist, who was called a prophet of the Most High because he went before the Lord and prepared the way. He told his people how to find a new and restored life through the forgiveness of their sin.

Praise you for your tender mercy, for the light of heaven which has dawned before us, giving light to us who live in darkness and in the shadow of death, guiding us on to a path of wholeness and well-being.[59]

DECLARE

I believe in God, the Father Almighty, maker of heaven and earth;
And in Jesus Christ his only Son our Lord;
> who was conceived by the Virgin Mary,
> suffered under Pontius Pilate,
> was crucified, dead and buried.
> He descended into hell.
> The third day he rose again from the dead.
> He ascended into heaven,
> and sitteth on the right hand of God the Father Almighty.
From thence he shall come to judge the quick and the dead.
I believe in the Holy Ghost,
> the Church universal,
> the communion of saints,
> the forgiveness of sins,

the resurrection of the body,
and the life everlasting. Amen.[60]

READ

As we approach God's message today, may this prayer help us see with fresh and new vision.

As we open the Scriptures this morning, may the words become your living word shaping our lives to be receptive to your instruction, inspiration, and calling. Help us be willing to obey: completely, immediately, and joyfully. In Jesus' name, we pray. Amen.

Slowly and prayerfully read today's selections as found in the Devotional Lectionary and/or in one or more of the passages below:

1 Samuel 12:16-25
Ephesians 6:1-9
Matthew 18:1-14

PRAY

Prayer of the Day

God Almighty, who sent your Son to us as a servant and made it possible for us to join your work in the world as servants, hear our prayer. We need your help, for we:

are slow to learn your values and virtues
in our upside-down culture;

too frequently forget your power and promises
to protect and accompany us;

are often prayer-less, working and striving
in the ways and means of our own best plans;

fail to make the most of our time,
wasting opportunities and time in trivial tasks and distractions.

We desire to serve you, our master and maker. Toward that end, we ask for:

the faith of Abraham, who left all that was familiar
to obey your voice;

the joy of King David, who, seeing your good work and will
fulfilled, moved his heart to praise;

the loyalty of Ruth, who chose Naomi's country and God
over an opportunity to return to her own;

the devotion of Mary, who pondered the moments and movements of her anointed Son, Jesus;

the love of the apostle John, who showed in word and deed that the love commands were the signature of God's family;

the boldness of the apostle Paul, who followed God's leading, showing and sharing the good news at the Spirit of God's prompting.

We ask that we might be made ultimately in the likeness of your Son, Jesus—full of mercy, kindness, love, patience, and willingness to obey your will. We ask that you send your Holy Spirit to come and cleanse, convict, convert, and consecrate our hearts, hands, and heads to be servants whose good is to do your will.

This we ask in your Son, our Savior's, most holy name, Jesus. Amen.

The Lord's Prayer

Closing Prayer

O God, you have taught us to keep all your commandments by loving you and our neighbors. Grant us the grace of your Holy Spirit, that we may be devoted to you with our whole heart and united to one another with pure affection, through Jesus Christ, our Lord, who lives and reigns with you and the Holy Spirit, one God, for ever and ever. Amen.[61]

BLESS

Glory to the Father, and to the Son, and to the Holy Spirit: as it was in the beginning, is now, and will be for ever. Amen.[62]

PREPARE

Find a comfortable spot and take some moments to relax. Breathe. When you are still, focus your attention on God and pray:

O God, you make us glad with the weekly remembrance of the glorious resurrection of your Son, our Lord. Give us this day such blessing through our worship of you that the week to come may be spent in your favor, through Jesus Christ, our Lord. Amen.

REMEMBER

The Lord Jesus, on the night he was betrayed, took bread, and when he had given thanks, he broke it and said, "This is my body, which is for you; do this in remembrance of me." In the same way, after supper he took the cup, saying, "This cup is the new covenant in my blood; do this, whenever you drink it, in remembrance of me." For whenever you eat this bread and drink this cup, you proclaim the Lord's death until he comes. (1 Corinthians 11:23-26)

May we remember that Jesus willingly walked to the cross and spread out his arms along that wood, offering his broken body and his spilled blood as a perfect sacrifice for the whole world. In these moments, may we express our gratitude for God willingly offering his Son to rescue and restore us to our intended created purpose.

Join your voice with the Church in praying this ancient prayer associated with Christ's holy meal:

Soul of Christ, sanctify me
Body of Christ, save me
Blood of Christ, inebriate me
Water from the side of Christ, wash me
Passion of Christ, strengthen me
O good Jesus, hear me
Within thy wounds hide me
Permit me not to be separated from thee
From the malicious enemy defend me
In the hour of my death call me
And bid me come unto thee
That I may praise thee with thy saints
Forever and ever.
Amen.[63]

When you are ready, continue the remainder of the prayer.

CONFESS

Merciful God, we admit that we need your help. We confess that
we have wandered from the straight and narrow path; we have done
wrong, and we have failed to do what is right. You alone can help and
rescue us.

Have mercy on us: wipe out our sins and teach us to forgive others.
Produce in us the fruit of the Holy Spirit, that we may live as followers
of Jesus. This we ask in the name of Jesus our Savior. Amen.

PSALM 150

Praise the LORD.

Praise God in his sanctuary;
praise him in his mighty heavens.
Praise him for his acts of power;
praise him for his surpassing greatness.
Praise him with the sounding of the trumpet,
praise him with the harp and lyre,
praise him with tambourine and dancing,
praise him with the strings and flute,
praise him with the clash of cymbals,
praise him with resounding cymbals.

Let everything that has breath praise the LORD.

Praise the LORD.

Pause. Be quiet and reflect on the psalm. If necessary, read through it
again.

PRAISE

Take my life, and let it be consecrated, Lord, to thee.
Take my moments and my days; let them flow in ceaseless praise.
Take my hands, and let them move at the impulse of thy love.
Take my feet, and let them be swift and beautiful for thee.

Take my voice, and let me sing always, only, for my King.
Take my lips, and let them be filled with messages from thee.
Take my silver and my gold; not a mite would I withhold.
Take my intellect, and use every power as thou shalt choose.

Take my will, and make it thine; it shall be no longer mine.
Take my heart, it is thine own; it shall be thy royal throne.
Take my love, my Lord, I pour at thy feet its treasure store.
Take myself, and I will be ever, only, all for thee.[64]

STOP

Re-enter the quiet and keep a few moments of silence before God, recognizing his presence and his work in our midst.

COMMIT

Teach us, dear Lord, to number our days,
that we may apply our hearts to your wisdom.
Oh, satisfy us early with your mercy,
that we may rejoice and be glad all of our days.
And let the beauty of the Lord our God be upon us
and confirm the work of our hands.
And let the beauty of the Lord our God be upon us
and confirm the work of our hands, dear Lord. Amen.

PRAY

Prayer of the Day

God Almighty, who sent your Son to us as a servant and made it possible for us to join your work in the world as servants, hear our prayer. We need your help for we:

are slow to learn your values and virtues
in our upside-down culture;

too frequently forget your power and promises
to protect and accompany us;

are often prayer-less, working and striving
in the ways and means of our own best plans;

fail to make the most of our time,
wasting opportunities and time in trivial tasks and distractions.

We desire to serve you, our master and maker. Toward that end, we ask for:

the faith of Abraham, who left all that was familiar
to obey your voice;

the joy of King David, who, seeing your good work and will
fulfilled, moved his heart to praise;

the loyalty of Ruth, who chose Naomi's country and God
over an opportunity to return to her own;

the devotion of Mary, who pondered the moments and movements
of her anointed Son, Jesus;

the love of the apostle John, who showed in word and deed
that the love commands were the signature of God's family;

the boldness of the apostle Paul, who followed God's leading,
showing and sharing the good news at the Spirit of God's
prompting.

We ask that we might be made ultimately in the likeness of your Son,
Jesus—full of mercy, kindness, love, patience, and willingness to obey
your will. We ask that you send your Holy Spirit to come and cleanse,
convict, convert, and consecrate our hearts, hands, and heads to be
servants whose good is to do your will.

This we ask in your Son, our Savior's, most holy name, Jesus. Amen.

Prompting: Ask God to show you someone who needs love, help, or
encouragement. Then try to find a way to demonstrate God's love,
encouragement, or service to this person anonymously. Leave a note
of encouragement or secretly complete an act of service that shows
kindness and love to the person, brings God glory, and is a pure offering of devotion to God on your part.

Try to complete this act of service in the spirit of the Scripture that
teaches us that "when you give to the needy, do not let your left hand
know what your right hand is doing, so that your giving may be in secret.
Then your Father, who sees what is done in secret, will reward you"
(Matthew 6:3-4).

Closing Prayer

And let the beauty of the Lord our God be upon us
and confirm the work of our hands.
And let the beauty of the Lord our God be upon us
and confirm the work of our hands, dear Lord. Amen.

BLESS

Thanks be to God, our maker; the Son, our Savior; and God, the Holy
Spirit who empowers the Church. Amen.

Sunday Prayer at Dusk

PREPARE

Return to a quiet and still posture of heart, mind, and body. When you are in a place of readiness, pray:

> Our Lord and our God, who has opened the way for us to be recipients of your grace and extended an invitation to participate in your mission of restoration, we invite you to receive the offering of our prayers as this day comes to a close. In your mercy, hear our prayers. Amen.

PRAISE

> We proclaim that you are a great God; we rejoice in your gift of life found in giving your Son, Jesus the Christ.

> We praise you for the mercy you have shown to us and to each generation.

> We praise you, Almighty God, because:
>> you have shown the strength of your arm
>> by scattering the proud in their conceit;

>> you have cast down the mighty from their high places
>> and lifted up the lowly;

>> you have filled those who hunger with the best thing
>> and sent away the wealthy with nothing;

>> you remembered and kept your promises to your people;

>> your promise and your mercy have extended from Abraham to Mary
>> and even to our generation.

> We proclaim that you are a great God; we rejoice in God our Savior! Amen.[65]

PSALM 22

> My God, my God, why have you forsaken me?
> Why are you so far from saving me,
> so far from the words of my groaning?
> O my God, I cry out by day, but you do not answer,
> by night, and am not silent.

Yet you are enthroned as the Holy One;
you are the praise of Israel.
In you our fathers put their trust;
they trusted and you delivered them.
They cried to you and were saved;
in you they trusted and were not disappointed.

But I am a worm and not a man,
scorned by men and despised by the people.
All who see me mock me;
they hurl insults, shaking their heads:
"He trusts in the LORD;
let the LORD rescue him.
Let him deliver him,
since he delights in him."

Yet you brought me out of the womb;
you made me trust in you
even at my mother's breast.
From birth I was cast upon you;
from my mother's womb you have been my God.
Do not be far from me,
for trouble is near
and there is no one to help.

Many bulls surround me;
strong bulls of Bashan encircle me.
Roaring lions tearing their prey
open their mouths wide against me.
I am poured out like water,
and all my bones are out of joint.
My heart has turned to wax;
it has melted away within me.
My strength is dried up like a potsherd,
and my tongue sticks to the roof of my mouth;
you lay me in the dust of death.
Dogs have surrounded me;
a band of evil men has encircled me,
they have pierced my hands and my feet.
I can count all my bones;
people stare and gloat over me.
They divide my garments among them
and cast lots for my clothing.

But you, O LORD, be not far off;
O my Strength, come quickly to help me.
Deliver my life from the sword,
my precious life from the power of the dogs.
Rescue me from the mouth of the lions;
save me from the horns of the wild oxen.

I will declare your name to my brothers;
in the congregation I will praise you.
You who fear the LORD, praise him!
All you descendants of Jacob, honor him!
Revere him, all you descendants of Israel!
For he has not despised or disdained
the suffering of the afflicted one;
he has not hidden his face from him
but has listened to his cry for help.

From you comes the theme of my praise in the great assembly;
before those who fear you will I fulfill my vows.
The poor will eat and be satisfied;
they who seek the LORD will praise him—
may your hearts live forever!
All the ends of the earth
will remember and turn to the LORD,
and all the families of the nations
will bow down before him,
for dominion belongs to the LORD
and he rules over the nations.

All the rich of the earth will feast and worship;
all who go down to the dust will kneel before him—
those who cannot keep themselves alive.
Posterity will serve him;
future generations will be told about the Lord.
They will proclaim his righteousness
to a people yet unborn—
for he has done it.

Pause. Be quiet and reflect on the psalm. If necessary, read through it
again.

CONFESS

Almighty God, maker of all things, judge of all people and nations, we admit and confess our many sins, which we have committed in thought, word, and action.

Pause now and remember and recount those sins that come to mind.

We sincerely repent and turn from our misdeeds. Have mercy on us, merciful God. For your Son our Lord Jesus Christ's sake, forgive us all that is past and come to our help that from now on we may serve and please you with lives that are renewed by your Holy Spirit, to the glory of your name. Amen.

DECLARE

One of the teachers of religious law was standing there listening to the debate. He realized that Jesus had answered well, so he asked, "Of all the commandments, which is the most important?"

Jesus replied, "The most important commandment is this: 'Listen, O Israel! The Lord our God is the one and only Lord. And you must love the Lord your God with all your heart, all your soul, all your mind, and all your strength.' The second is equally important: 'Love your neighbor as yourself.' No other commandment is greater than these" (Mark 12:28-31, NLT).

READ

As we open the Bible, we pray,

As we open the Scriptures this evening, may the words become your living word shaping our lives to be receptive to your instruction, inspiration, and calling. Help us be willing to obey: completely, immediately, and joyfully. In Jesus' name, we pray. Amen.

Slowly and prayerfully read today's selections as found in the Devotional Lectionary and/or in one or more of the passages below:

Jeremiah 30:1-11
Ephesians 5:13-26
Matthew 18:21-35

PRAY

Prayer of the Day

God Almighty, who sent your Son to us as a servant and made it possible for us to join your work in the world as servants, hear our prayer. We need your help, for we:

> are slow to learn your values and virtues
> in our upside-down culture;

> too frequently forget your power and promises
> to protect and accompany us;

> are often prayer-less, working and striving
> in the ways and means of our own best plans;

> fail to make the most of our time,
> wasting opportunities and time in trivial tasks and distractions.

We desire to serve you, our master and maker. Toward that end, we ask for:

> the faith of Abraham, who left all that was familiar
> to obey your voice;

> the joy of King David, who, seeing your good work and will
> fulfilled, moved his heart to praise;

> the loyalty of Ruth, who chose Naomi's country and God
> over an opportunity to return to her own;

> the devotion of Mary, who pondered the moments and movements
> of her anointed Son, Jesus;

> the love of the apostle John, who showed in word and deed
> that the love commands were the signature of God's family;

> the boldness of the apostle Paul, who followed God's leading,
> showing and sharing the good news at the Spirit of God's
> prompting.

We ask that we might be made ultimately in the likeness of your Son, Jesus—full of mercy, kindness, love, patience, and willingness to obey your will. We ask that you send your Holy Spirit to come and cleanse, convict, convert, and consecrate our hearts, hands, and heads to be servants whose food is to do your will.

This we ask in your Son, our Savior's, most holy name, Jesus. Amen.

Intercede

Lord Jesus Christ, you stretched out your arms of love on the hard wood of the cross, that everyone might come within the reach of your saving embrace.

So clothe us in your Spirit that we, reaching forth our hands in love, may bring those who do not know you to the knowledge and love of you; for the honor of your name. Amen.[66]

The Lord's Prayer

BLESS

Glory to the Father, and to the Son, and to the Holy Spirit: as it was in the beginning, is now, and will be for ever. Amen.[67]

PRAYERS AT DARK
(Between 9:00 p.m. and midnight)

Monday

PREPARE

Holy God,
Holy and Mighty,
Holy and Immortal,
have mercy on us.[1]

REQUEST

Lord Almighty, grant us a peaceful night and a perfect end. Amen.

CONFESSION

Almighty God, to you all hearts are open, all desires known, and from
you no secrets are hidden: cleanse the thoughts of our hearts by the
inspiration of your Holy Spirit, that we may perfectly love you, and
worthily magnify your holy name; through Christ our Lord. Amen.[2]

PSALM 25

To you, O Lord, I lift up my soul;
in you I trust, O my God.
Do not let me be put to shame,
nor let my enemies triumph over me.
No one whose hope is in you
will ever be put to shame,
but they will be put to shame
who are treacherous without excuse.

Show me your ways, O Lord,
teach me your paths;
guide me in your truth and teach me,
for you are God my Savior,
and my hope is in you all day long.
Remember, O Lord, your great mercy and love,
for they are from of old.
Remember not the sins of my youth
and my rebellious ways;
according to your love remember me,
for you are good, O Lord.

Good and upright is the Lord;
therefore he instructs sinners in his ways.

He guides the humble in what is right
and teaches them his way.
All the ways of the LORD are loving and faithful
for those who keep the demands of his covenant.
For the sake of your name, O LORD,
forgive my iniquity, though it is great.
Who, then, is the man that fears the LORD?
He will instruct him in the way chosen for him.
He will spend his days in prosperity,
and his descendants will inherit the land.
The LORD confides in those who fear him;
he makes his covenant known to them.
My eyes are ever on the LORD,
for only he will release my feet from the snare.

Turn to me and be gracious to me,
for I am lonely and afflicted.
The troubles of my heart have multiplied;
free me from my anguish.
Look upon my affliction and my distress
and take away all my sins.
See how my enemies have increased
and how fiercely they hate me!
Guard my life and rescue me;
let me not be put to shame,
for I take refuge in you.
May integrity and uprightness protect me,
because my hope is in you.

Redeem Israel, O God,
from all their troubles!

PRAISE

Sovereign Lord, as you have promised,
you now dismiss your servant in peace.
For my eyes have seen your salvation,
which you have prepared in the sight of all people,
a light for revelation to the Gentiles
and for glory to your people Israel.
(Luke 2:29-32)

Glory to the Father, and to the Son, and to the Holy Spirit:
as it was in the beginning, is now, and will be for ever. Amen.

PRAY

Intercede

Keep watch, dear Lord, with those who work, or watch, or weep this night, and give your angels charge over those who sleep. Tend the sick, Lord Christ; give rest to the weary, bless the dying, soothe the suffering, pity the afflicted, shield the joyous, all for your love's sake. Amen.[3]

The Lord's Prayer

Closing Prayer

Guide us waking, O Lord, and guard us sleeping, that awake we may watch with Christ, and asleep we may rest in peace. Amen.

Accompanying Prayer

Repeat and meditate upon this prayer as you drift off to sleep:

Lord, have mercy on me, a sinner.

Tuesday

PREPARE
Holy God,
Holy and Mighty,
Holy and Immortal,
have mercy on us.[4]

REQUEST
Lord Almighty, grant us a peaceful night and a perfect end. Amen.

CONFESSION
Almighty God, to you all hearts are open, all desires known, and from you no secrets are hidden: cleanse the thoughts of our hearts by the inspiration of your Holy Spirit, that we may perfectly love you, and worthily magnify your holy name; through Christ our Lord. Amen.[5]

PSALM 4
Answer me when I call to you,
O my righteous God.
Give me relief from my distress;
be merciful to me and hear my prayer.

How long, O men, will you turn my glory into shame?
How long will you love delusions and seek false gods?
Know that the LORD has set apart the godly for himself;
the LORD will hear when I call to him.

In your anger do not sin;
when you are on your beds,
search your hearts and be silent.
Offer right sacrifices
and trust in the LORD.

Many are asking, "Who can show us any good?"
Let the light of your face shine upon us, O LORD.
You have filled my heart with greater joy
than when their grain and new wine abound.
I will lie down and sleep in peace,
for you alone, O LORD,
make me dwell in safety.

PRAISE

Sovereign Lord, as you have promised,
you now dismiss your servant in peace.
For my eyes have seen your salvation,
which you have prepared in the sight of all people,
a light for revelation to the Gentiles
and for glory to your people Israel.
(Luke 2:29-32)

Glory to the Father, and to the Son, and to the Holy Spirit:
as it was in the beginning, is now, and will be for ever. Amen.

PRAY

Intercede

O God, your unfailing providence sustains the world we live in and
the life we live: watch over those, both night and day, who work while
others sleep, and grant that we may never forget that our common life
depends upon each other's toil; through Jesus Christ our Lord. Amen.[6]

The Lord's Prayer

Closing Prayer

Guide us waking, O Lord, and guard us sleeping, that awake we may
watch with Christ, and asleep we may rest in peace. Amen.

Accompanying Prayer

Repeat and meditate upon this prayer as you drift off to sleep:

Come, Holy Spirit; you are welcome.

Wednesday

PREPARE

Holy God,
Holy and Mighty,
Holy and Immortal,
have mercy on us.[7]

REQUEST

Lord Almighty, grant us a peaceful night and a perfect end. Amen.

CONFESSION

Almighty God, to you all hearts are open, all desires known, and from you no secrets are hidden: cleanse the thoughts of our hearts by the inspiration of your Holy Spirit, that we may perfectly love you, and worthily magnify your holy name; through Christ our Lord. Amen.[8]

PSALM 134

Praise the LORD, all you servants of the LORD
who minister by night in the house of the LORD.
Lift up your hands in the sanctuary
and praise the LORD.

May the LORD, the Maker of heaven and earth,
bless you from Zion.

PRAISE

Sovereign Lord, as you have promised,
you now dismiss your servant in peace.
For my eyes have seen your salvation,
which you have prepared in the sight of all people,
a light for revelation to the Gentiles
and for glory to your people Israel.
(Luke 2:29-32)

Glory to the Father, and to the Son, and to the Holy Spirit:
as it was in the beginning, is now, and will be for ever. Amen.

PRAY

Intercede

Guard all your household, Lord, through the dark night of faith, and purify the hearts of those who wait on you, until your kingdom dawns with the rising of your Son, Christ, the morning star. Amen.[9]

The Lord's Prayer

Closing Prayer

Guide us waking, O Lord, and guard us sleeping, that awake we may watch with Christ, and asleep we may rest in peace. Amen.

Accompanying Prayer

Repeat and meditate upon this prayer as you drift off to sleep:

Not my will, but thine be done, O Lord.

Thursday

PREPARE

Holy God,
Holy and Mighty,
Holy and Immortal,
have mercy on us.[10]

REQUEST

Lord Almighty, grant us a peaceful night and a perfect end. Amen.

CONFESSION

Almighty God, to you all hearts are open, all desires known, and from
you no secrets are hidden: cleanse the thoughts of our hearts by the
inspiration of your Holy Spirit, that we may perfectly love you, and
worthily magnify your holy name; through Christ our Lord. Amen.[11]

PSALM 17

Hear, O Lord, my righteous plea;
listen to my cry.
Give ear to my prayer—
it does not rise from deceitful lips.
May my vindication come from you;
may your eyes see what is right.

Though you probe my heart and examine me at night,
though you test me, you will find nothing;
I have resolved that my mouth will not sin.
As for the deeds of men—
by the word of your lips
I have kept myself
from the ways of the violent.
My steps have held to your paths;
my feet have not slipped.

I call on you, O God, for you will answer me;
give ear to me and hear my prayer.
Show the wonder of your great love,
you who save by your right hand
those who take refuge in you from their foes.
Keep me as the apple of your eye;

hide me in the shadow of your wings
from the wicked who assail me,
from my mortal enemies who surround me.

They close up their callous hearts,
and their mouths speak with arrogance.
They have tracked me down, they now surround me,
with eyes alert, to throw me to the ground.
They are like a lion hungry for prey,
like a great lion crouching in cover.

Rise up, O LORD, confront them, bring them down;
rescue me from the wicked by your sword.
O LORD, by your hand save me from such men,
from men of this world whose reward is in this life.

You still the hunger of those you cherish;
their sons have plenty,
and they store up wealth for their children.
And I—in righteousness I will see your face;
when I awake, I will be satisfied with seeing your likeness.

PRAISE

Sovereign Lord, as you have promised,
you now dismiss your servant in peace.
For my eyes have seen your salvation,
which you have prepared in the sight of all people,
a light for revelation to the Gentiles
and for glory to your people Israel.
(Luke 2:29-32)

Glory to the Father, and to the Son, and to the Holy Spirit:
as it was in the beginning, is now, and will be for ever. Amen.

PRAY

Intercede

Keep watch, dear Lord, with those who work, or watch, or weep this
night, and give your angels charge over those who sleep. Tend the sick,
Lord Christ; give rest to the weary, bless the dying, soothe the suffering, pity the afflicted, shield the joyous, and all for your love's sake.
Amen.[12]

The Lord's Prayer

Closing Prayer

Guide us waking, O Lord, and guard us sleeping, that awake we may watch with Christ, and asleep we may rest in peace. Amen.

Accompanying Prayer

Repeat and meditate upon this prayer as you drift off to sleep:

May I decrease and you increase, Jesus.

Friday

PREPARE

Holy God,
Holy and Mighty,
Holy and Immortal,
have mercy on us.[13]

REQUEST

Lord Almighty, grant us a peaceful night and a perfect end. Amen.

CONFESSION

Almighty God, to you all hearts are open, all desires known, and from
you no secrets are hidden: cleanse the thoughts of our hearts by the
inspiration of your Holy Spirit, that we may perfectly love you, and
worthily magnify your holy name; through Christ our Lord. Amen.[14]

PSALM 31:1-5

In you, O Lord, I have taken refuge;
let me never be put to shame;
deliver me in your righteousness.
Turn your ear to me,
come quickly to my rescue;
be my rock of refuge,
a strong fortress to save me.
Since you are my rock and my fortress,
for the sake of your name lead and guide me.
Free me from the trap that is set for me,
for you are my refuge.
Into your hands I commit my spirit;
redeem me, O Lord, the God of truth.

PRAISE

Sovereign Lord, as you have promised,
you now dismiss your servant in peace.
For my eyes have seen your salvation,
which you have prepared in the sight of all people,
a light for revelation to the Gentiles
and for glory to your people Israel.
(Luke 2:29-32)

Glory to the Father, and to the Son, and to the Holy Spirit:
as it was in the beginning, is now, and will be for ever. Amen.

PRAY

Intercede

O God, your unfailing providence sustains the world we live in and
the life we live: watch over those, both night and day, who work while
others sleep, and grant that we may never forget that our common life
depends upon each other's toil; through Jesus Christ our Lord. Amen.[15]

The Lord's Prayer

Closing Prayer

Guide us waking, O Lord, and guard us sleeping, that awake we may
watch with Christ, and asleep we may rest in peace. Amen.

Accompanying Prayer

Repeat and meditate upon this prayer as you drift off to sleep:

In your hands, mighty God, I rest.

Saturday

PREPARE

Holy God,
Holy and Mighty,
Holy and Immortal,
have mercy on us.[16]

REQUEST

Lord Almighty, grant us a peaceful night and a perfect end. Amen.

CONFESSION

Almighty God, to you all hearts are open, all desires known, and from
you no secrets are hidden: cleanse the thoughts of our hearts by the
inspiration of your Holy Spirit, that we may perfectly love you, and
worthily magnify your holy name; through Christ our Lord. Amen.[17]

PSALM 70

Hasten, O God, to save me;
O LORD, come quickly to help me.
May those who seek my life
be put to shame and confusion;
may all who desire my ruin
be turned back in disgrace.
May those who say to me, "Aha! Aha!"
turn back because of their shame.
But may all who seek you
rejoice and be glad in you;
may those who love your salvation always say,
"Let God be exalted!"

Yet I am poor and needy;
come quickly to me, O God.
You are my help and my deliverer;
O LORD, do not delay.

PRAISE

Sovereign Lord, as you have promised,
you now dismiss your servant in peace.
For my eyes have seen your salvation,
which you have prepared in the sight of all people,
a light for revelation to the Gentiles
and for glory to your people Israel.
(Luke 2:29-32)

Glory to the Father, and to the Son, and to the Holy Spirit:
as it was in the beginning, is now, and will be for ever. Amen.

PRAY

Intercede

We give thanks, O God, for revealing your Son Jesus Christ to us by
the light of his resurrection: grant that as we sing your glory at the
close of this day, our joy may abound in the morning as we celebrate
the Passover mystery; through Jesus Christ our Lord. Amen.[18]

The Lord's Prayer

Closing Prayer

Guide us waking, O Lord, and guard us sleeping, that awake we may
watch with Christ, and asleep we may rest in peace. Amen.

Accompanying Prayer

Repeat and meditate upon this prayer as you drift off to sleep:

Lord, increase my faith.

Sunday

PREPARE

Holy God,
Holy and Mighty,
Holy and Immortal,
have mercy on us.[19]

REQUEST

Lord Almighty, grant us a peaceful night and a perfect end. Amen.

CONFESSION

Almighty God, to you all hearts are open, all desires known, and from
you no secrets are hidden: cleanse the thoughts of our hearts by the
inspiration of your Holy Spirit, that we may perfectly love you, and
worthily magnify your holy name; through Christ our Lord. Amen.[20]

PSALM 91

He who dwells in the shelter of the Most High
will rest in the shadow of the Almighty.
I will say of the LORD, "He is my refuge and my fortress,
my God, in whom I trust."

Surely he will save you from the fowler's snare
and from the deadly pestilence.
He will cover you with his feathers,
and under his wings you will find refuge;
his faithfulness will be your shield and rampart.
You will not fear the terror of night,
nor the arrow that flies by day,
nor the pestilence that stalks in the darkness,
nor the plague that destroys at midday.
A thousand may fall at your side,
ten thousand at your right hand,
but it will not come near you.
You will only observe with your eyes
and see the punishment of the wicked.

If you make the Most High your dwelling—
even the LORD, who is my refuge—
then no harm will befall you,
no disaster will come near your tent.
For he will command his angels concerning you
to guard you in all your ways;
they will lift you up in their hands,
so that you will not strike your foot against a stone.
You will tread upon the lion and the cobra;
you will trample the great lion and the serpent.

"Because he loves me," says the LORD, "I will rescue him;
I will protect him, for he acknowledges my name.
He will call upon me, and I will answer him;
I will be with him in trouble,
I will deliver him and honor him.
With long life will I satisfy him
and show him my salvation."

PRAISE

Sovereign Lord, as you have promised,
you now dismiss your servant in peace.
For my eyes have seen your salvation,
which you have prepared in the sight of all people,
a light for revelation to the Gentiles
and for glory to your people Israel. (Luke 2:29-32)

Glory to the Father, and to the Son, and to the Holy Spirit:
as it was in the beginning, is now, and will be for ever. Amen.

PRAY

Night Prayer

Guard all your household, Lord, through the dark night of faith, and
purify the hearts of those who wait on you, until your kingdom dawns
with the rising of your Son, Christ, the morning star. Amen.[21]

The Lord's Prayer

Closing Prayer

Guide us waking, O Lord, and guard us sleeping, that awake we may
watch with Christ, and asleep we may rest in peace. Amen.

Accompanying Prayer

Repeat and meditate upon this prayer as you drift off to sleep:

Jesus, my light and my love.

EXPRESS PRAYER FORMS

Express Prayer at Dawn

PREPARE

O Lord, open my lips that my mouth may declare your praise.
O God, make speed to save us. O Lord, make haste to help us. Amen.

CONFESS

Most merciful God, we confess that we have sinned against you in
thought, word, and deed by what we have done and by what we have
left undone. We have not loved you with our whole heart; we have not
loved our neighbors as ourselves. We are truly sorry and we humbly
repent. For the sake of your Son Jesus Christ, have mercy on us and
forgive us, that we may delight in your will and walk in your ways to
the glory of your name. Amen.[1]

PSALM 95:1-7

Come, let us sing for joy to the LORD;
let us shout aloud to the Rock of our salvation.
Let us come before him with thanksgiving
and extol him with music and song.

For the LORD is the great God,
the great King above all gods.
In his hand are the depths of the earth,
and the mountain peaks belong to him.
The sea is his, for he made it,
and his hands formed the dry land.

Come, let us bow down in worship,
let us kneel before the LORD our Maker;
for he is our God
and we are the people of his pasture,
the flock under his care.

DECLARE

To whom shall we go?
You have the words of eternal life,
and we have believed and have come to know
that you are the Holy One of God.
Praise to you, Lord Jesus Christ,
King of endless glory.[2]

SMALL VERSE

Praise be to the God and Father of our Lord Jesus Christ! In his great mercy he has given us new birth into a living hope through the resurrection of Jesus Christ from the dead. (1 Peter 1:3)

PRAY

Dawn Prayer

Lord God, almighty and everlasting Father, you have brought us in safety to this new day: preserve us with your mighty power, that we may not fall into sin, nor be overcome by adversity; and in all we do, direct us to the fulfilling of your purpose; through Jesus Christ our Lord. Amen.[3]

The Lord's Prayer

Closing Prayer

O God, you have taught us to keep all of your commandments by loving you and our neighbor: grant us the grace of your Holy Spirit, that we may be devoted to you with our whole heart, and united to one another with pure affection; through Jesus Christ our Lord, who lives and reigns with you and the Holy Spirit, one God, for ever and ever. Amen.[4]

BLESS

Glory to the Father, and to the Son, and to the Holy Spirit: as it was in the beginning, is now, and will be for ever. Amen.[5]

Express Prayer at Daylight

PREPARE

This is the day the LORD has made;
let us rejoice and be glad in it.
(Psalm 118:24)

CONFESS

Merciful God, we admit that we need your help. We confess that
we have wandered from the straight and narrow path; we have done
wrong, and we have failed to do what is right. You alone can help and
rescue us. Have mercy on us: wipe out our sins and teach us to forgive
others. Produce in us the fruit of the Holy Spirit, that we may live as
followers of Jesus. This we ask in the name of Jesus our Savior. Amen.

PSALM 121 (NLT)

I look up to the mountains—
does my help come from there?
My help comes from the LORD,
who made heaven and earth!

He will not let you stumble;
the one who watches over you will not slumber.
Indeed, he who watches over Israel
never slumbers or sleeps.

The LORD himself watches over you!
The LORD stands beside you as your protective shade.
The sun will not harm you by day,
nor the moon at night.

The LORD keeps you from all harm
and watches over your life.
The LORD keeps watch over you as you come and go,
both now and forever.

COMMIT

Teach us, dear Lord, to number our days,
that we may apply our hearts to your wisdom.
Oh, satisfy us early with your mercy,
that we may rejoice and be glad all of our days.
And let the beauty of the Lord our God be upon us
and confirm the work of our hands.
And let the beauty of the Lord our God be upon us
and confirm the work of our hands, dear Lord. Amen.

PRAY

Daylight Prayer

Lord Jesus Christ, you stretched out your arms of love on the hard
wood of the cross, that everyone might come within the reach of your
saving embrace.

So clothe us in your Spirit that we, reaching forth our hands in love,
may bring those who do not know you to the knowledge and love of
you; for the honor of your name. Amen.

Closing Prayer

O God, you will keep in perfect peace those whose minds are fixed
on you for in returning and rest we shall be saved; quietness and trust
shall be our strength.[6]

BLESS

Glory to the Father, and to the Son, and to the Holy Spirit: as it was in
the beginning, is now, and will be for ever. Amen.[7]

Express Prayer at Dusk

PREPARE

Holy God, maker of all, be near.
Lord Jesus, forgiver and friend, hear our prayer.
Holy Spirit, light and life, dwell in us.
Three in One, you are welcome; come be our guest. Amen.

CONFESS

Almighty God, maker of all things, judge of all people and nations,
we admit and confess our many sins, which we have committed in
thought, word, and action. We sincerely repent and turn from our
misdeeds. Have mercy on us, merciful God. For your Son our Lord
Jesus Christ's sake forgive us all that is past and come to our help that
from now on we may serve and please you with lives that are renewed
by your Holy Spirit, to the glory of your name. Amen.

PSALM 141:1-4, 9-10

O Lord, I call to you; come quickly to me.
Hear my voice when I call to you.
May my prayer be set before you like incense;
may the lifting up of my hands be like the evening sacrifice.

Set a guard over my mouth, O Lord;
keep watch over the door of my lips.
Let not my heart be drawn to what is evil,
to take part in wicked deeds
with men who are evildoers;
let me not eat of their delicacies. . . .

Keep me from the snares they have laid for me,
from the traps set by evildoers.
Let the wicked fall into their own nets,
while I pass by in safety.

PRAISE

O gracious Light,
pure brightness of the everliving Father in heaven,
O Jesus Christ, holy and blessed!
Now as we come to the setting of the sun,
and our eyes behold the vesper light,
we sing your praise, O God: Father, Son, and Holy Spirit.

You are worthy at all times to be praised by happy voices,
O Son of God, O giver of life,
and to be glorified through all the worlds.[8]

DECLARE

One of the teachers of religious law was standing there listening to the debate. He realized that Jesus had answered well, so he asked, "Of all the commandments, which is the most important?"

Jesus replied, "The most important commandment is this: 'Listen, O Israel! The Lord our God is the one and only Lord. And you must love the Lord your God with all your heart, all your soul, all your mind, and all your strength.' The second is equally important: 'Love your neighbor as yourself.' No other commandment is greater than these." (Mark 12:28-31, NLT)

SMALL VERSE

For we do not preach ourselves, but Jesus Christ as Lord, and ourselves as your servants for Jesus' sake. For God, who said, "Let light shine out of darkness," made his light shine in our hearts to give us the light of the knowledge of the glory of God in the face of Christ. (2 Corinthians 4:5-6)

PRAY

Prayer at Dusk

Patient God, you await us lovingly even as we await your coming. Forgive our frequent drifting by disobedience away from you. Help us daily to put your words into action and to strive to live in peace and holiness, through the example of Jesus and the guidance of your Holy Spirit. Amen.[9]

The Lord's Prayer

Closing Prayer

Almighty and eternal God, grant that we may grow in faith, hope, and love; and so that we may obtain what you promise, make us love what you command, through Jesus Christ our Lord. Amen.[10]

BLESS

Glory to the Father, and to the Son, and to the Holy Spirit: as it was in the beginning, is now, and will be for ever. Amen.[11]

PART 3

Occasional Prayers

THE CHRISTIAN YEAR

For thousands of years Christians have observed the Christian calendar. Throughout the Christian year, we, as followers of Jesus, rehearse God's redemptive acts in our history and discover our place in his continuing story of restoration.

There are two halves to the Christian year: the first half is the Season of Feasts, while the second half has been referred to as Ordinary Time. The Season of Feasts focuses on walking through the "life of Jesus," which begins with Advent (beginning in late November) and ends with Jesus' ascension and the sending of the Holy Spirit observed in the feast of Pentecost (observed in late May/early June).

During the second half of the Christian year, referred to as Ordinary Time, we focus on becoming more devoted to Jesus and life in the kingdom, which Christ has instituted.

ADVENT

The Christian year begins with the season of Advent, which is a four-week period that starts four Sundays before December 25 and concludes on Christmas Eve. It is the season of repentance and remembrance in preparation for the celebration of the season of Christmas.

Advent comes from the Latin word *Adventus,* meaning "arrival or coming."

During this time, Christians focus on looking back at the promise of Jesus' first coming and anticipate his second coming as the king of glory.

Prayers of Preparation

During the season of Advent, you can pray any of the following prayers as a substitute for or supplement to the Opening Prayer at dawn, daylight, and dusk.

(1) Blessed are you, O Lord our God, ruler of the universe and maker of light and darkness. May Christ, the light of the world, be our new beginning, the hope of our lives, and the salvation that all of creation is longing to see; we ask this in the name of God our Creator, redeemer, and the giver of life. Amen.

(2) Blessed are you, O Lord our God, bright morning star who shines down light and life upon us through the message of the prophets and the coming of your beloved Son, Jesus. May our hunger for you and the gift of your Son grow within us this day, and at the dawn of his coming may we be found welcoming with joy his loving presence and the truth of the living word. Amen.

(3) Blessed are you, O Lord Jesus Christ, to whom we cry, "Blessed is he who comes in the name of the LORD" (Psalm 118:26). Allow us to join in the songs of praise with those in heaven and on earth who recognized your first coming and who anticipate your coming again. We pray this through the same name, Jesus Christ, our Lord. Amen.

(4) Blessed are you, O Lord our God, the one who is coming to gather together the people of God. May your Holy Spirit strengthen our minds and hearts that we might be always alert and fixed upon you, for you tell us our redemption is drawing near. Amen.

Closing Prayers

During the season of Advent, you can pray any of the following prayers as a substitute for or supplement to the Closing Prayer at dawn, daylight, and dusk.

(1) Lord Jesus, our light and our salvation, you alone are the one who has come to save us. We thank you for your coming and for your will to perform your saving work in us again. Rule us by your Holy Spirit, that from this point forward we may wait for none other and put our trust in nothing in heaven or earth except you alone, our Lord. Amen.[1]

(2) Eternal light, shine into our hearts; eternal goodness, deliver us from evil; eternal power, be our support; eternal wisdom, scatter the darkness of our ignorance; eternal pity, have mercy upon us, that with all our heart, mind, soul, and strength we may seek your face and be brought by your infinite mercy to your holy presence, through Jesus Christ, our Lord. Amen.[2]

(3) We praise and thank you, Creator God, for you have not left us alone. Each year you come to us, Emmanuel, God with us in a manger. Each time you come to us in the broken bread and the cup we share. In time or out of time you will be revealed and we shall see you face to face. Give us courage, God our strength, to see your Christ in all who suffer, to be hands to the helpless, food for the hungry, and rescue for the oppressed. Amen.[3]

(4) Almighty God, we give thee thanks for the mighty yearning of the human heart for the coming of a Savior and the constant promise of thy word that he was to come. In our own souls we repeat the humble signs of ancient men and ages and own that our souls are in darkness and infirmity, without faith in him who brings God to man and man to God. . . . O God, prepare thou the way in us now, and may we welcome anew thy Holy Child. Amen.[4]

CHRISTMAS

The word *Christmas* means "the mass of the Christ." Christmas is the most well-known and celebrated of all the Christian feasts. But the Christmas season, also called Christmastide, is more than one day; it begins Christmas Eve night and proceeds to the Sunday following January 6.

This season is one in which we celebrate the gift of Jesus coming as our Savior and also the gift of our own lives.

Prayer of Preparation

During the Christmas season, you can pray the following prayer as a substitute for or supplement to the Opening Prayer at dawn, daylight, and dusk.

Welcome, welcome, Jesus Christ, our infant savior, baby who makes every birth holy. May we, who, like the shepherds, have seen in your birth a new kind of love, witness to that love in our lives.[5]

Closing Prayer

During the Christmas season, you can pray the following prayer as a substitute for or supplement to the Closing Prayer at dawn, daylight, and dusk.

Blessed are you, O Lord, our God, for you have made our gladness greater and increased our joy by sending to dwell among us the wonderful counselor, the prince of peace. Born of Mary, proclaimed to the shepherds and acknowledged to the ends of the earth, your unconquered sun of righteousness gives light in darkness and establishes us in freedom. All glory in the highest be to you, through Christ, the Son of your favor, in the abiding presence of your Spirit, this day and forever and ever. Amen.[6]

LENT

Lent is the period of time between Ash Wednesday and Easter; it is a season of denial, fasting, and repentance in preparation for the celebration of the resurrection of Jesus Christ.

This forty-day period of preparation finds parallels in the Israelites' wandering in the desert for forty years and the forty days of Jesus' temptation in the wilderness as he prepared to launch his public ministry.

During Lent, Christians are to ready, cleanse, and renew themselves to remember and observe the great events of Jesus' last week, which Christians refer to as Holy Week.

Prayer of Preparation

During the season of Lent, you can pray any of the following prayers as a substitute for or supplement to the Opening Prayer at dawn, daylight, and dusk.

(1) Blessed are you, O Lord, our God; you are close to those who struggle and are tempted. As we practice the season of Lent, help us understand the meaning of Jesus' death and resurrection, and help us demonstrate it in the way we live. Amen.

(2) Blessed are you, O Lord, our God; you have revealed your kingdom to us. We pray that you will turn our hearts toward you as we practice Lent. Help us; by your mercy may we seek your kingdom and its values of love, mercy, and justice that we might become the people of God. Amen.

(3) Blessed are you, O Lord, our God, who sent us the gift of the Messiah. Help us be ready to celebrate the great mystery of Jesus' suffering and death offered on our behalf. Help our love grow, our devotion deepen, our faith increase, and our awareness of your presence heighten as the feast of the resurrection draws nearer. Amen.

(4) Blessed are you, O Lord, our God, who sent the prince of peace to reconcile us to creation, ourselves, one another, and you. O God, may we find our joy in your word this day and in your Son, who brings us new life. With faith and patience, may we faithfully continue our Lenten journey toward Easter. Amen.

(5) Father, help us be formed in the likeness of your Son, Jesus Christ, who willingly came to our world, lived a perfect life, and died that we

might live a new life. May we be filled with his never-ending love, nurtured by the truth of his living word, and guided through his perfect example. Amen.

Closing Prayers

During the season of Lent, you can pray any of the following prayers as a substitute for or supplement to the Closing Prayer at dawn, daylight, and dusk.

(1) Shepherd of Israel and of your Church, you were the pillar of cloud by day, their pillar of fire by night. In these forty days you lead us into the desert of repentance that in this pilgrimage of prayer we might learn to be your people once more. In fasting and service you bring us back to your heart. You open our eyes to your presence in the world and you free our hands to lead others to the wonders of your grace. Be with us in these journey days, for without you we are lost and will perish. To you alone be dominion and glory, forever and ever. Amen.[7]

(2) We thank you, Father, for those days in the desert when through prayer and fasting, Jesus discovered your will for his life and overcame the temptations of the evil one. Help us during these days of Lent to come close to you and to listen to your voice. Give us strength to overcome the temptation to please ourselves and live life without you. Teach us your way. For Jesus' sake. Amen.[8]

(3) Praise and glory to you, Jesus Christ our Saviour, for you do not call the righteous but us sinners to repentance. You draw us away from the easy road that would lead to our destruction. You call us instead to seek God's kingdom, to strive for what is right, and to lay up our treasure in heaven. Amen.[9]

(4) Christ Jesus, even when we can feel nothing of your presence you are always there. Your Holy Spirit remains constantly active in us, opening little ways forward to help us escape from our dead ends and to move us towards the essential of faith, and of trust. Amen.[10]

(5) O God, whose blessed Son steadfastly set his face to go to the city where he was to suffer and die; let there be in us this same devotion which was in him. Forgive us, we beseech thee, our many evasions of duty. We have held back from fear of men. We have ranked security and comfort higher than justice and truth, and our hearts condemn us. But thou, O Lord, who art greater than our hearts, have mercy upon us. Purge us from the fear that is born of self-concern. Beget in us the

fear that we may be found wanting in loyalty to thee and thy purpose of good for mankind. Fill us with the compassion of him who for our sake endured the cross; that we may be delivered from selfishness and cowardice; and that, dedicating our lives to thy service, we may be used of thee to help one another and to heal the hurt of the world; through the same Jesus Christ our Lord. Amen.[11]

HOLY WEEK

Holy Week is the final week of Lent and the week leading up to Easter, beginning with Palm Sunday. This week commemorates the last week of Jesus' life as recorded in the Scriptures and allows us to walk with him during this time: from his entry into Jerusalem, to his final meal, betrayal, trial, suffering, death on a cross, and burial in a borrowed tomb.

Traditionally, Christians have remembered these events with special observances: for instance, we remember the night of Jesus' final meal on Maundy Thursday and the events of Jesus' crucifixion on Good Friday.

Prayer of Preparation

During Holy Week, you can pray any of the following prayers as a substitute for or supplement to the Opening Prayer at dawn, daylight, and dusk.

(1) Blessed are you, O Lord our God, who set your face to go to Jerusalem to die on a cross that we might find relationship with you and life ever more. Guide us by your truth today and strengthen our lives through the power of your death that we can live united with you in your kingdom. We pray in the name of Jesus, King of kings and Lord of lords. Amen.

(2) God, as we walk through Holy Week, may we remember that beyond sin there is love inexhaustible, beyond death there is life unimaginable, beyond brokenness there is forgiveness incomprehensible, beyond betrayal there is grace poured out eternally. May we remember and give thanks. Amen.[12]

Maundy Thursday:

Blessed are you, O Lord our God. We praise you for you showed us love while we were yet sinners. May your example toward us inspire us to faithfully obey your new command given on this night you were betrayed, to love one another as you have loved us. Amen.

Good Friday:

> Blessed are you, O Lord our God, for you walked toward death on a cross, not as a victim but as a victor to defeat sin and death. On this day when you suffered as the sacrifice for our sin, make it a continual remembrance for us—our sins pardoned, nailed to your cross, buried in the grave, and remembered no more. May we be dead to sin and alive to Christ and fully embrace our place as children of the most high God. Amen.

Closing Prayer

During Holy Week, you can pray any of the following prayers as a substitute for or supplement to the Closing Prayer at dawn, daylight, and dusk.

(1) God, of your goodness give me yourself for you are sufficient for me. I cannot properly ask you anything less, to be worthy of you. If I were to ask less, I should always be in want. In you alone do I have all. Amen.[13]

(2) God, as we walk through this week we recognize it is not life as usual. This week we remember your last week on earth, which ended with your death on a cross and your being laid dead in a tomb. As we walk with you through this final week may we grow in holiness; may we deny ourselves, take up our crosses, and follow you. We long to grow in our trust in, love for, and devotion to you, our one true and living God the Father, Son, and Holy Spirit. Amen.

Maundy Thursday:

> God Almighty, on this day your Son, our Lord and Savior, gathered with his disciples to share in a final meal, which he commands his Church to reenact as an example of his love.

> On the eve of his betrayal and death, he commanded that we celebrate this meal as a remembrance of his new and eternal sacrifice on the cross. We pray that each time we partake of this meal, we might find fullness of love and life. May this be through our Lord Jesus Christ, who lives and reigns with you and the Holy Spirit, one God, forever and ever. Amen.

Good Friday:

> O sacred head, now wounded,
> with grief and shame weighed down,
> now scornfully surrounded

with thorns, thine only crown.
O sacred head, what glory,
what bliss, till now was thine!
Yet, though despised and gory,
I joy to call thee mine.

What thou, my Lord, hast suffered, was all for sinners' gain;
mine, mine was the transgression, but thine the deadly pain.
Lo, here I fall, my Savior! 'Tis I deserve thy place;
look on me with thy favor, vouchsafe to me thy grace.

My burden in thy passion,
Lord, thou hast borne for me,
for it was my transgression
which brought this woe on thee.
I cast me down before thee,
wrath were my rightful lot;
have mercy, I implore thee;
redeemer, spurn me not!

What language shall I borrow to thank thee, dearest friend,
for this, thy dying sorrow, thy pity without end?
O make me thine forever,
and should I fainting be,
Lord, let me never, never,
outlive my love for thee.[14]

EASTER

Easter is the observance of Jesus' resurrection from the dead. This fifty-day period begins on the Sunday following Holy Week and ends with the celebration that commemorates the sending of the Holy Spirit as recorded in Acts 2. The Easter season focuses on the renewal of all things, which results from Jesus' triumph over sin and death. Easter's date is not fixed but is based on the Sunday following the first full moon of spring (falling between March 22 and April 25).

Prayer of Preparation

You can pray the following prayer as a substitute for or supplement to the Opening Prayer at dawn, daylight, and dusk.

Christ is risen! He is risen indeed! We thank you, Almighty God, that you are risen from the dead. As ones who are risen with you, may our lives never deny this life that is eternal, this peace, hope, and joy! Praise to you, God of life, for you are stronger than death. Alleluia.

Closing Prayer

You can pray the following prayer as a substitute for or supplement to the Closing Prayer at dawn, daylight, and dusk.

> God our Father, Creator of all, today is the day of Easter joy. This is the morning on which the Lord appeared to men who had begun to lose hope and opened their eyes to what the Scriptures foretold that first he must die, and then he would rise and ascend into his Father's glorious presence. May the risen Lord breathe on our minds and open our eyes that we may know him in the breaking of bread, and follow him in his risen life. Grant this through Christ our Lord. Amen.[15]

PENTECOST

Pentecost is the time during which Christians remember the gift of the Holy Spirit and the birth of the Church as recorded in Acts 2. Pentecost is observed seven weeks after Easter and is also the last Sunday of the Easter season.

After Pentecost, the Christian year proceeds into ordinary time, during which we focus on becoming more devoted followers of Jesus and discovering our place in God's mission of restoration.

Prayer of Preparation

You can pray the following prayer as a substitute for or supplement to the Opening Prayer at dawn, daylight, and dusk.

> Almighty and ever-living God, you fulfilled the Easter promise by sending us your Holy Spirit. May that Spirit unite the races and nations on earth to proclaim your glory. Grant this through our Lord Jesus Christ, your Son, who lives and reigns with you and the Holy Spirit, one God, forever and ever. Amen.[16]

Closing Prayer

You can pray the following prayer as a substitute for or supplement to the Closing Prayer at dawn, daylight, and dusk.

> Most powerful Holy Spirit, come down upon us and subdue us. From heaven, where the ordinary is made glorious, and glory seems but ordinary, bathe us with the brilliance of your light like dew. Amen.[17]

The prayers that follow can be said on any occasion as stand-alone prayers or during your prayers at dawn or dusk.

Occasional Prayers that are specific to your current situation should be said between the Prayer of the Day and The Lord's Prayer.

PRAYERS OF PRAISE

Third-Century Hymn

May none of God's wonderful works keep silence, night or morning. Bright stars, high mountains, the depths of the seas, sources of rushing rivers: may all these break into song as we sing to Father, Son and Holy Spirit.

May all the angels in the heavens reply: Amen. Amen. Amen. Power, praise, honor, eternal glory to God, the only giver of grace. Amen. Amen. Amen.[1]

Te Deum

You are God: we praise you;
you are the Lord: we acclaim you;
you are the eternal Father: all creation worships you.
To you all angels, all the powers of heaven,
cherubim and seraphim, sing in endless praise:
holy, holy, holy Lord, God of power and might,
heaven and earth are full of your glory.

The glorious company of apostles praise you.
The noble fellowship of prophets praise you.
The white-robed army of martyrs praise you.
Throughout the world the holy Church acclaims you;
Father, of majesty unbounded,
your true and only Son, worthy of all worship,
and the Holy Spirit, advocate and guide.
You, Christ, are the king of glory,
the eternal Son of the Father.

When you became man to set us free
you did not shun the virgin's womb.
You overcame the sting of death
and opened the kingdom of heaven to all believers.
You are seated at God's right hand in glory.
We believe that you will come and be our judge.
Come then, Lord, and help your people,
bought with the price of your own blood,
and bring us with your saints
to glory everlasting.

Save your people, Lord, and bless your inheritance.
Govern and uphold them now and always.
Day by day we bless you.
We praise your name for ever.
Keep us today, Lord, from all sin.
Have mercy on us, Lord, have mercy.
Lord, show us your love and mercy;
for we put our trust in you.
In you, Lord, is our hope:
and we shall never hope in vain.[2]

You Are Holy

You are holy, Lord, the only God,
and your deeds are wonderful.
You are strong.
You are great.
You are the most high.
You are Almighty.
You, Holy Father, are King of heaven and earth.
You are Three and One, Lord God, all good.
You are good, all good, supreme good,
Lord God, living and true.
You are love. You are wisdom.
You are humility. You are endurance.
You are rest. You are peace.
You are joy and gladness.
You are justice and moderation.
You are all our riches, and you suffice for us.
You are beauty.
You are gentleness.
You are our protector.

You are our guardian and defender.
You are courage. You are our haven and our hope.
You are our faith, our great consolation.
You are our eternal life, great and wonderful Lord,
God Almighty, merciful Saviour.[3]

An Offering

I am giving thee worship with my whole life.
I am giving thee assent with my whole power.
I am giving thee praise with my whole tongue.
I am giving thee honour with my whole utterance.

I am giving thee reverence with my whole understanding.
I am giving thee offering with my whole thought
I am giving thee praise with my whole fervour.
I am giving thee humility in the blood of the Lamb.

I am giving thee love with my whole devotion.
I am giving thee kneeling with my whole desire.
I am giving thee love with my whole heart.
I am giving thee affection with my whole sense.
I am giving thee my existence with my whole mind.
I am giving thee my soul, O God of all gods.[4]

PRAYERS FOR GUIDANCE

The Breastplate

I bind unto myself today
the power of God to hold and lead,
his eye to watch, his might to stay,
his ear to hearken to my need;
the wisdom of my God to teach,
his hand to guide, his shield to ward,
the word of God to give me speech,
his heavenly host to be my guard.

Christ be with me, Christ within me,
Christ behind me, Christ before me,
Christ beside me, Christ to win me,
Christ to comfort and restore me.
Christ beneath me, Christ above me,
Christ in quiet, Christ in danger,

Christ in hearts of all that love me,
Christ in mouth of friend and stranger.

I bind unto myself the name,
the strong name of the trinity,
by invocation of the same,
the three in one, the one in three,
of whom all nature hath creation,
eternal Father, Spirit, Word:
praise to the Lord of my salvation,
salvation is of Christ the Lord.[5]

A Bright Flame Before Me

My dearest Lord,
be thou a bright flame before me,
a guiding star above me,
a smooth path beneath me,
a kindly shepherd behind me,
today and for evermore.[6]

Discernment of Thomas à Kempis

Grant me, O Lord, to know what is worth knowing,
to love what is worth loving,
to praise what delights you most,
to value what is precious in your sight,
to hate what is offensive to you.
Do not let me judge by what I see,
not pass sentence according to what I hear,
but to judge rightly between things that differ
and above all to search out and to do what pleases you,
through Jesus Christ our Lord.[7]

PRAYERS FOR MERCY

Lamb of God

O Lamb of God, who takest away the sin of the world,
look upon us and have mercy upon us;
thou who art thyself both victim and priest,
thyself both reward and redeemer,
keep safe from all evil
all those whom thou hast redeemed,
O Saviour of the world.[8]

The Jesus Prayer

Lord Jesus Christ, Son of God,
have mercy on me, a sinner.[9]

PRAYERS OF DEVOTION

A Life to Proclaim You

O gracious and Holy Father,
give us wisdom to perceive you,
intelligence to understand you,
diligence to seek you,
patience to wait for you,
eyes to behold you,
a heart to meditate upon you,
and a life to proclaim you,
through the power of the Spirit
of Jesus Christ our Lord. Amen.[10]

Prayer of Anselm

O Lord our God, grant us grace
to desire you with our whole heart,
that so desiring we may seek and find you,
and so finding you, may love you,
and loving you, may hate those sins
from which you have redeemed us.

PRAYERS FOR OTHERS

Prayer for All People

We beg you Lord,
to help and defend us.

Deliver the oppressed.
Pity the insignificant.
Raise the fallen.
Show yourself to the needy.
Heal the sick.
Bring back those of your people who have gone astray.
Feed the hungry.
Lift up the weak.
Take off the prisoner's chains.

May every people come to know
that you alone are God,
that Jesus is your child,
that we are your people, the sheep that you pasture.
Amen.[11]

Remember Your People

O God of all the nations of the earth, remember those who,
though created in your image, are ignorant of your love;
and, in fulfillment of the sacrifice of your Son, Jesus Christ,
let the prayers and labors of your Church
deliver them from false faith and unbelief,
and bring them to worship you;
through him who is the resurrection and the life
of all who put their trust in you, Jesus Christ, our Lord.[12]

New England Sampler Prayer

God bless all those that I love;
God bless all those that love me;
God bless all those that love those that I love
and all those that love those that love me.

For the Sick

Almighty God our Lord and great physician, graciously comfort your child, [name], in [his/her] suffering. Fill [his/her] heart with confidence that, though at times they may be afraid, they yet may put their trust in you, through Jesus Christ our Lord. Amen.[13]

PRAYERS IN TIMES OF DIFFICULTY

When You Don't Know How or What to Pray

O Lord, I do not know what to ask of thee. Thou alone knowest what are my true needs. Thou lovest me more than I know how to love thee. Help me to see my real needs which are concealed from me. I dare not ask either a cross or consolation.[14] I can only wait on thee. My heart is open to thee. Visit me and help me, for thy great mercy's sake. Strike me and heal me; cast me down and raise me up. I worship in silence thy holy will and thine inscrutable ways. I offer myself as a sacrifice to thee. I put all my trust in thee. I have no other desire than to fulfill thy will. Teach me to pray. Pray thou thyself in me. Amen.[15]

When Feeling Abandoned

O God, early in the morning I cry to you.
Help me to pray
and to concentrate my thoughts on you:
I cannot do this alone.

In me there is darkness,
but with you there is light;
I am lonely, but you do not leave me;
I am feeble in heart, but with you there is help;
I am restless, but with you there is peace.
In me there is bitterness, but with you there is patience;
I do not understand your ways,
but you know the way for me.

Restore me to liberty,
and enable me so to live now
that I may answer before you and before me.
Lord, whatever this day may bring,
your name be praised.[16]

For Trust in God

O God, the source of all health: so fill my heart with faith in your love, that with calm expectancy I may make room for your power to possess me, and gracefully accept your healing; through Jesus Christ our Lord. Amen.[17]

After a Catastrophe

Almighty God, have mercy. We know your thoughts are not our thoughts, and your ways are not our ways. In your wisdom you have made a world with the possibility of mighty waves, winds, fires, floods, and quaking ground.

At this time, help us trust you. Keep all of us and all who have been affected by this disaster from despair. Support us, and may we receive the comfort that comes only from your Holy Spirit. Assist those who attend to the injured and displaced, console those grieving, and protect the vulnerable. Empower your church, and bring hope and healing that all may find relief and restoration. We ask this through Jesus Christ our Lord. Amen.

PRAYERS FOR PEACE AND JUSTICE

Christ's Body

Christ has no body now on earth but yours; yours are the only hands with which he can do his work; yours are the only feet with which he can go about the world; yours are the only eyes through which his compassion can shine forth upon a troubled world. Christ has no body now on earth but yours. Amen.[18]

For Peace Among All

Grant, O God, that your holy and life-giving Spirit may so move every human heart, that barriers which divide us may crumble, suspicions disappear, and hatreds cease; that our divisions being healed, we may live in justice and peace; through Jesus Christ our Lord. Amen.[19]

For Orphans

Gracious God,
you remember all your children,
especially those who are left alone,
innocent victims of the acts of others.
Remind us of the orphans of this world,

that we may show special care and embrace them with your love.
Give them confidence in your parental guidance,
so they will find a home in your family of faith,
with brothers and sisters who follow Jesus Christ, your Son, our Lord.
Amen.[20]

PRAYERS FOR FAMILY

For Those We Love

Almighty God, we entrust all who are dear to us to thy never-failing care and love, for this life and the life to come, knowing that thou art doing for them better things than we can desire or pray for; through Jesus Christ our Lord. Amen.[21]

For Our Family

We give you thanks and praise, our God, for our parents, and brothers and sisters, whom you have allowed us to call our family. From these people we have learned to love and trust. In their company we have been found by you and have come to experience your love, grace, and forgiveness. We are grateful for the role they play in our lives.

We ask for your blessing, protection, provision, and care to watch over these loved ones and pray that our times together would be marked by your presence among us. May your hand continue to be over our families and over all those who helped us arrive at this place in our lives. Most of all we thank you for the privilege of being named in your family, God; through Jesus Christ our Lord. Amen.

PRAYERS FOR STUDENT LIFE

A Student's Prayer

Creator of all things, true source of light and wisdom, lofty source of all being, graciously let a ray of your brilliance penetrate into the darkness of my understanding and take from me the double darkness of sin and ignorance into which I have been born.

Give me a sharp sense of understanding, a retentive memory,
and the ability to grasp things correctly and fundamentally.
Grant me the talent of being exact in my explanations
and the ability to express myself with thoroughness and charm.

Point out the beginning, direct the progress, help in the completion. Through Christ, our Lord. Amen.[22]

For Our School

O eternal God, bless all schools, colleges, and universities and especially [name your school], that they may be lively centers for sound learning, new discovery, and the pursuit of wisdom; and grant that those who teach and those who learn may find you to be the source of all truth, through Jesus Christ our Lord. Amen.[23]

Before Studying

Loving God, I thank you for the privilege of learning and of attending school. Forgive me for taking education for granted. May I make the most of my opportunity to learn about the world and time in which you have placed me. May I take time now to study and honor you in my preparations. Grant me strength, attention, care, and discipline to do my best. With your grace, presence, and mercy may I study. Amen.

PRAYERS FOR CALLING AND WORK

Scottish Celtic Prayer

As the hand is made for holding and the eye for seeing,
you have fashioned me, O Lord, for joy.
Share with me the vision to find that joy everywhere:
in the wild violet's beauty;
in the lark's melody;
in the face of a steadfast man;
in a child's smile;
in a mother's love;
in the purity of Jesus.[24]

Consecration

O Christ, you take upon yourself all our burdens so that,
freed of all that weighs us down,
we can constantly begin anew to walk,
with lightened step,
from worry towards trusting,
from the shadows towards the clear flowing waters,
from our own will
towards the vision of the coming Kingdom.
And then we know,

though we hardly dared hope so,
that you offer to make every human being
a reflection of your face.[25]

ON VOCATION

Our God who has created us, we thank you for entrusting us with important and meaningful vocations. Forgive us for belittling work, for finding work menial, and for taking our work lightly.

Change our view; help us see our work as a provision from you and a way to find a joyful reward in serving and caring for the needs of others.

If we have taken up work that serves us rather than your purposes or have settled for work without listening for your call, forgive us.

May we listen carefully to your voice and find that place where our deep gladness and the world's deep hunger meet.

We ask in the name of him who faithfully answered the call, Jesus, our Lord and our Savior. Amen.[26]

PART 4

Appendices

Scripture Reading Plan[1]

Day	Dawn	Dusk
January		
1	Gen. 17:1-12; Col. 2:6-12; John 16:23-30	Isa. 62:1-5; Rev. 19:11-16; Matt. 1:18-25
2	Gen. 12:1-7; Heb. 11:1-12; John 6:35-42	1 Kings 19:1-8; Eph. 4:1-16; John 6:1-14
3	Gen. 28:10-22; Heb. 11:13-22; John 10:7-17	1 Kings 19:9-18; Eph. 4:17-32; John 6:15-27
4	Ex. 3:1-5; Heb. 11:23-31; John 14:6-14	Josh. 3:14—4:7; Eph. 5:1-20; John 9:1-12
5	Josh. 1:1-9; Heb. 11:32—12:2; John 15:1-6	Jonah 2:2-9; Eph. 6:10-20; John 11:17-27
6	Isa. 52:7-10; Rev. 21:22-27; Matt. 12:14-21	Isa. 66:18-23; Rom. 15:7-13; Ps. 100
7	Isa. 52:3-6; Rev. 2:1-7; John 2:1-11	Deut. 8:1-3; Col. 1:1-14; John 6:30-51
8	Isa. 59:15-21; Rev. 2:8-17; John 4:46-54	Ex. 17:1-7; Col. 1:15-23; John 7:37-52
9	Isa. 63:1-5; Rev. 2:18-29; John 5:1-15	Isa. 45:14-19; Col. 1:24—2:7; John 8:12-19
10	Isa. 65:1-9; Rev. 3:1-6; John 6:1-14	Jer. 23:1-8; Col. 2:8-23; John 10:7-17
11	Isa. 65:13-16; Rev. 3:7-13; John 6:15-27	Isa. 55:3-9; Col. 3:1-17; John 14:6-14
12	Isa. 66:1-23; Rev. 3:14-22; John 9:1-12	Gen. 49:1-12; Col. 3:18—4:6; John 15:1-16
13	Isa. 40:1-11; Heb. 1:1-12; John 1:1-20	Gen. 1:1—2:3; Eph. 1:3-14; John 1:29-34
14	Isa. 40:12-24; Eph. 1:1-14; Mark 1:1-13	Gen. 2:4-25; Heb. 1:1-14; John 1:1-18
15	Isa. 40:25-31; Eph. 1:15-23; Mark 1:14-28	Gen. 3:1-24; Heb. 2:1-10; John 1:19-28
16	Isa. 41:1-16; Eph. 2:1-10; Mark 1:29-45	Gen. 4:1-16; Heb. 2:11-18; John 1:29-42
17	Isa. 41:17-29; Eph. 2:11-22; Mark 2:1-12	Gen. 4:17-26; Heb. 3:1-11; John 1:43-51
18	Isa. 42:1-17; Eph. 3:1-13; Mark 2:13-22	Gen. 6:1-8; Heb. 3:12-19; John 2:1-12
19	Isa. 43:1-13; Eph. 3:14-21; Mark 2:23—3:6	Gen. 6:9-22; Heb. 4:1-13; John 2:13-22
20	Isa. 44:6-8, 21-23; Eph. 4:1-16; Mark 3:7-19	Gen. 8:6-22; Heb. 4:14—5:6; John 2:23-3:15
21	Isa. 44:9-20; Eph. 4:17-32; Mark 3:19-35	Gen. 9:1-17; Heb. 5:7-14; John 3:16-21
22	Isa. 44:24—45:7; Eph. 5:1-14; Mark 4:1-20	Gen. 9:18-29; Heb. 6:1-12; John 3:22-36
23	Isa. 45:5-17; Eph. 5:15-33; Mark 4:21-34	Gen. 11:1-9; Heb. 6:13-20; John 4:1-15

Day	Dawn	Dusk
24	Isa. 45:18-25; Eph. 6:1-9; Mark 4:35-41	Gen. 11:27—12:8; Heb. 7:1-17; John 4:16-26
25	Isa. 46:1-13; Eph. 6:10-24; Mark 5:1-20	Gen. 12:9—13:1; Heb. 7:18-28; John 4:27-42
26	Isa. 47:1-15; Heb. 10:19-31; John 5:2-18	Gen. 13:2-18; Gal. 2:1-10; Mark 7:31-37
27	Isa. 48:1-11; Gal. 1:1-17; Mark 5:21-43	Gen. 14:8-24; Heb. 8:1-13; John 4:43-54
28	Isa. 48:12-21; Gal. 1:18-2:10; Mark 6:1-13	Gen. 15:1-21; Heb. 9:1-14; John 5:1-18
29	Isa. 49:1-12; Gal. 2:11-21; Mark 6:13-29	Gen. 16:1-14; Heb. 9:15-28; John 5:19-29
30	Isa. 49:13-26; Gal. 3:1-14; Mark 6:30-46	Gen. 16:15—17:14; Heb. 10:1-10; John 5:30-47
31	Isa. 50:1-11; Gal. 3:15-22; Mark 6:47-56	Gen. 17:15-27; Heb. 10:11-25; John 6:1-15
February		
1	Isa. 51:1-8; Gal. 3:23-29; Mark 7:1-23	Gen. 18:1-16; Heb. 10:26-39; John 6:16-27
2	Isa. 51:9-16; Heb. 11:8-16; John 7:14-31	Gen. 18:16-33; Gal. 5:13-25; Mark 8:22-30
3	Isa. 51:17-23; Gal. 4:1-11; Mark 7:24-37	Gen. 19:1-23; Heb. 11:1-12; John 6:27-40
4	Isa. 52:1-12; Gal. 4:12-20; Mark 8:1-10	Gen. 21:1-21; Heb. 11:13-22; John 6:41-51
5	Isa. 52:13—53:12; Gal. 4:21-31; Mark 8:11-26	Gen. 22:1-18; Heb. 11:23-31; John 6:52-59
6	Isa. 54:1-10; Gal. 5:1-15; Mark 8:27—9:1	Gen. 23:1-20; Heb. 11:32—21:2; John 6:60-71
7	Isa 55:1-13; Gal. 5:16-24; Mark 9:2-13	Gen. 24:1-27; Heb. 12:3-11; John 7:1-13
8	Isa. 56:1-8; Gal. 5:25—6:10; Mark 9:14-29	Gen. 24:28-38; Heb. 12:12-29; John 7:14-36
9	Isa. 57:1-13; Heb. 12:1-6; John 7:37-46	Gen. 24:50-67; 2 Tim. 2:14-21; Mark 10:13-22
10	Isa. 57:14-21; Gal. 6:11-18; Mark 9:30-41	Gen. 25:19-34; Heb. 13:1-16; John 7:37-52
11	Isa. 58:1-12; 2 Tim. 1:1-14; Mark 9:42-50	Gen. 26:1-6, 12-33; Heb. 13:17-25; John 7:53-8:11
12	Isa. 59:1-21; 2 Tim. 1:15—2:13; Mark 10:1-16	Gen. 27:1-29; Rom. 12:1-8; John 8:12-20
13	Isa. 60:1-22; 2 Tim. 2:14-26; Mark 10:17-31	Gen. 27:30-45; Rom. 12:9-21; John 8:21-32
14	Isa. 61:1-9; 2 Tim. 3:1-17; Mark 10:32-45	Gen. 27:46—28:4; Rom. 13:1-14; John 8:33-47
15	Isa. 61:10—62:5; 2 Tim. 4:1-8; Mark 10:46-52	Gen. 29:1-20; Rom. 14:1-23; John 8:47-59
16	Isa. 62:6-12; 1 John 2:3-11; John 8:12-19	Gen. 29:20-35; 1 Tim. 3:14—4:10; Mark 10:23-31

Day	Dawn	Dusk
17	Isa. 63:1-6; 1 Tim. 1:1-17; Mark 11:1-11	Gen. 30:1-24; 1 John 1:1-10; John 9:1-17
18	Isa. 63:7-14; 1 Tim. 1:18—2:8; Mark 11:12-26	Gen. 31:1-24; 1 John 2:1-11; John 9:18-41
19	Isa. 63:15-64:9; 1 Tim. 3:1-16; Mark 11:27—12:12	Gen. 31:25-50; 1 John 2:12-17; John 10:1-18
20	Isa. 65:1-12; 1 Tim. 4:1-16; Mark 12:13-27	Gen. 32:3-21; 1 John 2:18-29; John 10:19-30
21	Isa. 65:17-25; 1 Tim. 5:1-22; Mark 12:28-34	Gen. 32:22—33:17; 1 John 3:1-10; John 10:31-42
22	Isa. 66:1-6; 1 Tim. 6:6-21; Mark 12:35-44	Gen. 35:1-20; 1 John 3:11-18; John 11:1-16
23	Isa. 66:7-14; 1 John 3:4-10; John 10:7-16	Prov. 1:20-33; 2 Cor. 5:11-21; Mark 10:35-45
24	Ruth 1:1-14; 2 Cor. 1:1-11; Matt. 5:1-12	Prov. 3:11-20; 1 John 3:18—4:6; John 11:17-29
25	Ruth 1:15-22; 2 Cor. 1:12-22; Matt. 5:13-20	Prov. 4:1-27; 1 John 4:7-21; John 11:30-44
26	Ruth 2:1-13; 2 Cor. 1:23—2:17; Matt. 5:21-26	Prov. 6:1-19; 1 John 5:1-12; John 11:45-54
27	Ruth 2:14-23; 2 Cor. 3:1-18; Matt. 5:27-37	Prov. 7:1-27; 1 John 5:13-21; John 11:55—12:8
28	Ruth 3:1-18; 2 Cor. 4:1-12; Matt. 5:38-48	Prov. 8:1-21; Philemon 1-25; John 12:9-19
29	Dan. 7:9-10; 2 Cor. 3:1-9; John 12:27-36	Mal. 4:1-6; 2 Cor. 3:7-18; Luke 9:18-27
March		
1	Ruth 4:1-22; 2 Cor. 4:13—5:10; Matt. 6:1-6	Prov. 8:22-36; 2 Tim. 1:1-14; John 12:20-26
2	Deut. 4:1-9; 2 Tim. 4:1-8; John 12:1-8	Prov. 9:1-12; 2 Cor. 9:6-15; Mark 10:46-52
3	Deut. 4:9-14; 2 Cor. 10:1-18; Matt. 6:6-15	Prov. 10:1-12; 2 Tim. 1:15—2:13; John 12:27-36a
4	Deut. 4:15-24; 2 Cor. 11:1-21; Matt. 6:16-23	Prov. 15:16-33; 2 Tim. 2:14-26; John 12:36b-50
5	Deut. 4:25-31; 2 Cor. 11:21-33; Matt. 6:24-34	Prov. 17:1-20; 2 Tim. 3:1-17; John 13:1-20
6	Deut. 4:32-40; 2 Cor. 12:1-10; Matt. 7:1-12	Prov. 21:30—22:6; 2 Tim. 4:1-8; John 13:21-30
7	Deut. 5:1-22; 2 Cor. 12:11-21; Matt. 7:13-21	Prov. 23:19-21; 2 Tim. 4:9-22; John 13:31-38
8	Deut. 5:22-33; 2 Cor. 13:1-14; Matt. 7:22-29	Prov. 25:15-28; Phil. 1:1-11; John 18:1-14
9	Deut. 6:1-15; Heb. 1:1-14; John 1:1-18	Prov. 27:1-12; Phil. 2:1-13; John 18:15-27
10	Deut. 6:16-25; Heb. 2:1-10; John 1:19-28	Prov. 30:1-4; Phil 3:1-11; John 18:28-38
11	Deut. 7:6-11; Titus 1:1-16; John 1:29-34	Hab. 3:1-15; Phil. 3:12-21; John 17:1-8

Day	Dawn	Dusk
12	Deut. 7:12-16; Titus 2:1-15; John 1:35-42	Ezek. 18:1-4, 25-32; Phil. 4:1-9; John 17:9-19
13	Deut. 7:17-26; Titus 3:1-15; John 1:43-51	Ezek. 39:21-29; Phil. 4:10-20; John 17:20-26
14	Deut. 8:1-20; Heb. 2:11-18; John 2:1-12	Gen. 37:1-11; 1 Cor. 1:1-19; Mark 1:1-13
15	Deut. 9:1-12; Heb. 3:1-11; John 2:13-22	Gen. 37:12-24; 1 Cor. 1:20-31; Mark 1:14-28
16	Deut. 9:13-21; Heb. 3:12-19; John 2:23—3:15	Gen. 37:25-36; 1 Cor. 2:1-13; Mark 1:29-45
17	Deut. 9:23—10:5; Heb. 4:1-10; John 3:16-21	Gen. 39:1-23; 1 Cor. 2:14—3:15; Mark 2:1-12
18	Deut. 10:12-22; Heb. 4:11-16; John 3:22-36	Gen. 40:1-23; 1 Cor. 3:16-23; Mark 2:13-22
19	Deut. 11:18-28; Heb. 5:1-10; John 4:1-26	Gen. 41:1-13; 1 Cor. 4:1-7; Mark 2:23—3:6
20	Jer. 1:1-10; 1 Cor. 3:11-23; Mark 3:31—4:9	Gen. 41:14-45; Rom. 6:3-14; John 5:19-24
21	Jer. 1:11-19; Rom. 1:1-15; John 4:27-42	Gen. 41:46-57; 1 Cor. 4:8-20; Mark 3:7-19
22	Jer. 2:1-13; Rom. 1:16-25; John 4:43-54	Gen. 42:1-17; 1 Cor. 5:1-8; Mark 3:19-35
23	Jer. 3:6-18; Rom. 1:28—2:11; John 5:1-18	Gen. 42:18-28; 1 Cor. 5:9—6:11; Mark 4:1-20
24	Jer. 4:9-28; Rom. 2:12-24; John 5:19-29	Gen. 42:29-38; 1 Cor. 6:12-20; Mark 4:21-34
25	Jer. 5:1-9; Rom. 2:25—3:18; John 5:30-47	Gen. 43:1-15; 1 Cor. 7:1-9; Mark 4:35-41
26	Jer. 5:20-31; Rom. 3:19-31; John 7:1-13	Gen. 43:16-34; 1 Cor. 7:10-24; Mark 5:1-20
27	Jer. 6:9-15; 1 Cor. 6:12-20; Mark 5:1-20	Gen. 44:1-17; Rom. 8:1-10; John 5:25-29
28	Jer. 7:1-15; Rom. 4:1-12; John 7:14-36	Gen. 44:18-34; 1 Cor. 7:25-31; Mark 5:21-43
29	Jer. 7:21-34; Rom. 4:13-25; John 7:37-52	Gen. 45:1-15; 1 Cor. 7:32-40; Mark 6:1-13
30	Jer. 8:4-7; Rom. 5:1-11; John 8:12-20	Gen. 45:16-28; 1 Cor. 8:1-13; Mark 6:13-29
31	Jer. 10:11-24; Rom. 5:12-21; John 8:21-32	Gen. 46:1-7; 1 Cor. 9:1-15; Mark 6:30-46
April		
1	Jer. 11:1-8; Rom. 6:1-11; John 8:33-47	Gen. 47:1-26; 1 Cor. 9:16-27; Mark 6:47-56
2	Jer. 13:1-11; Rom. 6:12-23; John 8:47-59	Gen. 47:27—48:7; 1 Cor. 10:1-13; Mark 7:1-23
3	Jer. 14:1-9; Gal. 4:21—5:1; Mark 8:11-21	Gen. 48:8-22; Rom. 8:11-25; John 6:27-40
4	Jer. 16:10-21; Rom. 7:1-12; John 6:1-15	Gen. 49:1-28; 1 Cor. 10:14—11:1; Mark 7:24-37

Day	Dawn	Dusk
5	Jer. 17:29-37; Rom. 7:13-25; John 6:16-27	Gen. 49:29—50:14; 1 Cor. 11:2-34; Mark 8:1-10
6	Jer. 18:1-11; Rom. 8:1-11; John 6:27-40	Gen. 50:15-26; 1 Cor. 12:1-11; Mark 8:11-26
7	Jer. 22:13-23; Rom. 8:12-27; John 6:41-51	Ex. 1:6-22; 1 Cor. 12:12-26; Mark 8:27—9:1
8	Jer. 23:1-8; Rom. 8:28-39; John 6:52-59	Ex. 2:1-22; 1 Cor. 12:27—13:3; Mark 9:2-13
9	Jer. 23:9-15; Rom. 9:1-18; John 6:60-71	Ex. 2:23—3:15; 1 Cor. 13:1-13; Mark 9:14-29
10	Jer. 23:16-32; 1 Cor. 9:19-27; Mark 8:31—9:1	Ex. 3:16—4:12; Rom. 12:1-21; John 8:46-59
11	Jer. 24:1-10; Rom. 9:19-33; John 9:1-17	Ex. 4:10-31; 1 Cor. 14:1-19; Mark 9:30-41
12	Jer. 25:8-17; Rom. 10:1-13; John 9:18-41	Ex. 5:1—6:1; 1 Cor. 14:20-40; Mark 9:42-50
13	Jer. 25:30-38; Rom. 10:14-21; John 10:1-18	Ex. 7:8-24; 2 Cor. 2:14—3:6; Mark 10:1-16
14	Jer. 26:1-24; Rom. 11:1-12; John 10:19-42	Ex. 7:25—8:19; 2 Cor. 3:7-18; Mark 10:17-31
15	Jer. 29:1-14; Rom. 11:13-24; John 11:1-27	Ex. 9:13-35; 2 Cor. 4:1-12; Mark 10:32-45
16	Jer. 31:27-34; Rom. 11:25-36; John 11:28-44	Ex. 10:21—11:8; 2 Cor. 4:13-18; Mark 10:46-52
17	Ps. 84; 1 Tim. 6:12-16; John 12:1-10	Ps. 42; Zech. 9:9-12; John 12:37-50
18	Jer. 12:1-17; Phil 3:1-14; John 12:9-19	Lam. 1:1-12; 2 Cor. 1:1-7; Mark 11:12-25
19	Jer. 15:10-21; Phil 3:15-21; John 12:20-26	Lam. 1:17-22; 2 Cor. 1:8-22; Mark 11:27-33
20	Jer. 17:5-18; Phil 4:1-13; John 12:27-36	Lam. 2:1-9; 2 Cor. 1:23—2:11; Mark 12:1-11
21	Jer. 20:7-18; 1 Cor. 10:14-17; John 17:1-26	Lam. 2:10-18; 1 Cor. 11:27-32; Mark 14:12-25
22	Gen. 22:1-14; 1 Pet. 1:10-20; John 13:36-38	Lam. 3:1-9, 19-33; Ps. 22; John 19:38-42
23	Job 19:21-27; Heb. 4:1-16; Rom. 8:1-11	Lam. 3:37-58; Ps. 31; Rom. 8:1-11
24	Ex. 12:1-14; Ps. 93; Luke 24:13-35	Isa. 51:9-11; Ps. 136; John 20:19-23
25	Jonah 2:1-10; Acts 2:14-32; John 14:1-14	Ex. 12:14-27; 1 Cor. 15:1-11; Mark 16:1-8
26	Isa. 30:18-26; Acts 2:36-47; John 14:15-31	Ex. 12:28-39; 1 Cor. 15:12-28; Mark 16:9-20
27	Micah 7:7-15; Acts 3:1-10; John 15:1-11	Ex. 12:40-51; 1 Cor. 15:29-41; Matt. 28:1-16
28	Ezek. 37:1-14; Acts 3:11-26; John 15:12-27	Ex. 13:3-10; 1 Cor. 15:41-50; Matt. 28:16-20
29	Dan. 12:1-4, 13; Acts 4:1-12; John 16:1-15	Ex. 13:1-2, 11-16; 1 Cor. 15:41-50; Luke 24:1-12
30	Isa. 25:1-9; Acts 4:13-31; John 16:16-33	Ex. 13:17—14:4; 2 Cor. 4:16—5:10; Mark 12:18-27

Day	Dawn	Dusk
May		
1	Isa. 43:8-13; 1 Pet. 2:2-10; John 14:1-7	Ex. 14:5-22; 1 John 1:1-12; John 14:1-7
2	Dan. 1:1-21; 1 John 1:1-10; John 17:1-11	Ex. 14:21-31; 1 Pet. 1:1-12; John 14:8-17
3	Dan. 2:1-16; 1 John 2:1-11; John 17:12-19	Ex. 15:1-21; 1 Pet. 1:13-25; John 14:18-31
4	Dan. 2:17-30, 1 John 2:12-17; John 17:20-26	Ex. 15:22—16:10; 1 Pet. 2:1-10; John 15:1-11
5	Dan. 2:31-49; 1 John 2:18-29; Luke 3:1-14	Ex. 16:10-22; 1 Pet. 2:11-3:12; John 15:12-27
6	Dan. 3:1-18; 1 John 3:1-10; Luke 3:15-22	Ex. 16:23-36; 1 Pet. 3:13—4:6; John 16:1-15
7	Dan. 3:19-30; 1 John 3:11-18; Luke 4:1-13	Ex. 17:1-16; 1 Pet. 4:7-19; John 16:16-33
8	Dan. 4:1-18; 1 Pet. 4:7-11; John 21:15-25	Ex. 18:1-12; 1 John 2:7-17; Mark 16:9-20
9	Dan. 4:19-27; 1 John 3:19—4:6; Luke 4:14-30	Ex. 18:13-27; 1 Peter 5:1-14; Matt. 3:1-6
10	Dan. 4:28-37; 1 John 4:7-21; Luke 4:31-37	Ex. 19:1-16; Col. 1:1-14; Matt. 3:7-12
11	Dan 5:1-12; 1 John 5:1-12; Luke 4:38-44	Ex. 19:16-25; Col. 1:24—2:7; Matt. 3:13-17
12	Dan. 5:13-30; 1 John 5:13-21; Luke 5:1-11	Ex. 20:1-21; Col. 1:24—2:7; Matt. 4:1-11
13	Dan. 6:1-15; 2 John 1-13; Luke 5:12-26	Ex. 24:1-18; Col. 2:8-23; Matt. 4:12-17
14	Dan. 6:16-28; 3 John 1-15; Luke 5:27-39	Ex. 25:1-22; Col. 3:1-17; Matt. 4:18-25
15	Gen. 18:22-33; 1 Pet. 5:1-11; Matt. 7:15-29	Ex. 28:1-4, 30-38; 1 John 2:18-29; Mark 6:30-44
16	Jer. 30:1-9; Col. 1:1-14; Luke 6:1-11	Ex. 32:1-20; Col. 3:18—4:18; Matt. 5:1-10
17	Jer. 30:10-17; Col. 1:15-23; Luke 6:12-26	Ex. 32:21-34; 1 Thess. 1:1-10; Matt. 5:11-16
18	Jer. 30:18-22; Col. 1:24—2:7; Luke 6:27-38	Ex. 33:1-23; 1 Thess. 2:1-12; Matt. 5:17-20
19	Jer. 31:1-14; Col. 2:8-23; Luke 6:39-49	Ex. 34:1-17; 1 Thess. 2:13-20; Matt. 5:21-26
20	Jer. 31:15-22; Col. 3:1-11; Luke 7:1-17	Ex. 34:18-35; 1 Thess. 3:1-13; Matt. 5:27-37
21	Jer. 31:23-25; Col. 3:12-17; Luke 7:18-35	Ex. 40:18-38; 1 Thess. 4:1-12; Matt. 5:38-48
22	Isa. 32:1-8; 2 Thess. 2:13-17; Matt. 7:7-14	Lev. 8:1-13, 30-36; Heb. 12:1-14; Luke 4:16-30
23	Jer. 32:1-15; Col. 3:18—4:18; Luke 7:36-50	Lev. 16:1-19; 1 Thess. 4:13-18; Matt. 6:1-6, 16-18
24	Jer. 32:16-25; Rom. 12:1-21; Luke 8:1-15	Lev. 16:20-34; 1 Thess. 5:1-11; Matt. 6:7-15

Day	Dawn	Dusk
25	Jer. 32:36-44; Rom. 13:1-14; Luke 8:16-25	Lev. 19:1-18; 1 Thess. 5:12-28; Matt. 6:19-24
26	Jer. 33:1-13; Rom. 14:1-12; Luke 8:26-39	Lev. 19:26-37; 2 Thess. 1:1-12; Matt. 6:25-34
27	Deut. 31:30—32:14; Rom. 14:13-23; Luke 8:40-56	Lev. 23:1-22; 2 Thess. 2:1-17; Matt. 7:1-12
28	Deut. 32:34-43; Rom. 15:1-13; Luke 9:1-17	Lev. 23:23-44; 2 Thess. 3:1-18; Matt. 7:13-31
29	Deut. 15:1-11; 1 Tim. 3:14—4:5; Matt. 13:24-34	Lev. 25:1-17; James 1:2-8, 16-18; Luke 12:13-21
30	Deut. 18:9-14; James 1:1-15; Luke 9:18-27	Lev. 25:35-55; Col. 1:9-14; Matt. 13:1-16
31	Deut. 18:15-22; James 1:16-27; Luke 11:1-13	Lev. 26:1-20; 1 Tim. 2:1-6; Matt. 13:18-23
June		
1	Deut. 19:1-7; James 5:13-18; Luke 12:22-31	Lev. 26:27-42; Eph. 1:1-10; Matt. 22:41-46
2	Ezek. 1:1-14; Heb. 2:5-18; Matt. 28:1-20	Dan. 7:9-14; Rev. 5:1-14; Ps. 113
3	Ezek. 1:28—3:3; Heb. 4:14—5:6; Luke 9:28-36	1 Sam. 2:1-10; Eph. 2:1-10; Matt. 7:22-27
4	Ezek. 3:4-17; Heb. 5:7-14; Luke 9:37-50	Num. 11:16-29; Eph. 2:11-22; Matt. 7:28—8:4
5	Ezek. 3:16-27; Eph. 2:1-10; Matt. 10:24-42	Ex. 3:1-12; Heb. 12:18-29; Luke 10:17-24
6	Ezek. 4:1-17; Heb. 6:1-12; Luke 9:51-62	Josh. 1:1-9; Eph. 3:1-13; Matt. 8:5-17
7	Ezek. 7:10-27; Heb. 6:13-20; Luke 10:1-17	1 Sam. 16:1-13; Eph. 3:14-21; Matt. 8:18-27
8	Ezek. 11:14-25; Heb. 7:1-17; Luke 10:17-24	Isa. 4:2-6; Eph. 4:1-16; Matt. 8:28-34
9	Ezek. 18:1-4; Heb. 7:18-28; Luke 10:25-37	Zech. 4:1-14; Eph. 4:17-32; Matt. 9:1-8
10	Isa. 11:1-9; 1 Cor. 2:1-13; John 14:21-29	Deut. 16:9-14; Acts 4:18-33; John 1:29-34
11	Deut. 11:1-12; Rev. 10:1-11; Matt. 13:44-58	Eccl. 1:2-22; Acts 8:26-40; Luke 11:1-13
12	Deut. 11:13-19; 2 Cor. 5:11—6:2; Luke 17:1-10	Eccl. 2:1-15; Gal. 1:1-17; Matt. 13:44-52
13	Deut. 12:1-12; 2 Cor. 6:3-13; Luke 17:11-19	Eccl. 2:16-26; Gal. 1:18-2:10; Matt. 13:52-58
14	Deut. 13:1-11; 2 Cor. 7:2-16; Luke 17:20-37	Eccl. 3:1-15; Gal. 2:11-21; Matt. 14:1-12
15	Deut. 16:18-20; 17:14-20; 2 Cor. 8:1-16; Luke 18:1-8	Eccl. 3:16—4:3; Gal. 3:1-14; Matt. 14:13-21
16	Deut. 26:1-11; 2 Cor. 8:16-24; Luke 18:9-14	Eccl. 5:1-7; Gal. 3:15-22; Matt. 14:22-36
17	Deut. 29:2-15; 2 Cor. 9:1-15; Luke 18:15-30	Eccl. 5:8-20; Gal. 3:23—4:11; Matt. 15:1-20

Day	Dawn	Dusk
18	Deut. 29:16-29; Rev. 12:1-12; Matt. 15:29-39	Eccl. 6:1-12; Acts 10:9-23; Luke 12:32-40
19	Deut. 30:1-10; 2 Cor. 10:1-18; Luke 18:31-43	Eccl. 7:1-14; Gal. 4:12-20; Matt. 15:21-28
20	Deut. 30:11-20; 2 Cor. 11:1-21; Luke 19:1-10	Eccl. 8:14—9:10; Gal. 4:21-31; Matt. 15:29-39
21	Deut. 31:30—32:14; 2 Cor. 11:12-33; Luke 19:11-27	Eccl. 9:11-18; Gal. 5:1-15; Matt. 16:1-12
22	Song of Sol. 1:1—2:3; 2 Cor. 12:1-10; Luke 19:28-40	Eccl. 11:1-8; Gal. 5:16-24; Matt. 16:13-20
23	Song of Sol. 4:1-11; 2 Cor. 12:11-21; Luke 19:41-48	Eccl. 11:9-12:14; Gal. 5:25—6:10; Matt. 16:21-28
24	Song of Sol. 7-8:7; 2 Cor. 13:1-14; Luke 20:1-8	Num. 3:1-13; Gal. 6:11-18; Matt. 17:1-13
25	Ex. 6:2-13; 7:1-6; Rev. 15:1-8; Matt. 18:1-14	Num. 6:22-27; Acts 13:1-12; Luke 12:41-48
26	1 Sam. 1:1-20; Acts 1:1-14; Luke 20:9-19	Num. 9:15-23, 10:29-36; Rom. 1:1-15; Matt. 17:14-21
27	1 Sam. 1:21—2:11; Acts 1:15-26; Luke 20:19-26	Num. 11:1-23; Rom. 1:16-25; Matt. 17:22-27
28	1 Sam. 2:12-26; Acts 2:1-21; Luke 20:27-40	Num. 11:24-35; Rom. 1:28-2:11; Matt. 18:1-9
29	1 Sam. 2:27-36; Acts 2:22-36; Luke 20:41—21:4	Num. 12:1-16; Rom. 2:12-24; Matt. 18:10-20
30	1 Sam. 3:1-21; Acts 2:37-47; Luke 21:5-19	Num. 13:1-3, 21-30; Rom. 2:25—3:8; Matt. 18:21-35

July

Day	Dawn	Dusk
1	1 Sam. 4:1-11; Acts 4:32—5:11; Luke 21:20-28	Num. 13:31—14:25; Rom. 3:9-20; Matt. 19:1-12
2	1 Sam. 4:12-22; James 1:1-18; Matt. 19:23-30	Num. 14:26-45; Acts 15:1-12; Luke 12:49-56
3	1 Sam. 5:1-12; Acts 5:12-26; Luke 21:29-36	Num. 16:1-19; Rom. 3:21-31; Matt. 19:13-22
4	1 Sam. 6:1-16; Acts 5:27-42; Luke 21:37—22:13	Num. 16:20-35; Rom. 4:1-12; Matt. 19:23-30
5	1 Sam. 7:2-17; Acts 6:1-15; Luke 22:14-23	Num. 16:36-50; Rom. 4:13-25; Matt. 20:1-16
6	1 Sam. 8:1-22; Acts 6:15—7:16; Luke 22:24-30	Num. 17:1-11; Rom. 5:1-11; Matt. 20:17-28
7	1 Sam. 9:1-14; Acts 7:17-29; Luke 22:31-38	Num. 20:1-13; Rom. 5:12-21; Matt. 20:29-34
8	1 Sam. 9:15—10:1; Acts 7:30-43; Luke 22:39-51	Num. 20:14-29; Rom. 6:1-11; Matt. 21:1-11
9	1 Sam. 10:1-16; Rom. 4:13-25; Matt. 21:23-32	Num. 21:4-9, 21-35; Acts 17:12-24; Luke 13:10-17
10	1 Sam. 10:17-27; Acts 7:44—8:1; Luke 22:52-62	Num. 22:1-21; Rom. 6:12-23; Matt. 21:12-22
11	1 Sam. 11:1-15; Acts 8:1-13; Luke 22:63-71	Num. 22:21-38; Rom. 7:1-12; Matt. 21:23-32

Day	Dawn	Dusk
12	1 Sam. 12:1-6, 16-25; Acts 8:14-25; Luke 23:1-12	Num. 22:41—23:12; Rom. 7:13-25; Matt. 21:33-46
13	1 Sam. 13:5-18; Acts 8:26-40; Luke 23:13-25	Num. 23:11-26; Rom. 8:1-11; Matt. 22:1-14
14	1 Sam. 13:19—14:15; Acts 9:1-9; Luke 23:26-31	Num. 24:1-13; Rom. 8:12-17; Matt. 22:15-22
15	1 Sam. 14:16-30; Acts. 9:10-18; Luke 23:32-43	Num. 24:12-25; Rom. 8:18-25; Matt. 22:23-40
16	1 Sam. 14:36-45; Rom. 5:1-11; Matt. 22:1-14	Num. 27:12-23; Acts 19:11-20; Mark 1:14-20
17	1 Sam. 15:1-3, 7-23; Acts 9:19-31; Luke 23:44-56	Num. 32:1-6, 16-27; Rom. 8:26-30; Matt. 23:1-12
18	1 Sam. 15:24-35; Acts 9:32-43; Luke 23:56—24:11	Num. 35:1-3, 9-15, 30-34; Rom. 8:31-39; Matt. 23:13-26
19	1 Sam. 16:1-13; Acts 10:1-16; Luke 24:13-35	Deut. 1:1-18; Rom. 9:1-18; Matt. 23:27-39
20	1 Sam. 16:14—17:11; Acts 10:17-33; Luke 24:36-53	Deut. 3:18-28; Rom. 9:19-33; Matt. 24:1-14
21	1 Sam. 17:17-30; Acts 10:34-48; Mark 1:1-13	Deut. 31:7-13, 24—32:4; Rom. 10:1-13: Matt. 24:15-31
22	1 Sam. 17:31-49; Acts 11:1-18; Mark 1:14-28	Deut. 34:1-12; Rom. 10:14-21; Matt. 24:32-51
23	1 Sam. 17:50—18:4; Rom. 10:4-17; Matt. 23:29-39	Josh. 1:1-18; Acts 21:3-15; Mark 1:21-27
24	1 Sam. 18:5-16, 27-30; Acts 11:19-30; Mark 1:29-45	Josh. 2:1-14; Rom. 11:1-12; Matt. 25:1-13
25	1 Sam. 19:1-18; Acts 12:1-17; Mark 2:1-12	Josh. 2:15-24; Rom. 11:13-24; Matt. 25:14-30
26	1 Sam. 20:1-23; Acts 12:18-25; Mark 2:13-22	Josh. 3:1-13; Rom. 11:25-36; Matt. 25:31-46
27	1 Sam. 20:24-42; Acts 13:1-12; Mark 2:23—3:6	Josh. 3:14—4:7; Rom. 12:1-8; Matt. 26:1-16
28	1 Sam. 21:1-15; Acts 13:13-25; Mark 3:7-19	Josh. 4:19—5:1, 10-15; Rom. 12:9-21; Matt. 26:17-25
29	1 Sam. 22:1-23; Acts 13:26-43; Mark 3:19-35	Josh. 6:1-14; Rom. 13:1-7; Matt. 26:26-35
30	1 Sam. 23:7-18; Rom. 11:33—12:2; Matt. 25:14-30	Josh. 6:15-27; Acts 22:30—23:11; Mark 2:1-12
31	1 Sam. 24:1-22; Acts 13:44-52; Mark 4:1-20	Josh. 7:1-13; Rom. 13:8-14; Matt. 26:36-46
August		
1	1 Sam. 25:1-22; Acts 14:1-18; Mark 4:21-34	Josh. 8:1-22; Rom. 14:1-12; Matt. 26:47-56
2	1 Sam. 25:23-44; Acts 14:19-28; Mark 4:35-41	Josh. 8:30-35; Rom. 14:13-23; Matt. 26:57-68
3	1 Sam. 28:3-20; Acts 15:1-11; Mark 5:1-20	Josh. 9:3-21; Rom. 15:1-13; Matt. 26:69-75
4	1 Sam. 31:1-13; Acts 15:12-21; Mark 5:21-43	Josh. 9:22—10:15; Rom. 15:14-24; Matt. 27:1-10

Day	Dawn	Dusk
5	2 Sam. 1:1-16; Acts 15:22-35; Mark 6:1-13	Josh. 23:1-16; Rom. 15:25-33; Matt. 27:11-23
6	2 Sam. 1:17-27; Rom. 12:9-21; Matt. 25:31-46	Josh. 24:1-15; Acts 28:23-31; Mark 2:23-28
7	2 Sam. 2:1-11; Acts 15:36—16:5; Mark 6:14-29	Josh. 24:16-33; Rom. 16:1-16; Matt. 27:24-31
8	2 Sam. 3:6-21; Acts 16:6-15; Mark 6:30-46	Judg. 2:1-5, 11-23; Rom. 16:17-27; Matt. 27:32-44
9	2 Sam. 3:22-39; Acts 16:16-24; Mark 6:47-56	Judg. 3:12-30; Acts 1:1-14; Matt. 27:45-54
10	2 Sam. 4:1-12; Acts 16:25-40; Mark 7:1-23	Judg. 4:4-23; Acts 1:15-26; Matt. 27:55-66
11	2 Sam. 5:1-12; Acts 17:1-15; Mark 7:24-37	Judg. 5:1-18; Acts 2:1-21; Matt. 28:1-10
12	2 Sam. 5:22—6:11; Acts 17:16-34; Mark 8:1-10	Judg. 5:19-31; Acts 2:22-36; Matt. 28:11-20
13	2 Sam. 6:12-23; Rom. 14:7-12; John 1:43-51	Judg. 6:1-23; 2 Cor. 9:6-15; Mark 3:20-30
14	2 Sam. 7:1-17; Acts 18:1-11; Mark 8:11-21	Judg. 6:25-40; Acts 2:37-47; John 1:1-18
15	2 Sam. 7:18-29; Acts 18:12-28; Mark 8:22-33	Judg. 7:1-18; Acts 3:1-11; John 1:19-28
16	2 Sam. 9:1-13; Acts 19:1-10; Mark 8:24—9:1	Judg. 7:19—8:12; Acts 3:12-26; John 1:29-42
17	2 Sam. 11:1-27; Acts 19:11-20; Mark 9:2-13	Judg. 8:22-35; Acts 4:1-12; John 1:43-51
18	2 Sam. 12:1-14; Acts 19:21-41; Mark 9:14-29	Judg. 9:1-21; Acts 4:13-31; John 2:1-12
19	2 Sam. 12:15-31; Acts 20:1-16; Mark 9:30-41	Judg. 9:22-25, 50-57; Acts 4:32—5:11; John 2:13-25
20	2 Sam. 13:1-22; Rom. 15:1-13; John 3:22-36	Judg. 11:1-11, 29-40; 2 Cor. 11:21-31; Mark 4:35-41
21	2 Sam. 13:23-29; Acts 20:17-38; Mark 9:42-50	Judg. 12:1-7; Acts 5:12-26; John 3:1-21
22	2 Sam. 14:1-20; Acts 21:1-14; Mark 10:1-16	Judg. 13:1-15; Acts 5:27-42; John 3:22-36
23	2 Sam. 14:21-33; Acts 21:15-26; Mark 10:17-31	Judg. 13:15-24; Acts 6:1-15; John 4:1-26
24	2 Sam. 15:1-18; Acts 21:27-36; Mark 10:32-45	Judg. 14:1-19; Acts 6:15—7:16; John 4:27-42
25	2 Sam. 25:19-37; Acts 21:37—22:16; Mark 10:46-52	Judg. 14:20—15:20; Acts 7:17-29; John 4:43-54
26	2 Sam. 26:1-23; Acts 22:17-29; Mark 11:1-11	Judg. 16:1-14; Acts 7:30-43; John 5:1-18
27	2 Sam. 27:1-23; Gal. 3:6-14; John 5:30-47	Judg. 16:15-31; 2 Cor. 13:1-11; Mark 5:25-34
28	2 Sam. 27:24—18:8; Acts 22:30—23:11; Mark 11:12-26	Judg. 17:1-13; Acts 7:44—8:1; John 5:15-29
29	2 Sam. 18:9-18; Acts 23:12-24; Mark 11:27—12:12	Judg. 18:1-15; Acts 8:1-13; John 5:30-47

Day	Dawn	Dusk
30	2 Sam. 18:19-33; Acts 23:23-35; Mark 12:13-27	Judg. 18:15-31; Acts 8:14-25; John 6:1-15
31	2 Sam. 19:1-23; Acts 24:1-23; Mark 12:28-34	Job 1:1-22; Acts 8:26-40; John 6:16-27

September

1	2 Sam. 19:24-43; Acts 24:24—25:12; Mark 12:35-44	Job 2:1-13; Acts 9:1-9; John 6:27-40
2	2 Sam. 23:1-7, 13-17; Acts 25:13-27; Mark 13:1-13	Job 3:1-26; Acts 9:10-19; John 6:41-51
3	2 Sam. 24:1-2, 10-25; Gal. 3:23—4:7; John 8:12-20	Job 4:1-6, 12-21; Rev. 4:1-11; Mark 6:1-6
4	1 Kings 1:5-31; Acts 26:1-23; Mark 13:14-27	Job 5:1-11, 17-27; Acts 9:19-31; John 6:52-59
5	1 Kings 1:32—2:4, 46; Acts 26:24-27:8; Mark 13:28-37	Job 6:1-15, 21; Acts 9:32-43; John 6:60-71
6	1 Kings 3:1-15; Acts 27:9-26; Mark 14:1-11	Job 7:1-21; Acts 10:1-16; John 7:1-13
7	1 Kings 3:16-28; Acts 27:27-44; Mark 14:12-26	Job 8:1-10, 20-22; Acts 10:17-33; John 7:14-36
8	1 Kings 5:1—6:1, 7; Acts 28:1-16; Mark 14:27-42	Job 9:1-15, 32-35; Acts 10:34-48; John 7:37-52
9	1 Kings 7:51—8:21; Acts 28:17-31; Mark 14:43-52	Job 10:1-9, 16-22; Acts 11:1-18; John 8:12-20
10	1 Kings 8:22-30; 1 Tim. 4:7-16; John 8:47-59	Job 11:1-9, 13-20; Rev. 5:1-14; Matt. 5:1-12
11	2 Chron. 6:32—7:7; James 2:1-13; Mark 14:53-65	Job 12:1-6, 13-25; Acts 11:19-30; John 8:21-32
12	1 Kings 8:65—9:9; James 2:14-26; Mark 14:66-72	Job 13:3-27; Acts 12:1-17; John 8:33-47
13	1 Kings 9:24—10:13; James 3:1-12; Mark 15:1-11	Job 14:1-22; Acts 12:18-25; John 8:47-59
14	1 Kings 11:1-13; James 3:13—4:12; Mark 15:12-21	Job 16:16-22, 17:13-16; Acts 13:1-12; John 9:1-17
15	1 Kings 11:26-43; James 4:13—5:6; Mark 15:22-32	Job 19:1-7, 14-27; Acts 13:13-25; John 9:18-41
16	1 Kings 12:1-20; James 5:7-20; Mark 15:33-39	Job 22:1-4, 21—23:7; Acts 13:26-43; John 10:1-18
17	1 Kings 12:21-33; Acts 4:18-31; John 10:31-42	Job 25:1-6; 27:1-6; Rev. 14:1-7, 13; Matt. 5:13-20
18	1 Kings 13:1-10; Phil. 1:1-11; Mark 15:40-47	Job 32:1-10; 33:19-28; Acts 13:44-52; John 10:19-30
19	1 Kings 16:23-34; Phil. 1:12-30; Mark 16:1-8	Job 29:1-20; Acts 14:1-18; John 10:31-42
20	1 Kings 17:1-24; Phil. 2:1-11; Matt. 2:1-12	Job 30:1-2, 16-31; Acts 14:19-28; John 11:1-16
21	1 Kings 18:1-19; Phil. 2:12-30; Matt. 2:13-23	Job 31:1-23; Acts 15:1-11; John 11:17-29
22	1 Kings 18:20-40; Phil. 3:1-16; Matt. 3:1-12	Job 31:24-40; Acts 15:12-21; John 11:30-44

Day	Dawn	Dusk
23	1 Kings 18:41—19:8; Phil 3:17—4:7; Matt. 3:13-17	Job 38:1-17; Acts 15:22-35; John 11:45-54
24	1 Kings 19:8-21; Acts 5:34-42; John 11:45-57	Job 38:18-41; Rev. 18:1-8; Matt. 5:21-26
25	1 Kings 21:1-16; 1 Cor. 1:1-19; Matt. 4:1-11	Job 40:1-24; Acts 15:36—16:5; John 11:55—12:8
26	1 Kings 21:17-29; 1 Cor. 1:20-31; Matt. 4:12-17	Job 41:1-11; Acts 16:6-15; John 12:9-19
27	1 Kings 22:1-28; 1 Cor. 2:1-13; Matt. 4:18-25	Job 42:1-17; Acts 16:16-24; John 12:20-26
28	1 Kings 22:29-45; 1 Cor. 2:14—3:15; Matt. 5:1-10	Job 28:1-28; Acts 16:25-40; John 12:27-36
29	2 Kings 1:2-17; 1 Cor. 3:16-23; Matt. 5:11-16	Esth. 1:1-4; Acts 17:1-15; John 12:36-43
30	2 Kings 2:1-18; 1 Cor. 4:1-7; Matt. 5:17-20	Esth. 2:5-8, 15-23; Acts 17:16-34; John 12:44-50

October

Day	Dawn	Dusk
1	2 Kings 4:8-37; Acts 9:10-31; Luke 3:7-18	Esth. 3:1—4:3; James 1:19-27; Matt. 6:1-6, 16-18
2	2 Kings 5:1-19; 1 Cor. 4:8-21; Matt. 5:21-26	Esth. 4:4-17; Acts 18:1-11; Luke 3:1-14
3	2 Kings 5:19-27; 1 Cor. 5:1-8; Matt. 5:27-37	Esth. 5:1-14; Acts 18:12-28; Luke 3:15-22
4	2 Kings 6:1-23; 1 Cor. 5:9—6:11; Matt. 5:38-48	Esth. 6:1-14; Acts 19:1-10; Luke 4:1-13
5	2 Kings 9:1-16; 1 Cor. 6:12-20; Matt. 6:1-6, 16-18	Esth. 7:1-10; Acts 19:11-20; Luke 4:14-30
6	2 Kings 9:17-37; 1 Cor. 7:1-8; Matt. 6:7-15	Esth. 8:1-8, 15-17; Acts 19:21-41; Luke 4:31-37
7	2 Kings 11:1-20; 1 Cor. 7:10-24; Matt. 6:19-24	Esth. 9:1-32; Acts 20:1-16; Luke 4:38-44
8	2 Kings 17:1-18; Acts 9:36-43; Luke 5:1-11	Hos. 1:1—2:1; James 3:1-13; Matt. 13:44-52
9	2 Kings 17:24-41; 1 Cor. 7:25-31; Matt. 6:25-34	Hos. 2:2-15; Acts 20:17-38; Luke 5:1-11
10	2 Chron. 29:1-3; 30:1-27; 1 Cor. 7:32-40; Matt. 7:1-12	Hos. 2:16-23; Acts 21:1-14; Luke 5:12-26
11	2 Kings 18:9-25; 1 Cor. 8:1-13; Matt. 7:13-21	Hos. 3:1-5; Acts 21:15-26; Luke 5:27-39
12	2 Kings 18:28-37; 1 Cor. 9:1-15; Matt. 7:22-29	Hos. 4:1-10; Acts 21:27-36; Luke 6:1-11
13	2 Kings 19:1-20; 1 Cor. 9:16-27; Matt. 8:1-17	Hos. 4:11-19; Acts 21:37—22:16; Luke 6:12-26
14	2 Kings 19:21-36; 1 Cor. 10:1-13; Matt. 8:18-27	Hos. 5:1-7; Acts 22:17-29; Luke 6:27-38
15	2 Kings 20:1-21; Acts 12:1-17; Luke 7:11-17	Hos. 5:8—6:6; 1 Cor. 2:6-16; Matt. 14:1-12
16	2 Kings 21:1-18; 1 Cor. 10:14—11:1; Matt. 8:28-34	Hos. 6:7—7:7; Acts 22:30—23:11; Luke 6:39-49

Day	Dawn	Dusk
17	2 Kings 22:1-13; 1 Cor. 11:2, 17-22; Matt. 9:1-8	Hos. 7:8-16; Acts 23:12-24; Luke 7:1-7
18	2 Kings 22:14—23:3; 1 Cor. 11:23-34; Matt. 9:9-17	Hos. 8:1-14; Acts 23:23-35; Luke 7:8-35
19	2 Kings 23:4-25; 1 Cor. 12:1-11; Matt. 9:18-26	Hos. 9:1-9; Acts 24:1-23; Luke 7:36-50
20	2 Kings 23:36—24:17; 1 Cor. 12:12-26; Matt. 9:27-34	Hos. 9:10-17; Acts 24:24—25:12; Luke 8:1-15
21	Jer. 35:1-19; 1 Cor. 12:27—13:3; Matt. 9:35-10:4	Hos. 10:1-15; Acts 25:13-27; Luke 8:16-25
22	Jer. 36:1-10; Acts 14:8-18; Luke 7:36-50	Hos. 11:1-11; 1 Cor. 4:9-16; Matt. 15:21-28
23	Jer. 36:11-26; 1 Cor. 13:4-13; Matt. 10:5-15	Hos. 11:12—12:1; Acts 26:1-23; Luke 8:26-39
24	Jer. 36:27—37:2; 1 Cor. 14:1-12; Matt. 10:16-23	Hos. 12:2-14; Acts 26:24—27:8; Luke 8:40-56
25	Jer. 37:3-21; 1 Cor. 14:13-25; Matt. 10:24-33	Hos. 13:1-3; Acts 27:9-26; Luke 9:1-17
26	Jer. 38:1-13; 1 Cor. 14:26-40; Matt. 10:34-42	Hos. 13:4-8; Acts 27:27-44; Luke 9:18-27
27	Jer. 38:14-28; 1 Cor. 15:1-11; Matt. 11:1-6	Hos. 13:9-16; Acts 28:1-16; Luke 9:28-36
28	Jer. 52:1-34; 1 Cor. 15:12-29; Matt. 11:7-15	Hos. 14:1-9; Acts 28:17-31; Luke 9:37-50
29	Jer. 39:11—40:6; Acts 16:6-15; Luke 10:1-20	Micah 1:1-9; 1 Cor. 10:1-13; Matt. 16:13-20
30	Jer. 44:1-14; 1 Cor. 15:30-41; Matt. 11:16-24	Micah 2:1-13; Rev. 7:1-8; Luke 9:51-62
31	Lam. 1:1-12; 1 Cor. 15:41-50; Matt. 11:25-30	Micah 3:1-8; Rev. 7:9-17; Luke 10:1-16

November

	Dawn	Dusk
1	Lam. 2:8-15; 1 Cor. 15:51-58; Matt. 12:1-14	Micah 3:9—4:5; Rev. 8:1-13; Luke 10:17-24
2	Ezra 1:1-11; 1 Cor. 16:1-9; Matt. 12:15-21	Micah 5:1-15; Rev. 9:1-12; Luke 10:25-37
3	Ezra 3:1-13; 1 Cor. 16:10-24; Matt. 12:22-32	Micah 6:1-8; Rev. 9:13-21; Luke 10:38-42
4	Ezra 4:7, 11-24; Philemon 1:1-25; Matt. 12:33-42	Micah 7:1-7; Rev. 10:1-11; Luke 11:1-13
5	Hag. 1:1—2:9; Acts 18:24-19:7; Luke 10:25-37	Jonah 1:1-17; 1 Cor. 10:15-24; Matt. 18:15-20
6	Zech. 1:7-17; Rev. 1:4-20; Matt. 12:43-50	Jonah 1:17—2:10; Rev. 11:1-14; Luke 11:14-26
7	Ezra 5:1-17; Rev. 4:1-11; Matt. 13:1-9	Jonah 3:1—4:11; Rev. 11:14-19; Luke 11:27-36
8	Ezra 6:1-22; Rev. 5:1-10; Matt. 13:10-17	Nahum 1:1-14; Rev. 12:1-6; Luke 11:37-52
9	Neh. 1:1-11; Rev. 5:11—6:11; Matt. 13:18-23	Nahum 1:15—2:12; Rev. 12:7-17; Luke 11:53—12:12

Day	Dawn	Dusk
10	Neh. 2:1-20; Rev. 6:12—7:4; Matt. 13:24-30	Nahum 2:13—3:7; Rev. 13:1-10; Luke 12:13-31
11	Neh. 4:1-23; Rev. 7:4-17; Matt. 13:31-35	Nahum 3:8-19; Rev. 13:11-18; Luke 12:32-48
12	Neh. 5:1-9; Acts 20:7-12; Luke 12:22-31	Zeph. 1:1-6; 1 Cor. 12:27—13:13; Matt. 18:21-35
13	Neh. 6:1-19; Rev. 10:1-11; Matt. 13:36-43	Zeph. 1:7-13; Rev. 14:1-13; Luke 12:49-59
14	Neh. 12:27-47; Rev. 11:1-19; Matt. 13:44-52	Zeph. 1:14-18; Rev. 14:14—15:8; Luke 13:1-9
15	Neh. 13:4-22; Rev. 12:1-12; Matt. 13:53-58	Zeph. 2:1-15; Rev. 16:1-11; Luke 13:10-17
16	Ezra 7:11-26; Rev. 14:1-13; Matt. 14:1-12	Zeph. 3:1-7; Rev. 16:12-21; Luke 13:18-30
17	Ezra 7:27-28, 8:21-36; Rev. 15:1-8; Matt. 14:13-21	Zeph. 3:8-13; Rev. 17:1-18; Luke 13:31-35
18	Ezra 9:1-15; 1 Pet. 1:1-12; Matt. 14:22-36	Zeph. 3:14-20; Rev. 18:1-14; Luke 14:1-11
19	Ezra 10:1-17; Acts 24:10-21; Luke 14:12-24	Joel 1:1-13; 1 Cor. 14:1-12; Matt. 20:1-16
20	Neh. 9:1-15; 1 Pet. 1:13-25; Matt. 15:1-20	Joel 1:15—2:2; Rev. 18:15-24; Luke 14:12-24
21	Neh. 9:26-38; 1 Pet. 2:1-10; Matt. 15:21-28	Joel 2:3-11; Rev. 19:1-10; Luke 14:25-35
22	Neh. 5:1-19; 1 Pet. 2:11-25; Matt. 15:29-39	Joel 2:12-19; Rev. 19:11-21; Luke 15:1-10
23	Neh. 6:1-19; 1 Pet. 3:13—4:6; Matt. 16:1-12	Joel 2:21-27; Rev. 20:1-15; Luke 15:11-32
24	Neh. 12:27-31; 1 Pet. 4:7-19; Matt. 16:13-20	Joel 2:28—3:8; Rev. 21:1-21; Luke 16:1-9
25	Neh. 13:4-22; Rom. 15:5-13; Matt. 16:21-28	Joel 3:9-17; Rev. 22:6-21; Luke 16:10-31
26	Isa. 1:1-9; 2 Pet. 3:1-10; Matt. 25:1-13	Amos 1:1-5, 13—2:8; 1 Thess. 5:1-11; Luke 21:5-19
27	Isa. 1:10-20; 1 Thess. 1:1-10; Luke 20:1-8	Amos 2:6-16; 2 Pet. 1:1-11; Matt. 21:1-11
28	Isa. 1:21-31; 1 Thess. 2:1-12; Luke 20:9-18	Amos 3:1-11; 2 Pet. 1:12-21; Matt. 21:12-22
29	Isa. 2:1-4; 1 Thess. 2:13-20; Luke 20:19-26	Amos 3:12—4:5; 2 Pet. 3:1-10; Matt. 21:23-32
30	Isa. 2:5-22; 1 Thess. 3:1-13; Luke 20:27-40	Amos 4:6-13; 2 Pet. 3:11-18; Matt. 21:33-46
December		
1	Isa. 3:1—4:1; 1 Thess. 4:1-12; Luke 20:41—21:4	Amos 5:1-17; Jude 1:1-16; Matt. 22:1-14
2	Isa. 4:2-6; 1 Thess. 4:13-18; Luke 21:5-19	Amos 5:18-27; Jude 1:17-25; Matt. 22:15-22
3	Isa. 5:1-7; 2 Pet. 3:11-18; Luke 7:28-35	Amos 6:1-14; 2 Thess. 1:5-12; Luke 1:57-68

Day	Dawn	Dusk
4	Isa. 5:8-17; 1 Thess. 5:1-11; Luke 21:20-28	Amos 7:1-9; Rev. 1:1-8; Matt. 22:23-33
5	Isa. 5:18-25; 1 Thess. 5:12-28; Luke 21:29-38	Amos 7:10-17; Rev. 1:9-16; Matt. 22:34-46
6	Isa 6:1-13; 2 Thess. 1:1-12; John 7:53—8:11	Amos 8:1-14; Rev. 1:17—2:7; Matt. 23:1-12
7	Isa. 7:1-9; 2 Thess. 2:1-12; Luke 22:1-13	Amos 9:1-10; Rev. 2:8-17; Matt. 23:13-26
8	Isa.7:10-25; 2 Thess. 2:13—3:5; Luke 22:14-30	Hag. 1:1-15; Rev. 2:18-29; Matt. 23:27-39
9	Isa. 8:1-15; 2 Thess. 3:6-18; Luke 22:31-38	Hag. 2:1-9; Rev. 3:1-6; Matt. 24:1-14
10	Isa. 3:1-13; Heb. 12:18-29; John 3:22-30	Amos 9:11-15; 2 Thess. 2:1-3, 13-17; John 5:30-47
11	Isa. 8:16—9:1; James 1:1-27; Luke 22:39-53	Zech. 1:7-17; Rev. 3:7-13; Matt. 24:15-31
12	Isa. 9:2-7; James 2:1-26; Luke 22:54-69	Zech. 2:1-13; Rev. 3:14-22; Matt. 24:32-44
13	Isa. 9:8-17; James 3:1-12; Mark 1:1-8	Zech. 3:1-10; Rev. 4:1-8; Matt. 24:45-51
14	Isa. 9:18—10:4; James 3:13—4:12; Matt. 3:1-12	Zech. 4:1-14; Rev. 4:9—5:5; Matt. 25:1-13
15	Isa. 10:5-19; James 4:13—5:6; Matt. 11:2-15	Zech. 7:8—8:8; Rev. 5:6-14; Matt. 25:14-30
16	Isa. 10:20-27; James 5:7-12; Luke 3:1-9	Zech. 8:9-17; Rev. 6:1-17; Matt. 25:31-46
17	Gen. 1:1—2:3; James 5:13-20; John 1:1-14	Zech. 9:9-16; Rev. 7:9-17; Matt. 26:6-13
18	Isa. 11:1-9; Eph. 6:10-20; John 3:16-21	Gen. 3:8-15; Rev. 12:1-10; John 3:27-36
19	Isa. 11:10-16; Rev. 20:1-10; John 5:30-47	Zeph. 3:14-20; Titus 1:1-16; Luke 1:1-25
20	Isa. 28:9-22; Rev. 20:11—21:8; Matt. 1:1-17	1 Sam. 2:1-10; Titus 2:1-10; Luke 1:26-38
21	Isa. 29:9-24; Rev. 21:9-21; Matt. 1:18-25	2 Sam. 7:1-17; Titus 2:11-3:8; Luke 1:39-48
22	Isa. 31:1-9; Rev. 21:22—22:5; Matt 2:1-12	2 Sam. 7:18-29; Gal. 3:1-14; Luke 1:49-56
23	Isa. 33:17-22; Rev. 22:6-11, 18-20; Matt. 2:13-18	Jer. 31:10-14; Gal. 3:15-22; Luke 1:57-66
24	Isa. 35:1-10; Rev. 22:12-17, 21; Luke 1:67-80	Isa. 60:1-6; Gal. 3:23—4:7; Luke 2:1-21
25	Zech. 2:10-13; 1 John 4:7-16; Luke 2:22-35	Micah 4:1-5; 5:2-4; Ps. 146; Phil. 2:5-11
26	2 Chron. 24:17-22; Ps. 116; Acts 6:1-7	Isa. 59:15-21; Ps. 148; Acts 7:59—8:8
27	Prov. 8:22-30; Ps. 34; 1 John 5:1-12	Ps. 121; Ps. 149; John 13:20-35
28	Isa. 49:23; Ps. 2; Matt. 2:19-23	Isa. 54:1-13; Ps. 150; Matt. 18:1-14
29	Isa. 12:1-6; Rev. 1:1-8; John 7:37-52	2 Sam. 23:13-17; 2 John 1-13; John 2:1-11

Day	Dawn	Dusk
30	Isa. 25:1-9; Rev. 1:9-20; John 7:53—8:11	1 Kings 17:17-24; 3 John 1:15; John 4:46-54
31	Isa. 26:1-6; 2 Cor. 5:16—6:2; John 8:12-19	1 Kings 3:5-14; James 4:13-17; 5:7-11; John 5:1-15

Guide to Christian Seasons

YEAR	Ash Wednesday (Lent)	Easter	Pentecost	Advent
2012	February 22	April 8	May 27	December 2
2013	February 13	March 31	May 19	December 1
2014	March 5	April 20	June 8	November 30
2015	February 18	April 5	May 24	November 29
2016	February 10	March 27	May 15	November 27
2017	March 1	April 16	June 4	December 3
2018	February 14	April 1	May 20	December 2
2019	March 6	April 21	June 9	December 1
2020	February 26	April 12	May 31	November 29
2021	February 17	April 4	May 23	November 28
2022	March 2	April 17	June 5	November 27
2023	February 22	April 9	May 28	December 3
2024	February 14	March 31	May 19	December 1
2025	March 5	April 20	June 8	November 30
2026	February 18	April 5	May 24	November 29
2027	February 10	March 28	May 16	November 28
2028	March 1	April 16	June 4	December 3
2029	February 14	April 1	May 20	December 2
2030	March 6	April 21	June 9	December 1
2031	February 26	April 13	June 1	November 30
2032	February 11	March 28	May 16	November 28
2033	March 2	April 17	June 5	November 27
2034	February 22	April 9	May 28	December 3
2035	February 7	March 25	May 13	December 2

Notes

Part 1: In the Beginning

1. Julie Andrews, "Do-Re-Mi," a song from *The Sound of Music*, directed by Robert Wise, 1965.

1. Lord, Teach Us to Pray

1. I recognize that it is not a case of either/or when it comes to prayer. One style of prayer is not superior to another. There is a place for both spontaneous prayer and fixed-hour prayer. I am trying to say that prayer is too often modeled and taught using only the model of spontaneous prayer.

2. Scot McKnight, *Praying with the Church* (Brewster, MA: Paraclete Press, 2006), 62-63.

3. Fixed-hour prayer goes by many different names. You may hear it referred to as: praying the hours, ordered prayer, the work of God, liturgy of the hours, praying with the church, the divine hours, and so on.

3. Before We Begin

1. A coracle is an oval-shaped boat made of a framework of willow rods covered by animal skin. It is a flat-bottomed, keel-less vessel that is powered with a paddle or a sail.

2. Esther de Waal, *The Celtic Way of Prayer* (New York: Doubleday, 1997), 2.

4. The Lord's Prayer

1. Referred to as the "Our Father" in some Christian traditions.

5. Week One: *Reflecting God's Character*

1. Northumbria Community, *Celtic Daily Prayer: Prayers and Readings from the Northumbria Community* (San Francisco: HarperCollins Publishers, 2002), 18.

2. Mary A. Lathbury, "Break Thou the Bread of Life," Public Domain, 1877. Verses 3 and 4 by Alexander Groves, Public Domain, 1913.

3. *St. Benedict's Prayer Book* (York, UK: Ampleforth Abbey Press, 1994), 56.

4. Ignaz Franz, trans. Clarence Walworth, "Holy God, We Praise Thy Name," Public Domain.

5. Ibid.

6. Ibid.

7. William Kethe, "All People That on Earth Do Dwell," Public Domain, 1561.

8. Thomas Ken, *The Doxology*, Manual of Prayers for the Use of the Scholars of Winchester College, Public Domain, 1674.

9. Charles Wesley, "And Can It Be That I Should Gain?" Public Domain, 1738.

10. Based on a prayer from: Glenstal Abbey, *The Glenstal Book of Prayer: A Benedictine Prayer Book* (Collegeville, MN: The Liturgical Press, 2001), 25.

11. Taizé Community, *Prayer for Each Day* (Chicago: GIA Publications, Inc., 1998), 118.

12. Charles Wesley, "And Can It Be That I Should Gain?" Public Domain, 1738.

13. Based on a prayer from *The Glenstal Book of Prayer*, 25.

14. Charles Wesley, "And Can It Be That I Should Gain?" Public Domain, 1738.

15. Based on a prayer from *The Glenstal Book of Prayer*, 25.

16. Prayer based on 1 John 1:5-9.

17. Edward Mote, "My Hope Is Built on Nothing Less," Public Domain, 1836.

18. The Apostles' Creed, developed between the 2nd and 9th centuries.

19. I am indebted to Scot McKnight's description of the New Testament people of God as found in *One Life: Jesus Calls, We Follow* (Grand Rapids: Zondervan, 2010), 103-4.

20. *Rerum, Deus, tenax vigor,* hymn attributed to St. Ambrose, AD 397.

21. I am indebted to Scot McKnight's description of the New Testament people of God as found in McKnight, *One Life,* 103-4.

22. *St. Benedict's Prayer Book,* 36.

23. An ancient Latin hymn, *Phos Hilaron,* Unknown Author from the Apostolic Constitutions, 3rd or 4th century.

24. William W. How, "O Word of God Incarnate," Public Domain, 1867.

25. I am indebted to Scot McKnight's description of the New Testament people of God as found in McKnight, *One Life,* 103-4.

26. *The Book of Common Prayer* (New York: Oxford University Press, 1990), 79.

27. Terry S. Taylor, "Be My Hiding Place," Zoom Daddy Music (BMI), 2002.

28. *The Book of Common Prayer,* 101.

29. Excerpt from *Te Deum Laudamus,* attributed to St. Ambrose.

30. Ibid.

31. Walter C. Smith, "Immortal, Invisible, God Only Wise," Public Domain, 1867.

32. Irenaeus, "The Rule of Faith" from *Against Heresies*, I:10:1.

33. William Kethe, "O Worship the King, All Glorious Above," Public Domain, 1561.

34. *Gloria Patri,* Author Unknown, Public Domain.

35. Frederick J. Schumacher (ed.), *For All the Saints: A Prayer Book for and by the Church,* vol. 3 (Dehli, NY: American Lutheran Publicity Bureau, 1995), 537.

36. "The Prayer of St. Francis," traditional. As prayed by Mother Teresa on the occasion of her address to the United Nations in 1985.

37. *Gloria Patri.*

38. Author's paraphrase of Luke 1:68-79; traditional prayer called the *Benedictus Dominus Deus.*

39. The Apostles' Creed, developed between the 2nd and 9th centuries.

40. *Gloria Patri.*

41. Based on a prayer found in The Church Society, *An English Prayer Book* (New York: Oxford University Press, 1994), 137-39.

42. Thomas Ken, *The Doxology.*

43. *Gloria Patri.*

44. Author's paraphrase of Luke 1:46-55; traditional prayer called *The Magnificat.*

45. Based on a prayer found in *The Book of Common Prayer,* 816.

6. Week Two: *Shaped by God's Mission*

1. Jamie Barnes, "Prayer of Confession," The Open Sourcebook, July 25, 2009, <http://theopensourcebook.org/2009/07/prayer-of-confession>.

2. Carl Boberg, trans. Stuart K. Hine, "How Great Thou Art," Public Domain, 1899.

3. Based on a prayer found in *The Book of Common Prayer,* 815.

4. Boberg, "How Great Thou Art."

5. Based on a prayer found in *The Book of Common Prayer,* 815.

6. Derald Daugherty and Steve Hindalong, "Sanctified," Never Say Never Songs (ASCAP), 1992.

7. Based on a prayer found in *The Book of Common Prayer*, 815.

8. Attributed to William Kethel, "All People That on Earth Do Dwell," Public Domain, 1561.

9. I am indebted to Henri Nouwen's insights as found in *Life of the Beloved: Spiritual Living in a Secular World* (New York: The Crossroad Publishing Company, 1994).

10. Schumacher (ed.), *For All the Saints*, 541.

11. Kethel, "All People That on Earth Do Dwell."

12. Charles Wesley, "Arise, My Soul, Arise!" Public Domain, 1742.

13. I am indebted to Nouwen's insights as found in *Life of the Beloved*.

14. Wesley, "Arise, My Soul, Arise!"

15. George Robinson and James Mountain, "I Am His and He Is Mine," Public Domain, 1876.

16. I am indebted to Nouwen's insights as found in *Life of the Beloved*.

17. The Anglican Church of Aotearoa, New Zealand, and Polynesia, *A New Zealand Prayer Book* (New York: HarperOne, 1997), 624.

18. Ibid.

19. Joseph A. Seiss, "Fairest Lord Jesus," Public Domain, 1873.

20. Wesleyan Holiness Study Project, *The Holiness Manifesto* (Azusa, CA: Eerdmans, 2006).

21. Brendan O'Malley, *A Celtic Primer: The Complete Celtic Worship Resource and Collection* (Harrisburg, PA: Morehouse Publishing, 2002), 61.

22. J. Philip Newell, *Celtic Prayers from Iona* (Mahwah, NJ: Paulist Press, 1997). 39.

23. Based on a prayer from: Schumacher, *For All the Saints*, 675.

24. Seiss, "Fairest Lord Jesus."

25. Longfellow, "God of the Earth, the Sky, the Sea."

26. Newell, *Celtic Prayers from Iona* (Mahwah, NJ: Paulist Press, 1997), 39.

27. Longfellow, "God of the Earth, the Sky, the Sea," Public Domain.

28. Newell, *Celtic Prayers from Iona*, 54.

29. William Williams, "Guide Me, O Thou Great Jehovah," Public Domain, 1771.

30. Newell, *Celtic Prayers from Iona*, 39.

31. Based on a prayer from *The Book of Common Prayer*, 827.

32. Newell, *Celtic Prayers from Iona*, 54.

33. Prayer based on Ephesians 3:14-19.

34. Jane E. Leeson, "Savior, Teach Me, Day by Day," Public Domain.

35. Prayer based on Ephesians 3:14-19.

36. Henry F. Lyte, "Praise My Soul the King of Heaven," Public Domain, 1834.

37. Prayer based on Ephesians 3:14-19.

38. Attributed to St. Benedict of Nursia; quoted by Olivia Warburton in *Hear Our Prayer: A Collection of Classic Prayers* (Peabody, MA: Hendrickson Publishers, 2004), 14.

39. *The Book of Common Prayer*, 79.

40. Fanny J. Crosby, "I Am Thine, O Lord," Public Domain.

41. Based on *A Scriptural Confession of Faith*, Advent Christian General conference (Accessed April 11, 2011) <http://www.adventchristian.org/Aboutus/Whatwebelieve/AScripturalConfessionofFaith/tabid/93/Default.aspx>.

42. Crosby, "I Am Thine, O Lord."

43. J. Wilbur Chapman, "Jesus! What a Friend for Sinners," Public Domain, 1910.

44. Schumacher (ed.), *For All the Saints*, 547.

45. J. Wilbur Chapman, "Jesus! What a Friend for Sinners," Public Domain, 1910.

46. Ibid.

47. Ibid.

48. Fanny J. Crosby, "Tell Me the Story of Jesus," Public Domain, 1880.

49. The International Congress on World Evangelization, *The Lausanne Covenant* (Lausanne, Switzerland: July 16-25, 1974), Section 6.

50. Based on a prayer from *A New Zealand Prayer Book*, 130.

51. Schumacher (ed.), *For All the Saints*, 557.

52. Thomas Ken, quoted in Warburton, *Hear Our Prayer*, 31.

53. Katherine Hankey, "I Love to Tell the Story," Public Domain, 1866.

54. Based on a prayer from *A New Zealand Prayer Book*, 130.

55. *Gloria Patri*, Author Unknown, Public Domain.

56. Benjamin R. Hanby, "Who Is He in Yonder Stall?" Public Domain, 1866.

57. Based on a prayer from *A New Zealand Prayer Book*, 130.

58. Ken, quoted in Warburton, *Hear Our Prayer*, 31.

59. Author's paraphrase of Luke 1:68-79.

60. The Apostles' Creed.

61. *The Book of Common Prayer*, 231.

62. *Gloria Patri.*

63. *Anima Christi,* Author Unknown, 14th century.

64. Francis R. Havergal, "Take My Life and Let It Be," Public Domain, 1874.

65. Author's paraphrase of Luke 1:46-55.

66. *The Book of Common Prayer*, 101.

67. *Gloria Patri.*

7. Prayers at Dark

1. Traditional prayer known as *Trisagion*, 5th century.

2. Traditional prayer known as *The Collect for Purity.*

3. *The Book of Common Prayer*, 134.

4. *Trisagion.*

5. *The Collect for Purity.*

6. *The Book of Common Prayer*, 134.

7. *Trisagion.*

8. *The Collect for Purity.*

9. The Monks of Glenstal Abbey, *The Glenstal Book of Daily Prayer* (Collegeville, MN: The Liturgical Press, 2008), 237.

10. *Trisagion.*

11. *The Collect for Purity.*

12. *The Book of Common Prayer,* 134.

13. *Trisagion.*

14. *The Collect for Purity.*

15. *The Book of Common Prayer,* 134.

16. *Trisagion.*

17. *The Collect for Purity.*

18. *The Book of Common Prayer,* 134.

19. *Trisagion.*

20. *The Collect for Purity.*

21. *The Glenstal Book of Daily Prayer,* 237.

8. Express Prayer Forms

1. *The Book of Common Prayer,* 79.

2. Northumbria Community, *Celtic Daily Prayer,* 18.

3. *The Book of Common Prayer,* 137.

4. Ibid., 231.

5. *Gloria Patri.*

6. Based on Isaiah 26:3 and 30:15.

7. *Gloria Patri.*

8. An ancient Latin hymn, *Phos Hilaron,* Unknown Author from the Apostolic Constitutions 3rd or 4th century.

9. Judith Sutera (ed.), *Work of God: Benedictine Prayer* (Collegeville, MN: The Liturgical Press, 1997), 22.

10. *An English Prayer Book,* 192.

11. *Gloria Patri.*

Part 3: Occasional Prayers
9. Prayers for Various Seasons

1. Martin Moller quoted in Schumacher (ed.), *For All the Saints,* 23.

2. Alcuin of York quoted in Warburton, *Hear Our Prayer,* 85.

3. *A New Zealand Prayer Book,* 526.

4. Samuel Osgood quoted in Schumacher (ed.), *For All the Saints,* 100.

5. *A New Zealand Prayer Book,* 527.

6. The Theology and Worship Ministry Unit for the Presbyterian Church (U.S.A.), *Book of Common Worship, Daily Prayer* (Louisville, KY: Westminster/John Knox Press, 1993), 49.

7. Ibid., 50.

8. *Alternative Service Book* quoted in Warburton, *Hear Our Prayer,* 90.

9. *A New Zealand Prayer Book,* 532.

10. *Prayer Each Day,* 70.

11. Ernest Fremont Tittle quoted in Schumacher (ed.), *For All the Saints,* 979.

12. Christine Sine, "Holy Week Prayer," GodSpace (Accessed on April 20, 2011) <http://godspace.wordpress.com/2011/04/19/holy-week-prayer>.

13. Attributed to Julian of Norwich, quoted in Schumacher (ed.), *For All the Saints,* 955.

14. Bernard of Clairvaux, "O Sacred Head, Now Wounded," Public Domain, 1153.

15. Schumacher (ed.), *For All the Saints*, 977.

16. Ibid., 1119.

17. Northumbria Community, *Celtic Daily Prayer*, 284.

10. Prayers for Various Situations

1. Author unknown.

2. From the 4th century; named after its opening words in Latin.

3. Attributed to St. Francis of Assisi (1181-1226).

4. An early Scottish prayer, Author Unknown.

5. Attributed to St. Patrick of Ireland (390-461).

6. Attributed to St. Columba of Iona (521-597).

7. Attributed to Thomas à Kempis (1380-1471).

8. Attributed to Irenaeus of Lyons, 2nd century.

9. Traditional prayer from AD 600.

10. Attributed to St. Benedict of Nursia (480-547).

11. Attributed to Clement of Rome, 1st century.

12. Attributed to Francis Xavier (1506-1552).

13. Based on a prayer from *The Book of Common Prayer*, 459.

14. Consolation in this context means: a comfort; a relief from hardship.

15. Metropolitan Philaret of Moscow (1782-1867).

16. Dietrich Bonhoeffer (1906-1945).

17. *The Book of Common Prayer*, 461.

18. Attributed to Teresa of Avila (1515-1582).

19. *The Book of Common Prayer*, 823.

20. *Book of Common Worship, Daily Prayer*, 444-45.

21. *The Book of Common Prayer*, 831.

22. Attributed to St. Thomas Aquinas (1225-1274).

23. *The Book of Common Prayer*, 824.

24. Alistair Maclean (1922-1987).

25. Brother Roger (1915-2005), founder of the Community of *Taizé*.

26. Based on: Frederick Buechner's *Wishful Thinking: A Seeker's ABC* (New York: Harper & Row, 1973), 122.

11. Scripture Reading Plan

1. Adapted from Daily Lectionary as found in *Book of Common Worship, Daily Prayer*, 461-506.

Recommended Resources

To explore the topic of fixed-hour prayer, I have found the following resource most helpful:

Scot McKnight, *Praying with the Church* (Brewster, MA: Paraclete Press, 2006).

To add greater variety to the observance of fixed-hour prayer, many have found that using various prayer books during different Christian seasons of the year is a helpful practice. I have used the following prayer manuals in my practice of fixed-hour prayer:

J. Philip Newell, *Celtic Prayers from Iona* (Mahwah, NJ: Paulist Press, 1997).

Northumbria Community, *Celtic Daily Prayer: Prayers and Readings from the Northumbria Community* (San Francisco: HarperCollins Publishers, 2002).

Frederick J. Schumacher (ed.), *For All the Saints: A Prayer Book for and by the Church.* 4 Volumes. (Dehli, NY: American Lutheran Publicity Bureau, 1995).

St. Benedict's Prayer Book (York: UK: Ampleforth Abbey Press, 1994).

Phyllis Tickle, *The Divine Hours.* 3 Volumes. (New York: Doubleday, 2000-2001).

Author's Acknowledgments

During the entire process of writing *Dawn to Dark*, I have had one person in view. It is for this reason that I dedicated this, my first book, to my daughter, Amelia. It is my greatest desire to pass on to her (as well as to my godsons, Cody Parson and Riley Bray-Jones) and to her generation not a dead ritual, but a way of prayer that stirs up a fiery passion and devotion for God and a practical and genuine kindness for our neighbors.

I hope through this manual I can pass on to others a little bit of the fire that has been gently and faithfully handed on to me by:

My parents, Roger and Dionne Jones, who taught me my first prayers and had me and my brothers and sister on the first or second pew for Sunday worship nearly every week.

My first youth pastors, Mark and Susie Robinson, who shared with our youth group not only the gospel but their whole lives (1 Thessalonians 2:8).

The professors at Messiah College who instilled a desire to be a part of and contributor to the upside-down kingdom that Jesus came to inaugurate, especially Dr. Randy Basinger and Dr. Terry Brensinger.

Three professors who taught me at Trinity Evangelical Divinity School and who still inspire me through their writing: Dr. Mark Senter, Dr. Gary Osbourne, and Dr. Scot McKnight.

Two pastors who marked my early years and who exemplified the mercy, kindness, and grace of our Lord: Rev. Roger Watts and Rev. Chuck Guth.

Carol Ina Ramsak, whose practical love and gentle way provided glimpses of Jesus for my wife and me during a dark season of our life.

Father Paul C. B. Schenck, who introduced me to fixed-hour prayer and the Christian heirloom that is *The Book of Common Prayer*.

To the Benedictine Sisters of Virginia and the Benedictine Pastoral Center in Linton Hall, Virginia, for the hospitality and space to be formed in the likeness of Jesus.

Chris Folmsbee, whose belief in me and encouragement helped me uncover new ways to contribute to God's kingdom.

Ross and Sonja Andrews, friendship personified.

Rick Rhoads, who understands why we have two ears and one mouth.

Project Renovation and the folks who have been a part of the Soul Thirst Retreats, where some of the material for *Dawn to Dark* was used in community for the first time.

Those who have recorded the "soundtrack of my life": Michael Roe and the 77's, Terry Taylor/Daniel Amos, The Flower Kings, Phil Keaggy, and Jeff Johnson.

The following authors who, though I don't know them, have left their mark: Leonard Sweet, Gary Thomas, Richard Foster, Kenda Creasy Dean, Robert Webber, and Esther de Waal.

Finally, and most importantly, I thank my wife. Her belief in me and encouragement of me have made me a better man. I know that because she is in my life I am richly blessed, far more balanced, kind, and human. Her faith in me when I have had doubts about my ability and capabilities has given me the courage to keep going. I love you, Lawren, and am thankful that you are beside me forever, from Dawn to Dark.